Maazungu

By

Samantha Kimambo

The English Maasai

ISBN : 978-0-9556857-1-2

© Copyright - Samantha Kimambo 2007

www.kimambo.com

This book is dedicated to the most bizarre, strange and amazing people I have ever met. My family.

Without you, there would be nothing to write.
Without you there is no pain or joy.
Without you there is no beginning, middle or end to the story.
Without you there is no life.

I am sorry.

I love you all.

Prelude To The Adventure

I found a space to sit down. This would not take long. The choice had already been made.

My choice; It felt good to think such a thing. I was doing this. Nobody, no man, no nothing was inflicting it on me. Soon I would be free.
Opening the tablet bottle, I smiled. Relief would soon come. Then I started. One lithium, two lithium, three lithium, four. Accompanied with tequila shots. These tablets had taken me so far into being like a zombie; they could have the rest of me.

I carried on taking them. At number ten, the tears started. I thought of my children, of how I had let them down in life. I hoped I wasn't doing that by my death also. My death. How had it come to this point? How had I got to this level? From being a normal mum of four, with a career, a family and a life, to this ghastly shell of a being, popping the last pills, ending her pathetic existence.
I had been so sure of what to do. I didn't want to hurt other people and decided the least painful way would be an overdose. Blood looks nasty. Jumping would leave squashed remains for other people to clear up. An overdose would be perhaps some vomit and a corpse. The much better option. I didn't want to hurt any more people.

11, 12, 13.

I started to feel light in my head. The effects coming. At least it wasn't going to hurt. Maybe I could just sleep and drift away into oblivion. Then I could rest. The pain would be over. I shut my eyes, breathing in my last sensations.

My mind would not stop bringing images of my children. I pictured myself pregnant with them, them as new born babies, of our once happy family life, of my sons, my daughters, growing from little helpless beings into the people they are today. Such beautiful children. I wondered what they would look like in the future. I knew their Father would be good to them. I knew they would have a normal life. Probably a much better one than with me around. Their Mum. The one who was seen as fun and adventurous, vibrant. The one who life had pretty much destroyed. The one they had not seen for 6 months. The tears would not stop falling.

14, 15, 16,

I didn't deserve them and there was no way I could have a future with them now. What could I do for them? I had gone from being Mum the adventurer, to Mum the wasted and infected. I would much prefer them to have a good memory of me. Not one of me falling away from them day by day.

17, 18, 19, 20.

My daughter. I could feel her. She was crying for me. She needed me. It was as if I could see her and feel her pain. Mine was insignificant. I pictured myself in her room. She was lying in bed. I reached out, she fell from my grasp.
I have to stop. I can't, it is done. I am slipping. I wanted to stop. I needed to see my daughter.

Stop the pills! Reaching for my phone, I pressed the last number redial. Who was it? My head was gone. I had no thoughts, and then the blackness came.

In the darkness I could see lights. Such beautiful lights. Begging me to come.
No. I tried to speak but no sound would come. I could only think. My children. What had I done? I thought of them, my life, and our lives. What had all gone so horribly wrong? Was this really the big adventure we had planned?

Chapter 1

We had done it. My family and I were standing in London Heathrow airport. Waiting to go airside. It had taken a long time to get to this point. Months of preparation, attempts of selling houses, family disputes, and endless arguments that it was not a crime to take your children to Africa. Finally, here we were, soon to be on the adventure of our lives.

I have always been an adventurous type of person, but somehow, in the every day show of life I put on, that part of me became submerged. Buried in my career and family, absorbed in the probably absurd notion, like most girls entering womanhood in the mid-nineties, that women really can have it all.

My work was as a freelance journalist, a job many perceive to be glamorous, which is of course one of the biggest career misconceptions in existence. Either that or I had never got into the glamorous side of journalism. Maybe there is a whole side to writing I have never seen, having been blinkered by the deadlines or more realistically, constantly trying to find work to enable me to even have a deadline!

It was through the combination of trying to fit everything into one life that I stumbled onto my future. I never planned to do my life. I was never the type of girl who sat with a personal planner and wrote her life schedule out. I have only ever been me. Sure I had some ambitions, but they were always 'off the scale', escapist even and never quite vocational based! When it was time for careers advice at school, I was the person who filled in the questions wrong, just to see what kind of job could be suggested for one who came across as a sociopath! The answer was of course 'social worker', which approximately 60% of the class got given. I guess the government had predicted the current shortage of trained Social Workers and thought it should plant some seeds into every 5th year student thinking about college. I guess all I ever really wanted to do was explore, and not regret my life. However I could not put that into words, and when I did express exploring as a career choice to my parents, the only reply was maybe you should work in a travel agents. Great. I never saw myself holding down a post selling packaged holidays in the local 'Lunn Poly'.

The only other thing I could do was write. I went on to study journalism.

At 17 I fell pregnant with my Son, 3 months before my 18th birthday he was born. At 19 I got married. I praised myself for not aspiring to do anything huge in life, because it would now be even more difficult to do. I wasn't wrong. From the age of 17 to 24 I was in constant production. I was either pregnant or recovering from pregnancy and birth. After my 4th child was born, I was sterilized. I could face no more of the constant baby cycle and certainly didn't want to risk another pregnancy.

My husband agreed with this. We were both still young and felt it was time to enjoy our lives and grow with our children. The baby machine had stopped.

With the close of this chapter in my life, I began to re-examine who I was and what I was doing. I was working freelance, balancing family and work quite well, and to the world, I probably looked successful and happy, but within me, I knew there was far more to Samantha then what was showing. I never felt real to myself. I performed well for other people, but to myself, I couldn't lie.
Who was I? What did I want? It was a question I couldn't answer very well. In some ways I had spent so long hiding from who I was, and the things which had happened to me as a child, that I probably forgot how to be real to myself. I don't know.

At 8 years old I watched something on T.V. It was an event which changed my life and thinking; a news report with Julia Somerville reporting the plight of the Ethiopian people due to famine. Something stirred in my heart as a result of that news. Ever since I watched it, the report and scenes have always stuck with me. At the time of the viewing, I remember having this urge to jump on a plane and go to

help. I recall telling my Mum what I was feeling, and I remember the pain in my heart when she replied "but, what can you do?"
The words struck deep in me, letting me feel as if I could do nothing.

I hate the words, "but what can you do?" As I sat going through a retrospect on my life, trying to work out the next steps, I asked myself the same question. But, what can I do? Within me I found the answer with a question. "What do I want to do?" I wanted to help. I looked at the pain around the world, and felt it. From natural disasters to famine, to war and conflict; I wanted to help the pain.

An Uncle of mine had recently formed a charity to assist an orphanage in Kenya. I was asked if I wanted to get involved. I did. Soon an opportunity to go to Kenya arose, and I took it.

The work at the orphanage was good. With every piece of assistance, I felt as if I was actually doing something in the world. In addition to the positive work for the children, working in this way helped me so much. It gave me a real value of self that I had never experienced before. Kenya opened up my eyes.

Not long after the first trip I was able to go again. Throughout this trip, I felt as if I wanted to do more than coming over every few months. I kept thinking about living here. About what it would be like to be able to work like this on an every day basis. On what I could really do to offer help. The ideas would not go away. I spoke with some local people on what they would like in their community, together we came up with a plan.

The residents I had spoken to really wanted computer education. We sat talking through what was wanted and needed, before coming up with the idea of a community based IT centre. This place would benefit the most disadvantaged in society, by giving them the chance of competing in the modern business world with IT education. The plan was for it to become self-sustaining. I was so excited by the thoughts swimming around my head, and felt it was so right to carry on with this thought path.

The concept of 'Future Foundations International' was born.
After the trip, I shared with my husband, Andy about the plans. Initially he found them too adventurous and risky. Andy has never been the most 'out of the box' person. His idea of adventure is a form of normality. Bless him! To shock him with where my thoughts were, left him reeling, although he was probably just thinking I was off on another of my 'things'. I often wondered how we got together. I mean I know HOW we got together but what on earth attracted our souls to join? I am a real alternative, 'out of the box', Guardian/anything reading thinker. He is a walking Arsenal almanac who thinks watching 'Have I Got News For You 'on a Friday night is adventurous! Oh we have talked about really doing life together, but the closest we seem to have got to 'doing life' was considering the consequence of feeling potentially homicidal, after a relationship breakdown 5 years into the marriage!

We spoke with people and began building the work of the charity in the UK. The plan was to ask for donations of computers and office equipment through local press, and ship them out to Kenya, ready for the school. The IT centre would receive its income from the students. Those who could pay would pay. Those who could not would have their lessons paid for by the school, who would receive it's money from the fee paying students and hopefully donations from supporters. 'Future Foundations International' would also initiate a community work/regeneration in a slum area. It was all very ambitious.

The first press campaign went very well and we received many computers. Some were unable to be used or were too weighty to ship out. Others were just fine. The garage we had hired for storing was soon full.

I had a friend who is a pastor in Kisumu, Kenya. A Mr.Tobias Abuoro. He was joining the work of 'Future Foundations International' and representing the Kenyan side. I had known Tobias and his wife, Beaty, since my first trip to Kenya. I had no reason to doubt them or their intentions. It was felt necessary for national people to be involved, as the work was due to be in Kenya. These two people had

a passion for helping their community. The last thing I wanted to do was to be seen as a 'big white woman' coming over and screaming for change. All I wanted to do was help and encourage empowerment and education, not to be seen to be doing it.
The more I worked on the projects, the more I wanted to go and actually do the work of them, I think for a few reasons. I wanted to oversee, really be a visible part of the team, and if I am perfectly honest with myself, the escape of over 4000 miles away seemed so tempting. Somewhere new. A new life? Every time I told someone of the forthcoming plans, I could feel my heart beat a little faster through desire. I knew I wanted to go and set up the work myself, however Andy was less than enthusiastic about the whole thing.

With a bizarre twist of circumstance, Andy lost his job. I saw this as a chance. A way we could get out and head on an adventure. With no job, we couldn't afford the mortgages, so the options, as I saw them, were to either find another job, or take some time out, sell the houses and go to Kenya to set up the projects!

Andy was not overly keen, but said he would think about it. We eventually decided to go to Kenya for two weeks, so he could see the place and make a decision based on what he had seen rather than what he did not know.

The trip went fine, and on the last day Andy agreed to come to Kenya for 1 year to live. I was very shocked as I was expecting a negative answer. We left Kenya, and headed back to the UK to make our plans and sell our house. Excitement filled my soul as I planned what was happening.

Of course nearly everybody in our families thought we had really gone mad this time. I mean this wasn't just being strange by painting your room alternative colours, or making your living freelance. This was really bizarre! Who on earth would want to give up their 3 bedroom semi in a leafy suburb of London to live *there*?

The majority of people thought I had pushed Andy into it, because I am the outwardly strong and vocal person in our relationship. Nearly everyone we told came out with the classic ' it's great for you but should you put your children through it'? Through what exactly, I wondered? Through wanting to share life with them instead of just dictate to them how to live? Through wanting to experience a new culture with them? Through wanting to be with them? I was ranging from bemusement to amusement and even anger at the attitudes of some people.

Why do we live in such a sanitised world of our own creation where our children have to conform to be accepted? Where we eat and only think about hunger and poverty on a year-to year basis when it's 'Comic Relief' time. Why do we not want our children to live and experience life, yet expect them to know so much about it? Why did we, as humans do this to ourselves?

Andy and I struggled on despite the accusations, and in some way, they spurned me on. I felt ashamed to know some of the people who were speaking to me, and it was truly a time when I saw my friends, family and associates in their true colours.
Our flights were booked for December 14th. We wanted to arrive a few weeks before the new school term in Kenya started, to enable the children to start to acclimatize to their new environment, before taking on the challenge of a new school.

Time flew by. In what seemed like a blur of days, it was December 13th. We rushed through ticked lists and agendas; there was nothing left to do. The house sale was left in the hands of the agent.

The morning of the 14th passed in absolute chaos. Nerves were edgy, children were excited, parents were crying. I couldn't wait to get to the point in which I am now standing! After what seemed like a very long 'goodbye' with enough parental tears to flood terminal 4, we joined the check in queue. We then walked through to air side. Doing it. Finally living an adventure and being fun! Finally raising our children how we wanted to when we first spoke about our idealism of parenthood and hopefully, finally being ourselves. This time couldn't come quick enough.

Chapter 2

It was decided that we would change some money from Pounds Sterling into Kenyan Shillings at the forex bureau on the air side section of Terminal 4. There was not a great deal of time before the plane was due to be boarded, but a simple exchange transaction would not take long. Andy headed off to find the bureau; I went with the children to find the gate for the aircraft. 10 minutes later Andy still hadn't arrived and I began to wonder where he could have gone? Sure, Terminal 4 is big and busy, but he knew where we were heading, and I could almost see the 'American Express' sign of the 'bureau du change', from where I was standing. The children and I were already at the gate we had arranged to go to. All of them were, by now, over excited, tired and very loud! I could see the other passengers seated in the waiting area by the gate watching us and in a strange burst of telepathy or recognition, I knew what they were thinking to themselves the uplifted eyes revealing wishes or prayers we did not get seated near them!

Life often presents strange encounters when you least expect them. Today I would experience one of them. Out of the blue, a friend I had not seen for 6 years appeared! Great. Doesn't that always happen at the most inopportune moments? At one of the most stressful times of my recent years, I am suddenly confronted with the woman I always thought of as Miss Perfect!

My friend Angela was always right, always pretty, always fun. She had a nice house, a good car, a good job and 2 normal children who probably had never used the moving walkway as a personal play thing, imagining it as an ocean swell, just crying out to be surfed. This was exactly what my little people were doing the moment I saw her.

Apparently Angela had called my house and my Mum had still been there. They chatted for a while before Mother had told us where we were off to that day, and as life would have it, Angela was now working for British Airways and was on shift that night, at T4! She had sought us out after Mum had given her our flight number, and here she was. Perfect Angela. I was happy to see her, but in some way regretted her choice to come and find me! I probably came across as a right mess.

We chatted a little then she had to go and get on with her job. As she left, she turned to face me and said "I envy you, I wish I could just do what you are doing". Then she walked away, leaving me in a state of confusion. Angela envied me? Perfect Angela envied me? Why? Why did she think I was enviable? I pulled the children off the walkway.

Andy finally returned from the money exchange. He joined us at the gate and immediately the children and I knew he was in a very bad mood. He had waited at the desk only to be told they didn't have enough Kenyan shillings to exchange the amount he wanted. So he only had a little money. I couldn't understand why he was so stressed over such a trivial thing. We didn't need money on the aircraft. There was no intention for either of us to buy any of the duty free items. The next place we would actually need cash would be in Kisumu. There was no problem, however Andy made it all into a massive problem and got into a right sulk.

We boarded the plane. The excited children found their chair numbers, having their inevitable arguments over window seats. Soon it was time to take off, and I knew that my children and I were there, on the plane, enjoying the anticipation. I looked at Andy, trying to read something on his current thoughts. He looked distant. For the first time in ages I wondered who he was.

The flight was very smooth, the children well behaved, and we all slept well despite feeling hungry because of the, um, food we were given! There is always a problem on airlines with 'special' diets. Why, if you are offered a 'special 'diet option does it rarely come as invited?

I know we are meant to appreciate the fact that at 35,000 ft altitude we are given something to eat, but why does it always come as inedible or nothing! In my family we are all vegetarian, and on every

flight we have taken together, there is always a missing veggie meal. When we book the flights we ask for the offered meal in a vegetarian option. At check in we re confirm we will be able to eat on the plane. But it is always the same when the time comes for the meals to be dished out! They are either not there, so we are offered beef instead! Or, alternatively, it is completely inedible and way off the range for a normal veggie
child or adult to want to eat. I know many vegetarian children and parents and despite the insistence of the said parents I believe there are very few who actually LIKE the lentil and 3 bean casserole type things they get given. It's more a taste they acquire through years of trying to get enough protein in their body. Why don't airlines offer more fun choices of food? Pizza, for example. I make a mental note to myself to write it on a suggestion card, then fall asleep, failing to write the card.

Oh well, the intention was there and I guess as a consequence of my inaction I will have to suffer more inedible or lost food!

We touched down in Nairobi at 06:30, thinking we would have enough time to connect to our inland flight, bound for Kisumu. However, by the time we got through immigration control and got our luggage it was 07:45. The flight for Kisumu took off at 08:10 and we had to get to the domestic airport. We rushed across the road to get to the other airport, and luckily managed to get on the flight.

It only takes 40 minutes to get to Kisumu from Nairobi. 40 minutes of stunning views as you fly over some of the Rift Valley and cross Lake Victoria. We landed in Kisumu, waited for everyone else to get off the plane, and then left the aircraft. Tobias and a friend of mine, Sandra was waiting for us with a matatu (small bus) to carry our things. I was surprised to find that Beaty was not waiting for us. We had become very close through the past few months, with daily e-mails and regular calls. I felt she was more of a Sister to me than a friend, so her absence was felt, but did not dampen the enjoyment of the moment.

Our house in Kisumu had been arranged by Tobias and Beaty. They had rented it on our behalf with our money. Photos of it had been sent to us, but their photographic skills were not great and we could not really see much of the house in them, except that it was large and white. It was so exciting as we drove through the pot-holed streets to be going somewhere completely new.
We soon arrived, dumped our things, and took in our new surroundings. The children were impressed with the size of the house and soon started settling in to playing in the garden and climbing trees. They squealed with excitement every time they saw a new animal or insect.

Many people come to greet us on the first day, which was tiring but fun. When night fell, and all the new people, except the guard had gone home I sat on the steps that led to the house and breathed. Allowing my breaths to relax my body, I felt calm and happy, soaking in the African night and sounds. Everything was going to be just fine. I could feel it. I was finally free.

The intention had been for my family and I to take a month to settle in before starting any work on the projects. However the day after my arrival I found myself in a slum area of Kisumu called Nyalenda, standing on some wasteland looking at a building which looked like a half finished tin hut!

Tobias had asked me to come and see this. It was a church. I was very shocked. I did not think we had started a church, I had sent some money for the registration of a community centre, but a church was not meant to be here. I asked why, and felt satisfied with the response. So, just got on with it. I couldn't shake the feeling that we were running before we were walking, and did not like the sense of miscommunication, however everybody was so enthusiastic for the projects and church and community work that I didn't feel as if I could stop it or dampen their feelings.

It seemed to me, on my previous trips to Kenya, that lack of motivation was a real key to the poverty level in the city. People had started to feel indifferent towards working. For unskilled labour, the pay was often low for very hard work, and there is a real aid dependency problem.

In the West we have spent so long giving out aid and help, it is now expected, and most seem to just wait for someone else to come along and help them, rather than help themselves. This was an attitude I wanted 'Future Foundations International' to try and combat, so to have a workforce and people around who were so motivated to help, was, I guess, inspiring.

Tobias had started the church with 3 other Pastors. Francis, Patrick, and Jeremiah. I didn't know any of them prior to my arrival in Kenya, which was something I was definitely not happy with. There is a certain element of church ministers who only seem to be in the job for the money. I wanted F.F.I to not have links to any such activity, so I was not amused when I found Pastors already involved in the work. I made my feelings known. Tobias assured me he had known these men for a long time, but still, it wasn't right. I had questions which were trying to get out, and alarm bells ringing, I just couldn't say them or work out exactly what I was thinking.

The work of the church was to help the community in a non-prejudiced way. Accepting all people and helping to regenerate the slum area we were situated in. Some of the money earned from the computer school would assist the church and slowly help build a better community centre. The community work began by starting to cook for the local street people twice a week; we then continued the program by offering studies, services, advice, counselling and support.
Just one month after our arrival, everything seemed to be going really well. The centre was growing, people were motivated, and our reputation of being accepting was throughout Kisumu. It all seemed good, but I still had some nagging questions at the back of my head, I struggled to work them out into what they really were.

As the church grew, so did the need for security in the tin hut. It may have just been a tin hut, but we had some belongings in there and

Kisumu is a violent city, with a massive misconception that wherever white people are, money is. It was decided that we should employ a guard to protect the church. The pastors made it known on the grapevine that we were looking for someone to work with us. There was much interest; we were soon inundated with people asking about the job. However none of them felt right. They all seemed to be a friend of a friend who needed a job, which was not the best option.

One afternoon I was sitting on a mat made of reeds, in the community centre, writing some notes, when I heard someone speak to me in Swahili. 'Here we go' I thought. I was trying to learn Swahili but the difference between what I thought I could say and what I could actually say was huge. I looked up to see 3 Maasai men above me. I knew they were Maasai from their distinctive clothes and hair. They spoke to me again and I managed to say "pole sio Swahili sana" which I think translated as " sorry not Swahili much". Of course it wasn't perfect but it said what they needed to hear!
One of them, who was taller than the rest and seemed to have an air of confidence about him, could speak a little English. He asked me "you job here?" A temptation to be pedantic came over me, which was nothing unusual. I thought better of it, as it would be lost in incomprehension. I said "yes" and asked them to come back later when someone who could speak Swahili was here. They agreed and went. I was left sitting on the mat wondering if they had understood I wanted them to come back later, or thought I had told them to sod off!
I surmised that time would tell and got back to my writing.

They did come back later, I was still alone, and this time I told them to wait. I felt there was something different about these people. I could not work out if it was the alternative nature of their style that was intriguing me or something else. I felt they would be good guards. They certainly looked fierce enough with their obviously died red hair, holes in ears, and big knifes on their sides!
Eventually Tobias and Francis came. They spoke with the Maasai and it turned out that it was one of them, called Benja, who was after a job. He gave a price he wanted, Tobias came to the other side of the

church, where I was seated to ask me about it. I wanted to employ him, he felt right, looked right and the price was good at 5000 ksh per month. So, Benja the Maasai was then employed as a guard at the 'Future Foundations International' community centre in Nyalenda. I was happy with the decision but little did I know how much it would come to affect me, my family and our lives later.

Chapter 3

The children started school at 'Kisumu Junior Academy', not long after our arrival in Kenya. Connor, 10, Xanthe, 8, and Tabitha, 3, settled into African school life very well.

Zachary, 5, struggled. For one month, every time he would arrive at school in the morning, he would cry. I felt awful, he felt awful. Zachary has never been the kind of boy who adjusts to change very well. He likes what he knows and he knows what he likes.

On the other hand, Connor and Tabitha are of the opposite disposition. They seem to thrive on the 'new'. I guess they have the confidence to cope with the changes of life and 'just be'.
Xanthe is Xanthe. She was enjoying the status of being the only Mzungu (white person) in school. Just being a Mzungu in Kenya seems to carry an enormous amount of street credibility, and for Xanthe, who had previously suffered bullying at her English school, this was fantastic.

Mzungu's carrying street cred. In East Africa was a realisation which surprised me. I always thought there would be some sort of distaste for us because of the Colonial times, but there wasn't much of that around. In fact I think there is less racism towards white people in East Africa then there is in the UK!

Zachary eventually settled down, and started to enjoy school life. This came as a relief to all of us. When family back in the UK asked us how the children were doing at school I couldfinally reply with the truth and say "fine" with clarity and honesty in my voice. Instead of the fine we all say, but never mean.

Family back home were all missing us. With every phone call came the question of "when are you coming home?" Nobody seemed to understand that we were here to do something and hopefully would be back when it was done. Often people only hear what they want to hear and only listen to what fits their idea of comfortable, and my life in Kenya was far from comfortable in a Western view. I understood that.

From my own personal point of view, I was absolutely loving Kenya. I felt alive and vibrant. I felt as if I was using myself to the best of my abilities. I felt challenged, needed, and happy. Life had finally come into me in a way that ignited every part of my being. I actually wanted to get up and work. I actually wanted to have problems to solve. I found my true self in serving others. I was actually being Samantha. Not a version of myself that fit in with other people's expectations. I was Sam and for once, I really liked her. I could look in the mirror, know who I was and what I was doing and feel a sense of pride and direction in my life.

Even being struck down with a dose of malaria could do little to dampen my enthusiasm for the work here. I finally felt as if I had a purpose in life.

Often, in life relationships have a 'see saw' effect going on. If you have ever looked or played on a see saw in a playground, you see they can bring such joy to the people riding it. If you look at the person who is being lifted up, the excitement on their face is often tremendous. They are having the feeling of rising and viewing the world from a different place. However, their companion has gone down low, and has to wait for the return of the other person until he can get high again. Life can sometimes be like a see saw. When some happiness comes in one area, another part of your life falls down. When one section falls down, another area rises, and so on.

My marriage is like a see saw. When one of us rides high, the other falls low. I have never understood why. I could never see why we could not rise together and fall together, isn't that what marriage is meant to be?

This time it was me who was up high and really enjoying life. I wanted Andy to be there with me, but all he did was draw further away. He hadn't fit very well into Kenya. Like Zachary, he takes a long time to adjust to change. I was aware of this before leaving

Europe and knew I would have to give him time. However, the longer the time went on, the more I felt he was not in my life.

Almost having excluded himself. I was having the time of my life, and he wasn't even with me in spirit. I was having the adventure we had both wanted. He was having himself. There were huge pains between us that neither of us could explain. All we could do was try and work through them, which is very hard when neither of you know what they really are! In what could be seen as selfish I decided to carry on, enjoy the life, wait for Andy, involve him more in the running of the projects and centre and try to have fun with the children. It seemed the best way forward. I certainly was not going to give up on my happiness and adventure. I had waited the first 27 years of my life to find my 'self '. I was not about to lose her now.

Ever since our arrival in Kenya, Connor had held a fascination for the Maasai people. He would look at them in the city, try to talk to them if he could, and just stare from the car in a kind of reverence. He was so thrilled to know that there were still warriors in this world. For a 10 year old boy, with an large liking for 'Lord Of The Rings' the discovery of real warriors with real swords was a very wonderful one!

I had told Connor about the employment of a Maasai guard at the community centre. Of course, he kept pestering me to go and meet him. I declined as I wanted to know them a bit longer before allowing them some sort of access to my children. I knew nothing about these people, only that they have a fearsome reputation.

The time came when I could not find a reason to delay Connor meeting them. Benja had been working with us for 3 weeks, he seemed a nice guy, so one day while on the way back from school, I stopped at the tin hut, telling Connor and Xanthe they were going to meet a real Maasai! Something which excited them immensely. We walked into the community centre, full of expectation, only to find no one there! The children were a little deflated by this, I told them we could stay a little while and see if he turned up. Which he did, in abundance!

When Benja finally walked through the gap in the metal which acted as a door, he had five other Maasai with him. The look on Connors face was of pure shock mixed with delight. His eyes were wide with a little fear and surprise. His body language was open and ready to know these people. Xanthe just stared for a while and came to stand with me, she was not sure what to say, and she felt safer just watching.

Connor didn't really care if he couldn't speak the language; he went straight into trying to! Something I will forever admire him for. At school all of the children were having Swahili lessons, so a little restricted conversation between Connor and the Maasai was possible. The afternoon passed quickly in immense fun. We had all joined in trying to talk to each other, which had left to a lot of laughing, though over what I am not quite sure! Were we laughing at what was being said or at each other? It didn't really matter, the cement of friendship was being laid with our laughter ,and we all elated with the joy of the sensation of 'new'. Connor asked Benja if he could teach him to be a Maasai. Benja laughed and agreed. It was arranged that Connor would come after school tomorrow for a lesson in how to use bow and arrow. I think he saw himself as some kind of 'Legolas' in red!

As we left, my children seemed satisfied. We had all made some new friends from a new culture, named Benja, Matayo, Cosmos, Laata and Joseph. The Maasai had made some Mzungu friends who taught them that contrary to popular opinion, Mzungus do know how to laugh! My heart ached with happiness and a longing for these kinds of exposures to keep happening to my family and myself.

One of the things I had desired on leaving the UK was to acquire the ability to speak Swahili. I was having some lessons from friends and seemed to be picking it up quite well, well enough to make myself known and hold a basic conversation at least. Andy and I had both Agreed, that when we arrived in Africa, we would learn both the local and national languages. It was important to our sense of belonging to the local community.

On the night of the day Connor and Xanthe first met the Maasai, I lay in bed and for once in my life, and I congratulated myself. I was doing it. Really doing it. Speaking a new language to people of many different cultures and tribes. Having an adventure and enjoying my life. My heart was happy. I then turned over to put my arm around Andy. He was already asleep.

Sadness shot through me taking away the previous happiness. What was happening to us? Why was he not truly with me? Why did he come if he was going to be like this? I felt really pushed away from him. I wanted to share all of these things with him. It had always been both of our plans to really "do" life. To travel and to see new cultures, learn new languages. 10 years previously I can remember us saying that when the children are grown we would do this sort of thing. It had come sooner than that, so where was the problem? Why was he like this? Why was he pushing me away? I closed my eyes and felt the wetness of the tears come. In the moment of my rise on the see saw, he had gone down, and it appeared he had even got off.

The house we were living in during our stay in Kisumu was a large ex colonial house. If we had been the people arranging the accommodation, I do not believe I would have rented such a house. When I stood in the community centre talking to my people, I sometimes felt hypocritical. Here I was teaching people from a slum community that we are all one, and then I would go home to my large walled house with a big compound in the posh part of town. I didn't like it, I felt segregated from my work, which in some psychological way was good for enabling a mental distance between home and work, but I couldn't shake off the thought that by living in such accommodation I was a hypocrite. Until the tenancy agreement expired, I could do precious little about it. With living in such a house, we had to have guards present 24 hours. Being a Mzungu is target enough, but a Mzungu in a large house with a car is almost an invitation to be burgled in Kisumu!

Our day guard was Peter, our night guard, Douglas. Douglas was a man of whom the whole family connected with. We liked him very much and felt he was part of us. Peter however, I struggled with. There didn't seem to be anything really wrong with him, but he just didn't feel right. I would often come home from work and feel as if people had been in my house, when no one was there. One day we all returned to find no one in the compound guarding the house! 10 minutes later Peter strolls down the pot holed path that lead to the compound, he had been to the local kiosk! Great guard!

Situations such as that kept happening. We would come home and often find Peter in the house, just coming out of the house or nowhere near the house! Something had to be done, as our security was of the utmost importance it was decided we would sack him, with 2 months pay in his hand so he would not have a problem to his family while he looked for a new job. This seemed fair to us, and even Peter, when the time came to let him go, was grateful of how we did it. The reason we were so generous to him was that we didn't want repercussion's of his departure to fall on our family, thinking it would be best to keep him as a friend.

Now Peter had gone we had to find a quick replacement. Douglas was given the opportunity of working either in the day or night, he chose the day. So we had to find a suitable night guard. The obvious place to ask was Benja. I was very happy with how he worked at the Church, and thought he might know someone of a similar disposition to himself. He did. The next day, he brought Samwel to meet us. Samwel, also a Maasai had a very likable feel to him. He was taller than Benja, with much more effeminate looks. High cheek bones, beautiful deep set eyes, and the most amazing full lips. If he wasn't a Maasai I would have sworn they had had collagen injections in them.

Samwel had long braided hair, which I admired. I stroked his hair in admiration, got a hand full of red dye! He offered to do my hair like his, I accepted, so he did! I sat on the floor, between the legs of a tall and beautiful Maasai having my hair braided by him. It was certainly the most bizarre interview situation I had ever been involved in!

Needless to say, but I will anyway, Samwel got the job. It wasn't just his hairdressing skills which endeared him to the whole family. It was his whole feel. He was a good man, and that was exactly what we were looking for.

Life at home passed smoothly enough. I wasn't there much in the day, spending my time between the projects and church. At night I would come home, just in time to catch up with Douglas before he finished his shift, then I would spend time with the family. The distance between Andy and I was growing. Every evening, when the children went to bed, he would just turn the play-station on. If I tried to speak to him, he wouldn't want to chat or be very responsive. So I spent time with Samwel, learning Maasai, enjoying the evening air sounds and fantastic electrical storms.

Samwel and I soon became very close. It might sound strange, but he was like my Sister. I had never been blessed with a Sister in my life. I had an older Brother who was awful. I had always wondered what having a Sister would be like. Samwel seemed to fill that gap for me.

We could sit for hours and speak about absolute crap, I could laugh and joke around. When I was sad, I would cry on him. When he was sad, he could cry on me, which was something new for him. Maasai men, especially the ones of the 'Moran' age set are not meant to show emotion like tears. With me, Samwel could show anything.

I even spent one evening teaching him how to put a condom on! Douglas had told me he had seen Samwel at the 'stage'. This was the bus station in Kisumu, which is a notorious hangout for prostitutes. I was a bit shocked at this and asked Samwel, and he denied it of course, but was it likely he would have told me if he was going to them for gratification? It didn't feel right to preach to him, so I thought the best thing I could do was ask him if he was being safe. Samwel wasn't sure what I meant by 'safe', so the next day I went and bought him some condoms!

I gave him the packet in the evening, just after he started work, and he looked confused. He didn't know what they were. Later the same evening, I went outside armed with a banana and a condom, for visual effect. He knew what they were for after that!

The 'Moran' age set in Maasai is a time of life after youth and before man. It is the warrior stage, when the duties of the young men are traditionally to protect their people and cattle.
As the world has changed, there is not so much need for the Morans in their home villages. Cattle raids are now rare, and the whole system of life is changing. The Morans who are surplus to the village often go out to find work to support their families. The families will generally be their parents and younger siblings. It is possible for Morans to marry, but it is frowned upon unless there is a child involved. Morans should marry when they are no longer Morans and the warrior stage of the Maasai age sets has finished. As a rule, when a young boy has been circumcised and healed from the wound, he can go to the 'Manyatta' camp to learn about being a Moran. He then becomes a Moran from around the age of 16-18, until
around 35.

Samwel was 30 years old. He had to come to find work in Kisumu to support his Mother and Brothers. His Father had died a few years previous leaving behind 4 wives and many children! On one of our long discussions we got on to the subject of polygamy. Initially Samwel had said it was a good thing and when he was a Mzee (the stage after Moran) he would marry around the same number of wives his Father had. He could see from my face I was horrified! While I do think in some circumstances, polygamy is justified, it should only be for the restoration of a nation. Not for pleasure. I explained my opinion to Samwel, who was confused by it. I went further into an example, and asked him if he would like to leave as many children Fatherless as his Dad had? He said "No". I then explained that in my opinion you should only have what you can provide for. To bring many children into the world and
not be able to feed or educate them was irresponsible, because if you died, how would they eat? He then agreed with me.

This became one of many conversations between Samwel and I where we educated each other, and learned so much. He was as fascinated about Mzungus as I was about Maasai.

Something was wrong at the church. I still had the questions that I could not find the words for. I still had some nagging doubts that would not go away. The uneasiness kept growing and I began to realise that something was amiss.

Tobias was constantly asking for money for church issues. Most of the financial side of the church had been left to Francis and Tobias. I didn't question much, as everything seemed legitimate. The books were in order and receipts were produced.

One morning, I was sitting in the church with Benja and Matayo. Benja had finished work a few hours previously, but hadn't left the tin hut yet. We were all enjoying each others company when Matayo asked "how much do you pay Benja"? I told him that was between Benja and myself, but Benja said it was OK and told him he gets paid 4000 ksh per month. I thought and remembered, then told him he didn't! He gets 5000 ksh per month, I knew because I paid it! We had a small argument and Benja became very angry. He realised that he was getting 1000 less than he should have been and I was paying 1000 more than he was getting! But where was it going? I thought back to who had negotiated the deal, it was Tobias and Francis. There lay the answer.

I paid Benja the difference of what he had not received, then asked him to not say anything. I wanted to see what happened at the end of the month. How much would I be asked for?

The end of the month came and along with it a demand for 5000 ksh, for the guards at the church. I shared with Beaty what had transpired and asked her to keep quiet, while I found out what was going on. I only revealed what had happened regarding the guards wages, but in truth I had so many questions going through my head.

I knew I had to be discreet and careful if I wanted to find the answers. The discovery of the discrepancy with Benja's wages had made me suspect every financial transaction.
I had my suspicions over Francis, as it was he who had negotiated directly with Benja. Tobias just translated into English for my benefit what Francis had told him, but as far as I could see at the time, he had no actual conversation with Benja.

The day after I told Beaty what was going on, Tobias came to me and said he had some problems with Francis and perhaps we should let him go. I told him "no, not yet. I was aware of something, but let us find out what it is first". He agreed, and then quite by surprise announced he had to go to Mombasa, to sort out something regarding the work of 'Future Foundations International'.
Rather shocked, I asked what it was. To which he replied "I have a friend in immigration there, who has said there is someone trying to get you kicked out of Kenya, I want to go and see what he is saying."

He then proceeded to ask for the fare. I agreed. I was reluctant, but with some quick thinking, agreed to pay up, for my own benefit.

When Tobias was speaking to me, I knew he was lying. Even if he had a contact in immigration with such absurd allegations, there are rules and systems to follow. Not clandestine meetings at a seaside resort. However, a few weeks without Tobias around would allow me to poke my nose in a few more places. By now I was suspicious of everyone.

I shared with Andy what was happening and told him of my plans to search for the truth. He said he would help me, he also reminded me that he had never liked Tobias and had always had suspicions over him. Great. Just what I needed to hear! I also told my friend Sandra, who was volunteering at a local orphanage. Sandra knew both Francis and Tobias, but had recently fallen out with one of them. She agreed to help us in any way she could as long as her name would not be mentioned. The work began. For the first time since our

arrival, it was good to see Andy get his teeth and enthusiasm into something.
Though what he was getting involved in was not quite what either of us wanted to be the spark for his motivation!

We began the work, and it was absolutely awful. Just by scratching the surface we unleashed a whole can of worms. Everywhere we looked, every receipt we chased up, nearly every transaction which had taken place was wrong. EVERYTHING. The whole registration of 'Future Foundations' was fake. The government receipts were counterfeit; the land we had paid a deposit on was not ours or even the persons who had sold it to us, the existence of
'Future Foundations' in Kenya was false. What was going on?

By a process of time and elimination we could work out that it was Tobias who had been responsible for this. Francis may have been involved in some of the activities, but the main culprit was Mr. Abuoro. I felt sick. Absolutely sick to my stomach. This man that I loved, trusted, respected, and served with was a fake? A con man? No, surely this couldn't be true. Could there be some sort of illogical explanation?

Andy and I went to the police with our findings. They decided there was a case against this man and opened a file. The problem now was that he was in Mombasa, and all we could do was wait for his arrival.

On Sunday 6th March 2004 at 8 am I received a call from Tobias, telling me that his coach was nearly pulling into Kisumu. I called the police who arranged to pick him up. Andy and I had to arrange to meet him, with the police parked close by, and then they would arrest him. It all seemed so dramatic and with a heavy heart, I arranged to meet Tobias by Barclays Bank in Kisumu.

When we got there he was already there, and so was the undercover police wagon. He was oblivious to the car he was standing next to and who it contained! Andy and I got out of the Pajero and walked up to greet him. Feeling scared, because I knew what was going to happen next. I hugged him, as that would be my normal way of greeting Tobias.

Then the police opened the door of their vehicle brandishing their guns in his direction. The name Tobias Abuoro was shouted out loud. He responded then they arrested him.

Call me old fashioned if you will, but I always thought after arresting somebody they should be handcuffed and placed with the police then accompanied back to the police station in the police car. Tobias was arrested, then handcuffed, then placed into OUR car, then driven back to the police station! The Kenyan police budget doesn't run into the cost of providing many cars! So there we were, the man accused of defrauding us, handcuffed and flanked by two armed police officers, in our car! We had to drive them to the police station. It is a situation I can laugh at now, but at the time I felt a mixture of angry and sad.

We arrived at the police station, where Tobias was taken to a cell. He would be questioned the following morning. I still had time for church, though I had changed my teaching time to allow for my early morning police action. I decided it would be better if I went to speak to the other pastors about what had just happened instead of waiting for them to hear through the super speed and twisted grapevine which Kisumu has! I also wanted to gauge Francis reaction, as he was still very suspicious in my eyes. The pastors, all of them, were genuinely surprised by the news I brought. Though they had been aware something was not right, and even gave me more evidence in the case against Tobias. Everything was false, even down to the amounts we paid in the church for the hire of the chairs. He not only defrauded me, he defrauded the church and in effect his very own community.

The next day at the police station, Andy and I were witness to the questioning of Tobias Abuoro. As soon as he walked in the room, we knew we were going to need as much proof of everything as possible. Thankfully there was so much concrete evidence. The very first words Tobias came out with were "it's a set up." Everybody in the room just laughed. Eventually Tobias could not deny the truth any longer and admitted his guilt.

At that stage, Beaty turned up in the police room. Much to my surprise, she came to defend Tobias, asking for this to be treated as a church matter and not a criminal one. The police asked me for my decision on that. I refused. Dodgy pastors have been ripping off people for long enough. I had an opportunity to stand up and with actions show that this was not acceptable. I wanted justice. I refused for this to be taken as a church or community centre issue. Tobias was led back to the cell.

I looked at Beaty and suddenly something clicked together in my mind about her. It was her who I had first met, Beaty, who I had befriended. She who knew many things about how 'Future Foundations' was run and how much money was involved. Her who asked for money for things which I later found out did not exist. She who had gone to Nairobi to register the organization with the authorities. It was Beaty also. How did I manage to overlook it? I accused her, she denied it of course, but it was now so obvious. They were in it together. My 'Sister' and her husband had ripped off the organization and my family of a whopping 2 million ksh in total. I felt absolutely ill and very responsible.

Chapter 4

The amazing thing about many churches and pastors in Kenya is that they are full of bullshit! Oh, don't get me wrong, not ALL of them. Though I had noticed since my arrival in Kisumu, how wrong much of the teaching is. The truth is, Christianity is such a simple faith with a simple set of rules. Why do they need to complicate it so very much? The answer to that question lies within the collection plate. Confusion and guilt often lead to people feeling they are not doing enough. If a dodgy pastor can make enough people feel guilty or fill them with strange teachings based on misrepresentation of the Bible, then he can be a very rich man indeed!

'Future Foundations International' has it written into the constitution that transparency and honesty were essential to the core of the organization. It was now time to put that into practise.

I had been advised by one of the Pastors to not say anything to the congregation regarding Tobias, but if somebody asked to know something, then speak to them. I couldn't do that. I didn't want to be seen as the community centre sweeping things under the carpet (not that this place could ever afford a carpet, all we had was mud floors and a few reed mats) I had to be seen to be owning up to the situation and be accountable for what was happening. The Sunday after Tobias was arrested; I stood before the congregation and gave a teaching on trust, broken trust and repairable trust. Somewhere, somehow in its content, I managed to speak about Tobias and offer to answer questions on a personal basis if anybody needed it.

Often, I felt as if I was winging it, which in reality I was! I know I am able to teach, but it didn't make me know all, or even the right things to say. After that Sunday morning teaching I had so much feedback on how well I deal with things and how inspirational it was to hear someone admit things are going wrong sometimes. Which came as a bit of a shock to me as I have never thought of myself as inspirational? I couldn't be inspirational. I was just me. Sam, the realist idealist, the person with no plan, no perfect future, no personal pension, and nothing that could be presented as Western normality in her life! How could that be inspirational?

The cessation of Tobias and Beaty's involvement with 'Future Foundations International' left a big hole in the rota. We simply did not have enough people to cover all the work, studies and services. I didn't want to get anyone else involved or even interested in leadership just yet. That would have to come much later. We had to make do with the people we did have, and luckily we had a good team of volunteers, willing to assist. The religious studies and services were arranged between Francis, Patrick, Jeremiah and myself. It soon became apparent that I would be doing the lion's share of the work. Both Francis and Patrick said they wanted to learn from me while I was there, because one day I would return to the UK. I agreed to run the majority of studies for 2 months. The services were on a fairer rota; the only other meeting was early morning counselling, which nobody seemed eager to head up, quite understandably as it started at 05:00am!

In the absence of anyone else offering to run the early mornings, I did. I have never been a great one for waking up in the mornings, so it was almost comical when I announced to Andy what I would be doing! Much to my surprise, I really enjoyed getting up for the early morning session. During the walk to the centre there would be hardly anyone else around, I had the opportunity to see Nyalenda in a different way and how it came alive in the morning. I was able to chat to some very disturbed and sad people right in their moments of despair, early in the morning, when no one else was open or available, there was a place to come and talk things through.

When nobody came, I would sit and chat to Benja, and try to learn Ki-Maasai. The early Morning Prayer time soon became my most enjoyable part of the day. Not only was I helping people, I was having fun and being educated.

With the increase of my Maasai lessons, I soon had the ability to speak this language. I could hold conversations and was very quickly able to speak more fluently in Ki-Maasai than in Swahili! This gave me an amazing amount of 'brownie points' with the local Maasai people who by this time had come to regard me as a friend to them and their tribe.

One March evening, Benja came to my home. There was a problem with one of the Maasai, a young man named Daudi. He was in Kisumu working at his job of a night guard. A notorious Kisumu gang had beaten him severely. The other Maasai who were with him had ran off to raise some people. Doing a kind of 'round robin' for the others who were working in Kisumu. Some Maasai rushed to where Daudi worked, only to find the gang had gone, leaving Daudi beaten and in a terrible condition. Benja had been in the group. He and had taken Daudi to the local hospital, where the nurses had given him a measly paracetamol and sent him on his way! He had been vomiting all day; Benja had remembered I could do some basic medical procedures, from lessons we had held at the community centre, he decided to come and find me.

We went to the place where Daudi was, and I instantly knew this was beyond me. I had a first aid kit, but there is little a band-aid can do for severe and open head injuries. I knew he had to get to hospital, but not the district one. It had to be the one I attended, where he would actually get care. I called Andy and asked him to come with the car. We took Daudi to the hospital, where he received quick medical attention and had a stay of 5 days, before coming home to convalesce with us at my house.

The crime against Daudi had been a racist one. One of the problems in Kisumu is tribalism. There are many tribes of people in Kenya, and they do not all get on well. I did think, that in this day and age, and with Kenya being the 2nd most developed country in Africa, tribalism would have gone, and to some extent it has. However, in Kisumu it is rife. The Luo are the local tribe of Nyanza, the province where Kisumu lies.

Luo seem particularly proud of their tribe and are quick to claim any misunderstanding as a tribal or racist slight, even if it was not based on such things. The Luo and the Maasai in Kisumu, do not have a particularly good relationship. There were many problems between them, especially among the youths, many of whom believed that the Maasai were taking their jobs. In some way you could see where the young Luo were basing their argument, as many Maasai did come to Kisumu to look for work. There were certainly sparks of discontent on a daily basis between these two tribes.

The Maasai who came to know the church soon discovered they were among friends. When word got around about Daudi being helped in the Mzungu/Rich African's hospital this attracted many more of them to find out more about us. Often they would come to the church in the daytime to sleep, in the night time to speak to Benja, and even to the services. Every morning, from around 6 am, when those who had worked through the night as guards would be finishing their shifts, the church would become a meeting place for the Maasai. It was not unusual to come to the church after dropping the children to school and find as many as 40 Maasai sitting around speaking and singing. It was a wonderful sight and experience, which shocked and eventually pleased many of the local residents.

One Sunday evening, it was my turn to teach the revival service. I wanted to try and combat the tribal feelings that were still coming up so my subject was on racism and tribalism. Rather than teach, I wanted people to acknowledge how they felt. I walked around the church and gave everyone a piece of paper. On it, they were asked to write which tribe they least liked. It was anonymous, and I just collected the bits of paper. I then asked if they really knew why they disliked these people? Was it a tribal thing or had the whole tribe truly done some something to upset them? It sure got people thinking and we really broke some barriers that night. The next week we had more people from more differing tribes.

By the beginning of May we had people from the Kikuyu, Luo, Luyah, Kisii, Maasai and Turkana tribes attending church regularly. We were really doing what we had come to do.

Reaching out in a non prejudiced way to all people. I felt a sense of achievement. It had taken a lot of work, a lot of time, a lot of sacrifice, but we had got to this point and it felt so good!

Connor had, by May, become very good with the bow and arrow. Nearly every day after school he would go to the church to practise. It was normally Benja who would teach him, though often the other Maasai would come and join in the lessons. It was so good watching Connor and these people become friends. The Maasai clothed him in their red clothes before starting. It was the most unlikely of combination of friendship, a young Mzungu boy and a group of Maasai warriors.

Connor was given the Maasai name of ' Matangoti ', and much to his delight, the Morans wanted to move away from working on the bow and arrow into the sword. Joseph asked if they could give him some of his own red enkarash (cloths) to wear, and a sword, but I said " No".

In one of my early morning conversations with Benja, he had explained to me that they have to earn the sword. I didn't want my Son to take an easy option, so I said to Joseph, "let him earn it". The Maasai liked this idea and began talking in 'too fast to comprehend' Ki- Maasai about what he should do. This subject had obviously excited them. The sounds coming from them and the body language was very animated and wonderful to watch.

Eventually Matayo came up with a suggestion. He asked me if Matangoti go to Manyatta with them", I didn't know what he was talking about, I had heard of Manyatta before from Samwel, but I asked him to explain in detail. Matayo said "Manyatta is a camp for Morans (the warriors). All Morans have a Manyatta. It's where we stay. Many of us go outside for work. Once a year we all meet up. The Maasai who have left for work come back and have their celebration, eat meat, and shave their hair off".

I still didn't truly understand what it was, but I wanted it! Seeds of excitement were growing in me. Gosh! A real tribal gathering! How great that would be for Connor. I asked a few more details like where? Why? When? Then I was also asked to come along. Oh my God! I almost screamed in excitement. I was so thrilled. So ecstatic! Connor and I were invited to go to somewhere Mzungus don't get to go, as the guests of the people who belong there. This was the dream coming true!

I told them "yes"! My excitement got the better of me, and I didn't wait to ask Andy until I gave them the answer. I thought he would be so pleased also, which thankfully he was!

For me, as a journalist, the opportunity to go to such a place was amazing. The writing I could do the photo's I could take! The money I could earn and experience I could have. I had never had anything like this come my way. If I did get any work I normally had to chase it, or write it first and just pray it got accepted! My career had always been a constant struggle of finding work, finding stories and finding childcare, and now this had just come my way. I wasn't going to let it go.

Manyatta would take place in Tanzania, in July. We would leave towards the end of June because nobody knows the exact date until it is set by the Maasai Oloibian (spiritual leader and elder).

Preparations for the trip took a long time. It was not really the journey to Manyatta which was hard to work out, it was making sure everything we had set up in Kenya would run smoothly in my absence. I knew the computer side of the project would be O.K. However, I did have some concerns over the projects. The community centre was far more human than the school, more vulnerable, more open to problems. I realised that this was a testing time for me.

The centre is not mine; it belongs to the community of Nyalenda. The situation with Tobias had affected me deeply, and in some ways I think I was involved in the projects too much, in some kind of attempt to stop anything similar happening again. I knew I needed to be able to let go and see how the others worked without me. This was that time.

I also realised I had some big concerns over home, and if anything was going to stop me going it would be this. The situation between Andy and I was getting ever more distant. I knew I was spending a long time at work every day, but instead of joining me, he would stay away. The sense of togetherness had gone from our relationship. Andy did want me to go to Manyatta; he could see the financial potential in doing so. However, he didn't like the Maasai. When Andy was first introduced to our new friends, he did not even try to communicate with them. This led to their relationship getting off on the wrong foot. The thing with Maasai is you simply do not get a second chance. Andy had his and blew it. Since then, the atmosphere between them was tense. He found them primitive and rude. They found him disrespectful. The Maasai thought of me as a kind of Mother figure to them. Andy found this bizarre and became jealous of the time I spent with them. I couldn't get enough of my time with them.

It was not really Andy's fault. He is on a very different wavelength to them and their culture. To them, you prove yourself once. You don't you fail. Andy just likes to take his time to know people first.
I had to spend time at the community centre/church, and I enjoyed spending time with the Maasai. In fact the more intolerable and distant my home situation became, the more I wanted to be with the Maasai, where I felt loved, respected, valued and most of all, happy.

It was not even just me. It was my first born. Connor and Andy have always had a problematic relationship. Connor is a very outspoken and opinionated young boy. In some ways that is our fault. We have raised him to speak out. The thing is, you cannot raise your children to have an opinion and use it, then when they do, decide it is not in order for them to speak out in such a way!

The Maasai had accepted Connor as one of their own, an action which Andy finds bizarre, not in the least because he probably wonders why anyone would want to take Connor as he is, as one of their own. I guess that kind of says it all about the state of their Father - Son relationship at that time.
It is a very difficult situation and very painful for Connor. He has found such acceptance with the Maasai for who he is. Not for who someone wants him to be. I truly understand that and in some way I have encouraged his relationship with the Maasai to become as deep as it has, because of how his relationship with his Dad is. My Son needs affirmation from strong male figures. He is not getting it from his Dad, but it has come from the most unlikely source, and I welcomed it.

The time span between the invitation to Manyatta and the time to go, meant I had the opportunity to learn more Ki-Maasai. Samwel had sent a message to a Maasai named 'Laizer Soitoti 'from his home village of Olbalbal to come to Kisumu and help me. Laizer had been to school and could speak good English, meaning he would be able to teach me more coherently than the others, also, I would be able to learn how to write in Maasai. Laizer arrived in Mid-May. We soon got to the task of study. Though it became easier for me, because I was taken ill for 2 weeks, and had to rest as much as possible. Resting meant bed rest, which meant boring days not doing much. My Maasai friends came round every day and amused me no end. They were such good companions to have around. They were my family.

Chapter 5

June 20th finally came along, and with it the time for the journey to Tanzania. I thought I would be gone for around 1 month to 6 weeks, but was not sure. The days were busy. Connor and I had been given some Maasai cloth as a gift from Benja, so we could wear similar clothes to them. We both had 3 pieces of cloth measuring about 1.5 meters each, blue and red in colour. They were so beautiful and I felt honoured to be given them, though, the way they wear their enkarash was not quite right for me! Adorning yourself in 3 pieces of rectangle material tied on the shoulders was not quite my thing, not least because every time I moved my breasts would be on display! It didn't seem appropriate. Being the only Mzungu in a crowd of Maasai would be attention enough for me, I didn't want to attract anything extra!

I asked local fundi (tailor), Christine, if she could make me a simple long dress from one of the pieces of material, then I would wear the other 2 tied up in the traditional way. This would allow me to keep my dignity while still looking the part. She made it, and it worked. When I tried on the dress and enkarash, I was stunned by my appearance. I didn't look like myself. I didn't even feel like I knew the reflection very well, but I loved what I saw. I was not a traditional Mzungu, I was not a traditional Maasai, I was somewhere in-between. A Maazungu? That's what I was. I spoke the words out loud to the woman in the mirror and let the sound of them sink into my heart. Realisation came, that I had found my true self in that moment. I suddenly knew who I was. Samantha the Maazungu. I delighted in my revelation and felt lifted with it. No wonder I had never felt like I truly fit into Mzungu life, I belonged
to a different tribe!

When other people saw me in my Maasai clothes, they were surprised! It was either a reaction of delight or discontent, but I didn't let either opinion bother me. I felt happy, and that was what mattered. In fact I was so thrilled with the first dress, I asked the fundi to make me more before I left for Tanzania, which she did. By the time I left, I had a few changes of Maasai dresses and materials, which was a relief as I wasn't sure how or when or how often I would be washing my clothes. In fact, I didn't even know how to wash my clothes, but I thought we'd just work on that when the time comes! Surely the Maasai must wash their enkarash somewhere, I would just follow their lead, which was pretty much my whole approach to this trip!

Leaving Kisumu was easy. I guess that might sound harsh. When you are a Mother of 4, society has this perception that every moment you are away from them, you are pining for them. I am either a particularly horrid Mama, or honest enough to admit I do not feel that way. I do love my children very, very much, but I also enjoy missing them. Any relationship can become strained if you see too much of the other part of it and lose yourself in it. I like my children seeing me as a Mum who does life, and not a Mum who is always around just to meet their needs. I do actually have a lot of respect for Mum's who stay at home with their children, but it is not something I could ever do either financially or emotionally. When I am not with my children, I miss them to the point of hurting, and for me that is healthy. It shows me some kind of measure of the depth of my love for them and also helps keep our relationship fresh. I like that.

The last day was a bit tense between Andy and I. We knew this little bit of physical distance could be good for us, but saying 'goodbye' is never easy, even if it is just for 6 weeks! Also, as I was packing, the house became inundated with Maasai. It became the temporary meeting place, which was enough to really annoy Andy. He felt my last day should have been sacred for my family, not them. I agreed with him, but I couldn't evict them, they were my travelling companions and protectors. What could I say? Night fell and it was time to go. I bid the children "goodbye" at our home, and went to the car. My youngest child, Tabitha wanted to come to the bus station with us, so she did. She was a little tearful, but understood Mummy had to go to Tanzania.

I stepped onto the Akamba bus in Kisumu bus terminal with 9 of our Maasai friends, and Connor, who was now refusing to be called

Connor, and only responded to the name Matangoti! We got seated. I was sitting next to Benja. Connor was next to Samwel in the seats behind us. Joseph, Julius, Lucas, Laizer, Laata, Daudi, and Karam, were dotted around the bus. This was due to be the longest road trip I had ever been on! We were taking the bus from Kisumu all the way to Arusha, I had never been a great fan of coach travel, but this one was going to be very different for all of us. There was an air of expectation that just hung over the group. This time was special and we were buzzing with life, hope and a desire to truly live our lives. As we left, Benja grabbed my hand and squeezed it. He was as excited to be bringing a Mzungu home with him as I was to be going home.

The first step of the journey from Kisumu to Nairobi went well. At Nairobi we had to change coaches. In-between the changeover we had the promise of food at the incorrectly named 'fast and friendly' cafe at the bus station. Fast and friendly? I think someone must have been high or deluded when they wrote that sign! Slow and miserable would have been far more apt! Anyway, we got our free food slop which came as part of our tickets. Connor and I went to the loo which costs an extortionate 10 shillings for the privilege of peeing in a dirty toilet!

We then headed out to get our connecting coach. Our next stop would be Namanga, a border between Kenya and Tanzania. It didn't take as long as I thought it would to get there. The time on this coach was just flying by. After Namanga, our next stop was Arusha. Everyone was in such good spirits, I can honestly say
that this journey was my most unlikely enjoyable journey ever.
In Arusha we stopped at a petrol station. I thought we were getting fuel, but it turned out that this was the Akamba stop in Arusha! We all tumbled off, grabbed our bags and went nowhere. There was no place to go. It was a bit confusing, as all of us had expected to be at least in the town centre, and here we were, in a bloody petrol station on a main road, surrounded by bags, looking like the most unlikely combination of travellers ever!

The next stage of the journey was to be long. There were no buses, so between us we all chipped in and decided to hire a 4x4 and driver. Laizer and Benja went into the town to try and find a car, leaving the rest of us sitting on our rucksacks in the petrol station. Fantastic! Welcome to Tanzania Sam!

After around 2 hours, they returned with a driver and land cruiser. Everyone was by now hungry and eager to eat or get on with the journey. We decided to do both. The driver wanted to fuel up and get some supplies, Connor and I used this opportunity to change some currency and get some food before starting on our way.

My first impression of Arusha was one of disappointment. I don't really know why, but in my mind I had built up a mental image of Tanzania as being somewhere very green or very arid. To be confronted with the concrete of a large town, chases away such imaginings and blasts them into reality! Arusha is a busy town, filled with people trying to live and work. Just like any other town in the world. Of course you have the pleasure of being in the shadow of Mount Meru, but aside from that, there really isn't that much exceptional or different about Arusha.

However, as you leave the town and start to head out, I could start to see what the fuss is all about. Open plains of nothing. Little groups of houses dotted here and there and many people wandering, heading somewhere at no particular pace or place. It seemed just wonderful! We drove from Arusha to Karatu, and then stopped for a break to pick up some more supplies. I was told by Laizer that there would be nothing available to eat where we were heading, so it was better for us to stock up a little now. I listened to his advice, but I was also a little apprehensive to take it up. I wanted to be accepted by the Maasai family of Benja, and I wondered if it was appropriate for me to turn up with my own type of foods and supplies? On the other hand, I wondered if it was right for my son and I to risk possible starvation if there really was nothing available. I chose to get the supplies!

The next part of our journey was from Karatu to Kimba, crossing through into the Ngorongoro conservation area. At the gate we had to pay over 160,000 tsh to get through. Laizer told the gatekeeper we should only be 4 days, however we knew we were going to be longer.

I was so shocked at this cost. At this rate, my money would not last the trip. We stayed overnight at Kimba, at a lodge. When the other Maasai who were staying in Kimba saw Connor and I in our Maasai clothes they greeted us so enthusiastically. This was my first night in Maasai-land, with Maasai who did not know me, and they had welcomed Connor and I. Not seeing us as tourists, but as their visitors. There is a big difference between the two, and I only wanted to be considered a visitor.

The night was as comfortable as could be expected in a double room, containing 2 single beds and 8 people! Julius and Karam were close to their boma (home) in Kimba, and decided to walk home from the lodge. So, there we were, 8 people, 2 beds, and a lot of laughter. It was so funny. We all stank and were sweaty from the travelling, the only bathroom was outside and contained only a bucket of cold water, the toilet was a smelly hole in the ground you had to squat over! The Maasai were quite used to sleeping all squashed up, but we Mzungus were shocked and amused by the novelty of it!

It was fortunate that we had all been tired out from the travelling, because despite the accommodation, none of us had any trouble in sleeping. I awoke early in the morning, and found Benja's arm draped over mine and Samwel's leg over mine. If I was not with these guys, I would have been offended. But I was with them, and it was fine. I knew nothing was meant by it. These people were my friends. The best friends I have ever had in my life. I lay in the bed, listening to their breathing and enjoying the still of the moment, though it didn't last for long because Connor woke up with his usual declaration of "I'm hungry".

Connor is always hungry. Fact. Connor is extremely hungry in the morning. Bigger fact. I decided we should try to get washed and dressed before the Maasai woke up, and find something to eat. I manoeuvred my way out of the position I was sharing with Benja and Samwel, found our clothes and wash things and left the bedroom to go to the bathroom. The morning air hit us like a slap in the face! It was so cold! I think I had been expecting a warm temperature - but this was freezing and wet! My wash was going to be a very short one!

Connor and I found food in the kitchen of the lodge. One by one the rest of the Maasai ventured out of the bedroom and into the food room. Eventually we had all eaten and were ready to continue the journey.

I was extremely excited today, as I was going to get my first ever real look at the Serengeti. Sure I had seen it on TV, but this was reality, and there is no match for real time viewing. The plan of action was that we would drive across the Serengeti, through the Ngorongoro conservation area dropping off people as we went past their relevant bomas. (homesteads).

The temperature had risen and visibility was good. This morning, when I first woke, Kimba had been coated in a sea of mist, but now we could see for miles and miles. The drive was fantastic. There was so much to see in a land of nothing! It was thrilling and exhilarating, and I was part of it. We saw so many animals, had such good company, met great people at the bomas, and shared immense fun. Connor spent a lot of the journey with his head out of the roof of the land cruiser. Though he had to occasionally come in, thanks to the dust of the plains. He had pleasures in his eyes that I had never seen before, he was alive with his view, so was I. To share this with my son was just amazing and an absolute blessing to my soul. By the time afternoon came, we had been to all of the bomas we were meant to go to. The last place to go was our destination. Piaya. Piaya was the home village of Benja. It was remote. A good 6 hours drive from Kimba.

Not everybody had got out at their Bomas, they had greeted relatives and friends, but decided to journey on with us. I guess we were either good company, or they were so amused by the Mzungu going to stay in the mud hut, they thought they'd come for the laugh!

Piaya sits on top of a hill. It is a village in a wilderness with no electricity and no water. As we approached it I could feel the pull of destiny. I am never sure what that truly means. It is easy to feel destiny and make crazy life changing decisions based on that emotion. Or on the other hand it is easy to feel the pull of destiny and ignore it for fear of life changing situations! I wasn't sure why or perhaps I didn't really want to think on it at that time, but it was there, magnetizing me as we entered into the steep final climb of our journey to Piaya.

The car erupted with the noise of the Maasai signing a homecoming song. It sounded absolutely great, and I even knew what to sing! I looked at Connor to see he was not joining in. He had gone pale and quiet. I didn't need to ask him to know what he was feeling, not because of any great telepathic link, more like recognition of emotion! He was nervous. The nerves he had were ripping through my stomach also. Here we were, Mzungu in a real Maasai place. A place that tourists are not normally allowed to stay, hundreds of miles from anything we could even consider normal. What were we doing? I knew his questions, they mirrored mine. The car stopped.

The Maasai piled out and were greeted by their friends and family. Benja disappeared! I wasn't sure what to do. Should I get out?

Would a woman be allowed to be so assertive in Maasai culture? Could a woman go and introduce herself? I realised that whatever I thought I knew about what I was doing, I should have known more! So I sat there. Connor did also, it was like we both had superglue stuck to our bums!

Benja returned, and asked us to get out of the car. We did. Connor and I were then led to the chiefs office, which was basically a mud hut with a wooden door.

In Maasai culture, all visitors must be verified, allowed and welcomed by the chief. He addressed us in Swahili. Fast Swahili. Great! Here I was, wanting to make a good impression with the chiefs of the village, so they could allow us to stay a while, and I couldn't even understand what he was saying! Aaaaagh! I asked him to speak a little slower, which seemed to make him angry.

Laizer, who was fluent in English, Maasai and Swahili, then, stepped in to translate for me.

The meeting at the chiefs office took ages. I felt like Connor and I were cattle on display. New elders and leaders of different Maasai families kept coming to see us and give their opinion as to whether we could stay or not. Some agreed some didn't. It was awful. If the big chief man said "no" then we would have to leave. Simple as that. All the journey and expectations would have been for nothing. I prayed.

Finally we got an answer. We could stay! I was so excited. But, there was a big downside. When Laizer came back with the translated report, he told me that the chiefs of the village had only said we could stay for 4 days; because that was the duration the conservation area authority had been paid for. I felt sick at the thought of it, but was too excited to be here, to let it get to me. Whatever will be, will be, I said. Then picked up my bags to follow Benja towards his boma.

After the long journey, I was grateful of the opportunity to walk, even if it was up a big hill, laden with bags! It was a wonderful view, over the Piaya hills and beyond. I felt truly blessed to see such things.

The boma of Pilaso was nigh. Pilaso is Benja's Mum. His Dad's name was Oloingolalle, but he was dead, so the homestead becomes known by the Mother's name. We had arrived at our mud huts. Inside the Engang there were 6 huts and one enclosure for sheep/goats.

My first reaction on seeing the mud huts up close was of surprise at how small they were! I wasn't sure if I and my hips were going to fit in the door! But I did. We did. And we soon began to settle down.

Sadly, Pilaso was not home. We had not been able to announce our arrival. Piaya is out of signal for mobile phones, which meant nobody had a clue we were coming. Pilaso had left the village for a week or so to go and visit a relative. Benja was disappointed at this as it meant Connor and I were unwelcomed by the boma owner, which was not a good thing in this culture.

We did, however get a wonderful welcome from another elder of the boma. An old man, of whom I never found out his real name.

When Connor and I first met him, we thought he didn't like us. He had come to his home boma to find us Mzungus there. He started muttering in what came across as an angry tone, it was a bit scary. He then spat on his hand, lifted his head in pure Whitney Houston from the bodyguard style, and said in perfect English "Take My Hand". Oh my God!

I didn't know what to do. If I took his hand I got my own palm covered with his gob. If I didn't accept it, I risked offending him. I took his hand, and this small act seemed to earn me acceptance from the rest of the resident Maasai there.

From that day, until this, this man is known as "Take my Hand", he has no other name from me!

The next few days passed in a state of bliss. In the day I would spend time exploring, writing, reading or playing with the young Maasai children. In the evening we would eat and then sing songs before going to sleep on the simple but effective bed. I liked life in Piaya very much, but I was only able to spend a small bit of time there, thanks to the conservation authority.

'Take my Hand' and I got on great. He would seek me out just to spit on me! I knew that this was a blessing from him to me, but it was bloody gross! The younger Maasai, especially those who had travelled outside of the village for work, and come into contact with other cultures, knew that spitting was not the same in Maasai as it was in other tribes. I mean, if I walked down Oxford Street gobbing at people, I'd probably get arrested! It was so funny, and I must admit, I did start coming into the boma a different way, so I didn't walk past his hut! Just in case.

I loved our stay in Piaya. I met some fantastic people and truly saw another way of living life. Sadly, it was soon time to leave. I vowed to come back. Next time, I hoped it would be for much longer. On the morning of our departure we had to arrange for the local transport to take us back out of the conservation area.
Now, the only two types of local transport in Piaya are a donkey or a bright blue Bedford CF truck! The donkey might be good, but she was never going to make it all the way across the Serengeti, so we had to see if the truck driver would give us a lift. Luckily he agreed, for a price of course!

The truck was ready people were coming to say "Goodbye" the chiefs came to bid me farewell, but I felt a bit miffed at them! Surely they could have spoken to the authority and got me in for longer? Laizer had told me they would only speak to them if I paid them a sum of 5 million shillings! A sum I didn't have and even if I did, wouldn't pay.

The back of the truck had filled up with passengers all getting a free lift at my expense. I didn't really mind, it seemed like good environmental and financial sense to me, and if I had to get somewhere one day, and had little money, I hoped there would be a truck available.

Chapter 6

Journeying from Piaya in a bright blue Bedford CF was no joke, yet for something that was no joke it was certainly one of the funniest things I have ever done! Connor and I were sitting in the front cab with the driver, sitting next to us was Benja. Approximately 20 Maasai were in the back. It was so bumpy and I did have a concern over the people seated there. If I was sitting on a seat which allegedly had springs, how on earth must they be feeling? Standing in the back of a truck with nothing to grab on to, and nowhere to sit their bums.

The driver seemed an amiable kind of guy. He didn't speak much English, but he did speak Maasai quite slowly, so I was able to understand most of the conversation. I didn't actually make it known I knew what was being said. Benja seems to assume I do not know what he is saying to other Maasai, as they do speak very fast to each other, and often come out with the most bizarre sayings, which have been passed down for generations through their tribe, and seem to make no sense in translation. However, the longer I spend time with them, the more I understand, especially if the pace of conversation is slowed down.

Most of what was being said in the front of the truck was the kind of 'how are you and how are your cows?' topic, which seems to be the main underlay of every conversation Maasai have. Though there were some interesting bits to be heard, especially when the driver asked what was the relationship between Benja and I. To which he replied she is going to be my wife! My what? Oh my God!

I squeezed his hand quite painfully, I wanted to do something to let him know that I knew what he had just said. He realised and just gave me this mischievous smile. I wouldn't question him with the driver there, so I let it go, ready to be brought up and dispelled when the time was right.

As we journeyed back across the Serengeti, the landscape transfixed me once more. In my mind, the words of Benja were running through. I knew he had meant them in jest, I thought he had said them either as a joke or perhaps to shock the driver, but still, I kept going over them. Benja and I had always been very firm friends, was I getting the wrong end of the stick? Did he see more in the friendship than there was? I have had many friendships destroyed by the fact that the male they were with saw me as something other than a friend.

In fact, I am incredibly naïve at friendships with men. I always assume they are after a good companionship where we can mutually understand and be friends with the opposite gender. To date it has never worked, and often ended in tears.

The words of Benja had re awoken everything I had first felt towards him and suppressed within me. Sure, I was probably reading more into it than there was, but that was me. Think things through and analyze words until they do actually mean something. Off the cuff comments have never been of my understanding!

I loved Benja, as a friend. However I also had to admit to myself that there was a strong attraction to him within me. I felt it during the time we spent together at the church. The first occasion I met him, I was in awe. It wasn't an awe that knocks you off your feet from being stunningly attractive, because he isn't. It was more of an admiration, a desire to want to know that person very well. To find out what it is that makes you and they tick. Though if I had a sound track to my life, the moment I met Benja would be best portrayed with the song "Never Tear Us Apart". Not because we were together, but there's a wonderful lyric that goes "I was standing, you were there, and 2 worlds collided". Because ours did.

In my life, Benja had to fit into the friendship category, as I was married, he was Maasai and I was Mzungu. Three big factors that would put off anyone considering starting a relationship; so friendship it would have to be. That was enough for me.

I would rather have him as a friend than as a friend than a nothing in my life. I let my thoughts drift here and there. Fantasising realising, idealising, and then sleeping. Though quite how one can manage to sleep in the truck which was hammering across the Serengeti is a mystery!

Our destination for tonight was to be another Maasai boma in a place called Olduvai. Olduvai, Kanjiro. A 'Cultural Boma'. This is where Maasai live there normal - ish lives, and tour companies bring round tourists to show them how the tribe are living and what they do.

In some ways it works, as the Maasai have a steady stream of people who are eager and willing to buy their handcrafts and beadwork. On the downside though, they are on display.

Every 4x4 which turns up expect to have some dancing and singing to watch, and while dancing and singing is a normal part of the Maasai everyday life, it doesn't just happen at anytime of day! In a normal boma you wouldn't find an Nkitok (wife) busy feeding her baby then suddenly passing the child to a Koko (Grandmother) as she feels like a dance! In Kanjiro you do, but not because the dance is felt like, it is more needed to help generate an income for these people.

The marketing of the Maasai is huge. In all Maasai land, from Kenya to Tanzania, they are marketed and sold as a tourist attraction. Yet the sad thing is they do not receive anything like the amount of income that they help to bring in to their relevant countries. Of course the influx of tourists mean they have the opportunity to sell their work, but in relation to what the tourists bring to the rest of the tourism industry, it is a very small percentage which
actually feeds back into the Maasai people.

We had stopped at Kanjiro on our journey to Piaya. I was happy to go back there, and see some of the people I had met once more. On arrival, I met Benja's Grandmother, who invited us to stay in her hut for the night.

The hut was much the same as the other Maasai homes I had stayed in at Piaya, the only difference was that now I knew what to expect, and didn't let the size or condition of the hut bother me one bit! Benja and Samwel went missing not long after we arrived at Olduvai, leaving Connor and I to chat with people. I was in desperate need of a hair wash, so went outside into the wilderness that surrounds the boma armed with my bottle of mineral water and shampoo!
Pouring the water over my upside down head was a wonderful cleansing sensation; the small things in life are definitely the best. Being able to wash my hair was such a sensation to me that day. I had felt filthy and dirty from the travelling and dust, but to be able to release that dirt and feel half human again was so good! Much to my surprise when I lifted my head to the correct position again, I had attracted a small crowd of Maasai! They were fascinated with how Europeans wash their strange hair. It was quite surreal. There I was, nothing but a boma in sight, with shampoo foam all over me, being watched by people. So funny.

After my spectator filled hair-wash I went back into the boma, and into Koko Benja's hut. A woman entered the hut not long after me and introduced herself as Benja's Sister. I was pleased to meet some more of his family. Here, in Kanjiro I had already met more people related to Benja than in his home village. We tried to chat a little, then she pointed to her wrist. On it was a piece of metal wrapped round and round. She asked in Swahili if I would like one. She said it would be a gift, so I said "yes", feeling quite pleased with myself that I had been given a gift. So, I sat down, she got the metal, and started wrapping it around my arm, slowly and precisely, telling me this kind of Maasai adornment is called a 'mambo'.

When my mambo was finished, I was thrilled with it. I thanked her profusely for my 'gift' she then held out her hand and asked for 20,000 shillings! A gift? That's not a gift! I was surprised, but not wishing to offend her, I just told her to speak to Benja when he came back, and that I had no money. Great! So, my gift was actually my purchase? It was very funny, but I also let a doubt creep into my mind. What was it these people were after? Did they really like me? Was I really a visitor to them? Or, did they view me much the same as they view other white people. An opportunity to earn money? I had no answer. Benja returned a few hours later, his Sister found him as soon as he arrived. There was a small argument, he then paid her only 5000 tsh! I guess I was the opportunity to earn money for her. I could understand it, but in some way it left me feeling a bit sad and even sick in my stomach. Was my perception wrong?

In the evening time, after the dancing and singing, Connor and I returned to the hut of Koko. We were exhausted and hungry. In great need of rest and food. There had not been any food offered here, not even the little rice portions, like we had been given at Piaya. The hospitality of Olduvai was fake. Oh they knew how to welcome visitors. It was their job, but the usual Maasai hospitality has been warped and corrupted by the expected money which visitors should bring.

I felt sad once more, and for the first time since leaving Kisumu, let my mind drift back to the people I am from and with. I wondered how Andy was doing. Why did I only want to be with him when I was not with him? Why when I was with my husband did I long to escape him? I cried. What were the other children up to? I cried. The tiredness and emotions of the day consumed me.

I was still awake when Benja came back into the hut, and I still had tears streaming down my face. Connor was asleep. I pretended to be asleep. Benja laid down next to me and asked if I was awake. I didn't answer for fear of him knowing I was crying. I wanted to tell him all of my fears and feelings at that point. I wanted some comfort for the pain I was feeling, but I couldn't bring myself to, so I just lay there, on my side with my back to him and my front facing Connor. He put his arms over me and pulled himself closer to me. I could feel his breath on my neck, which was comforting. His breathing slowed and became deeper. So did mine. We were drifting off to sleep together, Just before he went to sleep, Benja said in a whisper 'nakupenda . I love you. I cried silent tears of recognition. My heart was elated, I knew I was matching and accepting his love.

My conscience felt as if I was already betraying a deeply held moral, just by accepting these feelings. With an excited heart and a tired mind, I fell to sleep.

That night, we all slept very well. So well, that we woke up a bit late. Today we were due to leave Kanjiro and head for the town of Karatu. The only way we could do this was by the bus, of which there was 1 due. However, no-one knew at what time it was meant to be coming! Someone had suggested it could be there at 10 a.m. another had said at 4p.m. If we didn't get this bus, we would have to stay another night in Olduvai, which was not something I wanted to do.

A group of 10 of us set off to get to the bus stop. Only 7 were actually going to Karatu, this was Connor, I, Samwel, Benja, Laizer, Bobby and Cushion head! Bobby was not Bobby's real name, it was a name Connor had given to him. Cushion head had the same pleasure, as Connor named him according to the mass of hair which sat on his head resembling a cushion!

The walk to the bus stop was breathtaking. We were walking on the Serengeti floor. The actual plain. Not hidden away in a car, it was under our feet. At one point, giraffes were almost joining us on the trek. I looked to my left and saw some giraffe heads peering out of a bush. It was simply amazing. I have always had such a special affection for giraffes, and have forever been fascinated by them. To spend my morning walking with some of them and other animals filled my heart and soul to the point of bursting with happiness.

Connor walked ahead of me with Samwel. Laizer and I trailed behind the rest of the whole group, who were marching ahead with familiarity of surroundings forcing a complacency to come over them. I looked to the rest of the people and saw Benja turn to look for our location. As he looked, I smiled. Not that he would see it being so far ahead of me. I was smiling. For the first time in my life I felt completely happy and at peace with who I was and what I was doing. For the first time in my life I knew who I was. The plains felt like a roofless home and my companions felt like a family should.

I thought of my biological family. I had never felt so close to them as I did to the Maasai. I have never felt as if I belonged to them. I used to be convinced I was adopted, because of the sense of difference I felt from them. It was as if God had given me a 2nd family to heal my past hurts.

When I was 5 years old I had been abused by a family member, something I had never managed to tell my parents. I had told Andy about it, but I could never tell them, the distance was always too great and I feared they would never believe me. Then time went on, and somehow these things never got said. You learn to survive, live and shut up.

The morning I was in the Serengeti, I realised I had learned how to survive, live and start to recover. I was finally home and the relief was immense.

After trekking for 7 km's we came to the, erm, bus stop! It was actually a junction of the tourist road which thousands see the Serengeti from every year. Overlooking us was a mountain. Behind us were plains. Around us were animals hiding and the occasional tour car driving by. When the tour cars saw us Mzungus sitting on the side of the road with the Maasai, they stared and gawped out of the windows! At first it was funny, and then it became tiring. I began to realise what it must be like for the Maasai.

They are, without doubt, one of the most recognisable tribes in the world. The image of them is identifiable to most in Europe and America, in fact, many of the tourists come to Africa with the purpose of seeing them in their home lands of Kenya and Tanzania. But being stared at is no fun. All eyes on you to appease a tourist criteria is almost derogatory. I can understand westerners wanting to see these people, but to stare with such aggression I cannot. Westerners trampling through the cultural bomas and delighting in the Maasai has truly changed the Maasai people, and the directions they are taking.

Their whole world is now different and even beginning to fit the criteria set as standard by government offices. The true Maasai people are diminishing slowly into the rest of the world. And all the people could do was stare.

The bus came at about mid-day. The sun was at the point of getting very hot, climbing aboard the degenerated old wreck of a bus that was attempting to go on these roads, was actually a welcome relief! Of course I had doubts over whether we would make it to our destination or not, but hey, what other choice was there? It was this or nothing!

Laizer and Benja had decided that the best place for us to go would be Karatu. Karatu was a town with a phone signal, it was also close enough for us to get in and out of the conservation area when we could. This area seemed like a good idea, so Karatu it was. We had passed through here on the way to Piaya, I remembered seeing a hotel which offered internet facilities. At least I could finally communicate with my husband and children!

There is a small house which is rented by some Maasai who work in Karatu, we would be allowed to stay there a few nights while we sorted out where we would stay for the rest of the trip. There was nothing in the house, just a few mattresses inside, and some blankets hung to trees drying in the wind outside. I was struck by its simplicity and functionality. All it did was provide shelter and warmth. Nothing more - nothing less. By comparison, if you went into most people homes in the U.K. you would be confronted by a barrage of shit that we convince ourselves we need! When we don't. We only need to live. We need to survive. That's all. The rest of life is a comfort or a want.

Having the right shade of paint will not make you live any longer or shorter. Wearing the right kind of clothes will not add extra days to your life. If our life ends with nothing, then why on earth do we spend our lives accumulating stuff we do not need and even living lives that only carry value in terms of what material somebody has accumulated?

Standing inside the bare house in Karatu, surrounded by the 4 empty walls, western life no longer made any sense to me.

Connor and I got on well at the house in Karatu. We were able to stay as long as we wanted there, which came as a relief, because my money was running low. All of the gate fees and early trip out of Piaya had left a massive hole in my purse. I had to ask Andy to send me some money via Western Union, which thankfully he did!

I did have to get back into Ngorongoro and hopefully to Piaya, so I could get enough material for a story and some photos. As much as I was enjoying my trip here, I had to keep grounding myself with the reality that I came here to do a job! I wrote to the Ngorongoro Conservation Area Authority. I even tried to send messages to the chiefs of Piaya via Laizer, who said he knew them very well, and that they had even been to Karatu while we were there. I asked him to arrange a meeting, which he assured me he would. It turned out that all I could do was wait for the relevant people to get back to me.

It was not time spent in vain, as I quickly started to make friends and acquaintances in the town. I even began teaching as a guest speaker at a local church, which was great, though quite what they made of a liberal teacher who is actually a Pagan I would never know!
Living in the Maasai house was a real education for me. We had visitors all the time, my language skills were improving, and also my understanding of the social dynamics of the Maasai tribe.

Benja and I had never spoken about the night in Olduvai. I had also never mentioned that I had understood what he had told the truck driver on the route from Piaya to Olduvai. We seemed to just know the depth of each others feelings and in some way acknowledge that there was a boundary there that no one should cross. The more I got to know him, the closer I felt to him. I didn't need to get physical with him, though it could have easily happened at any point. I just needed to feel close to him, to know he was there. Sure, I fantasized about him, but those thoughts and daydreams were kept between me and my notebook! As a writer, I have always found a massive relief from writing.

Exploring a physical relationship in my notes was enough for me at that point, and wouldn't do anyone any harm.

One day, Benja had gone on one of his disappearing trips, leaving Connor and I with Samwel and Laizer. Rather unexpectedly, I became sick. Without warning, I developed a fever and very intense stomach pains. I did have an ongoing untreated problem, however this pain was far different. I started vomiting and feeling very dizzy. I began to think I had Malaria again. I had contracted it in Kenya and the symptoms I was feeling were very similar. It was just awful, and was made worse by the fact that at the time I fell sick, Benja's Mum turned up for a visit! I had never met Pilaso before, as she had not been in when we went to Piaya, and my worst possible time for meeting her would have been at the time I did. Benja arrived back at the house in Karatu with his Mum. I could have cried! I felt half dead, and almost wished there was a stone for me to crawl under and go! How could I impress this respected Maasai woman when I was feeling so low and sick? I needn't have even thought about it. When Benja and Pilaso saw how sick I was, they immediately got me to a Dr. who diagnosed Malaria, gave me treatment, and sent me home to rest. This rest was the most fun I had ever had. Sharing it with Pilaso who was not your average 60 year old, was great. She was funny, intelligent and soon became a firm friend in my heart. She asked me to come to Piaya. I told her I would love to, and then relayed the trouble we had experienced at the hands of the chiefs and the NCAA. She became very angry and told me she was going to sort it out. I wondered what she could do, but thanked her for her assistance. I was grateful of anything she could do, but I did doubt it would be much.

I had little money left and time was getting on. I was 3 weeks into the trip, half way through, and nothing had gone to plan. Nobody could tell us exactly when Manyatta would be, and I was getting anxious to get some material for my writing. All my notebooks contained were my desires and fantastical thoughts, nothing solid, good, or worth a sale. We had to go back in and get some material, even if it did mean paying the gate fee again.

Chapter 7

My money situation was getting worse. I had to ask Andy for extra money, which considering the fact I knew he was short in Kenya, was very hard to do. Things were not going to plan at all here, and if I didn't get the work done, I wouldn't earn any more money in the foreseeable future.

Andy transferred some more money through Western Union. The office in Karatu was closed, also the one in Ngorongoro. Though to go there wouldn't make good financial sense, as I would have to cross the gate and pay the fee in order to get the money, which would probably only just cover the gate fee, the only other place I could go to was Arusha. A three hours drive just to get a money transfer! I was not expecting to stay long, so I left Connor with Samwel, Laizer, Bobby and Cushionhead. Benja, I went to Arusha with promises of returning that night. However, when we got there, the Western Union was closed, so we had to stay overnight and wait for it to open the next morning.

We found a hotel which is used mainly by Maasai. It was called ' Katimakatano' and offered a few lodging rooms behind it's dubious restaurant. The accommodation was very basic, the noise level big, but the price fantastic, so we stayed!

In the evening, I became hungry and told Benja I was going out to get some food. Benja was a Moran, which in Maasai culture means he shouldn't ever eat alone, but should also not eat in front of a young woman. As I was a Mzungu and married, I didn't think there was a problem, however here, he didn't want to get grief from the other Maasai who did not know us or the history of our friendship. I chose to go to a different hotel to get my beans and rice.

One of the most bizarre things about my acceptance into the Maasai tribe which has endeared me to them further is the level of tolerance we have of each other. What I mean by this is, I am a sworn Vegetarian! I haven't eaten meat since I was 11 years old and the Maasai are big meat eaters. In fact, they live on milk and meat! Many people in Kisumu thought they would force me into meat, but the Maasai is a tribe who accept you as you are and if you show them and their way respect, they will try to understand you and your way. Being a lacto ovo vegetarian did give me some kudos though, as I was able to drink milk and be with them at their times of togetherness and sharing. If I had been back into my Veganism days, which do occasionally creep into my life, I think I would have struggled a lot more! My food option in most of the places we stayed was either rice, ugali, or rice and beans. I had become used to the taste of nothing which came with such food, so was just grateful of the opportunity to eat something!

I enjoyed my rice and beans, then headed back to Katimakatano. When I walked through the door, I had a shock. Sitting at a table with Benja were the chiefs of Piaya village! There was an empty plate in the centre of them, which I could see from the juices still remaining, had contained meat of some kind. It was a big surprise to see them, and I wasn't really sure how I should play the situation. Should I walk up and greet them or should I wait to be called over by them?

Despite what my personal opinion of them was, these people were the chiefs of Benja's home village, and I would hate to be the cause of a problem to his family by being rude to them. Benja noticed me not long after I walked through the door. Of course he would, because whenever I walked through an entrance I had the effect of drawing most people's attention to me. It was not because of my stunning looks or anything like that, it was more due to the fact here I was, a Mzungu, in a non Mzungu part of town, wearing Maasai clothes and speaking to Maasai people in Ki-Maasai.

I was not your usual kind of guest in Tanzania, that much was for sure! I walked up to the table, greeted everybody. The executive chair of Piaya then asked me to sit down. Which I did. He asked me why I left Piaya? Why was he asking me that? He knew why I left Piaya, and he and his ' team' were responsible for my departure with their demands of 5 million shillings before they could assist me with the conservation area authority. I felt quite angry, but tried to hide my feelings and told them that I could not afford their assistance, and only had 4 days where I could officially stay within the conservation area, so despite the fact that I did not want to leave Piaya, I had to. The chief looked at me, and said in slow Maasai that the village of Piaya was not in the conservation area. It was just over the boundary line! I gasped. He went on to say that they had never made any such financial demands and was very disappointed when I left. They also told me that Pilaso had been to them complaining about their alleged treatment of me, this was what had alerted them to the problem. I was dumbfounded. I had been in the office with them and Laizer when they had said these things. Why were they now saying it was not true? I looked at them for signs of lying or bad body language, there was none. I asked them if this was true, they repeated again that it was. Then something finally clicked in my mind; Laizer. The officers of Piaya had not told me that there was a problem. They had told Laizer, who being the only Maasai in the group to speak English, had translated everything that had been said in that office for me.

Could it be that he had lied and translated what he wanted to say? But why would he do that? Why would he want to leave Piaya? I told Benja and the chiefs what I was thinking. The chiefs then told me that Laizer had said many things about me to them, including a report that I was going to be his wife very soon! We carried on talking, sharing the things that Laizer has said to both sets of people over the past month. It turned out that nearly everything was untrue. It was a time of revelation, which was awful, but also managed to have a positive effect. As a result of this evening and the conservation with the chiefs, I was officially welcomed to Piaya at any time I wanted to go there. I was officially accepted into the Maasai village of Piaya.

The chiefs left Katimakatano. Benja and I went to our room. There were 2 beds available, but we both climbed into the 1 bed and talked about what had transpired. This was the first time Benja and I had been alone for more than a few minutes since our arrival in Tanzania. There was always Connor or other Maasai around, normally sleeping in close proximity to us. In some ways, it was good for us to have

others around, because the temptation to actually do something physical relating to the love we felt was hanging over us like an expectant cloud ready to burst. The air was so tight and heady we both knew what we wanted. His hands started to touch me, and I wanted to respond so much, but I couldn't. I said 'no '. He tried again, and again I refused. I got out of that bed and into the other one, where I held his hand across the gap. Tears came to me and with a heavy heart I spoke to him. I told him I loved
him so much, but right now I cannot do anything. I told him I adored him, but I was married and couldn't cheat on Andy. I had cheated on Andy already in this marriage, with a one night mistake. It still haunted me now that I had done this, it was 5 years ago, but still there, and I couldn't help noticing how the situation between Andy and I was the same. We had grown so very apart, just like when that happened. I inwardly applauded myself for my resolve this time. I truly did learn my lesson. Benja took my hand, which snapped me out of my thoughts.

He stared at me, then said he understood. I knew it was not what either of us wanted, my heart was in love with him, my body wanted him, but somehow I managed to grab on to my morality and not give in.

Benja looked at me, breathed deep, and spoke to me in Swahili. He said he wanted to tell me what he was feeling and what he wanted from me. He told me there was no other woman he wanted to be with, that he wanted me to be his wife and after Manyatta when he finished being a Moran and was allowed to marry, his desire was to have me. He went on to say that he knew I was married and had a husband, but he also knew I was not in love with that man
and that I was not being treated well.

This was wrong. Andy has always treated me well. We might not communicate, I might not be happy and feel very single in a marriage, but he has never mistreated me. Not in the conventional sense of a marriage mistreatment anyway. I have never been beaten. He works hard around the house, he provides for me, the sex was fantastic, yet, there was something huge missing from our lives. It was once there, had now gone, and didn't seem to be coming back. What did Benja mean by mistreat? What did he know? I asked him to explain what he meant. To which he replied "if you love someone you want to be with them and work with them. You don't hurt your child with bad words; you don't make your wife feel like she has no love."

His words permeated me with their truth, but I didn't say anything in response. This was not his issue to discuss with me. I felt relieved that the pressure of feelings between Benja and I had been exposed between ourselves. We now knew that our feelings were reciprocated by each other. At least if nothing ever happened, we would have not felt this love as a one-way thing. It may only come to exist in our minds and daydreams, but we now knew the truth, and that was refreshing. Though the reality was that, these thoughts and desires were impossible. I told Benja not to wait for me. That he should find someone else to marry after Manyatta.

I remembered that Maasai had arranged marriages so I asked where his intended Nkitok was? He told me Pilaso had a few ideas, but when she saw Benja and I together she knew how he felt towards me. He told me she would accept me as a Wife and Daughter. I smiled, it was a beautiful thought, but one which could not be. Benja took my hand once more and told me he would wait until after Manyatta to speak to me on this again. Until then we should just enjoy the friendship and being with each other. I couldn't agree more. He asked me to come back to his bed. I did. And we lay together, both being tempted, both wanting more, but both respecting and not giving in. The last thought which popped into my head before falling asleep in his arms, was one of regret for having such morals. If I was a 'normal' person, I would have given in to infidelity. Right now I craved normality!

Chapter 8

Laizer! I was so angry with Laizer. My first thought when I woke up the next morning was of him. How could he have caused so much trouble? Why had he created such problems for us? Did he really dislike us this much?

It is always disturbing when somebody you consider to be a friend lets you down. You question your perception on people and how you take them into your fold. You question every other friend you have made.

I tried to think of a logical answer to why this would happen, but I couldn't. There wasn't one. I felt so let down and the longer I thought on it the angrier I became.

I picked up the money transfer which was the whole reason I was in Arusha, and left for Karatu. This money would be my last. There was nothing more available after this. I had wasted so much time and money on this trip. My expected budget had gone out of the window, and I had nothing to show for it, because of Laizer and his lies. If this money didn't get me to the right locations for material for the story than I would have no story and would have to let possibly the best lead I have had during my career as a freelance journalist
slip through my fingers.

I sat on the matatu heading back to Karatu. Benja was with me, but we were hardly speaking. We both had so much swimming round our heads, and were both very angry!

In a positive sense, I now had the freedom to go to Piaya whenever I wanted. Though, as I had heard nothing from the NCAA, I would still have to pay the extortionate rate they charge all Mzungu. When we got back to Karatu, we went straight to the house to find Laizer. He had gone, which surprised us. Samwel then explained that one of the chiefs of Piaya had arrived back in Karatu earlier than us, and had seen him.

They had a large argument before Laizer backed down and walked away. He told Samwel he was going home, and that was it.
In some ways I felt cheated of my 'moment of truth' in other ways I was relieved. At least he was not here and could do no more damage. There were only around 3 weeks left of the trip,
I planned to enjoy them, hopefully see Manyatta, get photos, a good story and go back to my other children.

The day after arriving in Karatu from Arusha with the extra money, we went back to the Ngorongoro gate, trying to pass through it to go to Piaya. I told the rangers that this time I knew the boundary, and would only be paying for a day, because all I wanted to do was go through the conservation area, not be in it. They agreed. I realised that I was doing exactly what I should have been doing all along. If I had not allowed Laizer to speak on my behalf, I wouldn't have had such problems with him. I guess the easiest way to see mistakes is with hindsight. I made a promise to myself that from that moment on, with my knowledge of Swahili and Maasai; I would do all of the important contacts myself. That way, only I could be blamed of things went wrong!

Night was falling, so instead of carrying on the 6 hour journey to Piaya, we decided to stay at Kimba. The other Maasai who were staying at the Kimba lodge, informed us that the chiefs of Piaya and Loliondo districts had still not set a date for Manyatta. I was initially a little worried to hear this, because with time running out on us, I knew there was a real possibility I might not make it to Manyatta. If I didn't see the celebration, I would have to try and find
another angle to write from, which wouldn't pose too much of a problem. Living and being with these guys was certainly unusual enough and wonderful enough to write about and the amount of fantastic photo opportunities I was having, I could have enough work to sustain me for a while.

Despite the Manyatta news, I felt optimistic and enthusiastic. Whichever way this trip worked out, I would make something good come from it. That was for sure.

I spent an enjoyable evening in Kimba, sharing stories with the Maasai, relishing them and their company. I even managed to buy a few small gifts for people, as there are some stalls at Kimba. I thought it wise to buy them now before I ran out of money again, so I did. Nothing spectacular, just a few bead necklaces for my Daughters. There was also a guy coming round selling bows and arrows. Connor asked for one, but I said "no", because it wasn't the kind of thing I thought I should be spending my money on. Connor was upset at this. Benja had heard us and asked me if he could get it for Connor as a gift. I said "yes", as long as Connor could be responsible with it. He got the bow, with 6 arrows and a quiver to contain them.

The smile which came from him was so full and honest. It felt good to see Connor so happy.

I had a lesson to learn. There is a very large difference between what I consider as responsible behaviour, and what my son does. Oh I know, he is an 11 year old boy, whose biggest idol is Legolas from 'Lord of the Rings', but that shouldn't have given us too much difference in the understanding of what we expect as responsible.

In fact, as the next morning came to show, my Son's level of understanding of the word responsible is completely bipolar to mine!

I woke up to find arrows everywhere! The lodge at Kimba might not have much in the way of furniture, but whatever surfaces it did have, seemed to have either an arrow in it or a hole/scratch where one had been! Oh my God! The door was covered and looked like a dart board. The bed was broken where Connor had been carving it with a Maasai sword. The damage was immense, and just when I thought it could not get any worse, I opened the room door to go to the outside bathroom, to see marks on a car, which was owned by the proprietor of Kimba lodge. Just fantastic. Bloody great. I was almost speechless, and then I saw the hotel owner coming towards me. His face was like a stone and said it all. He was absolutely livid.
All I could do was apologise and get Connor to do the same. Of course we had to pay the bill for damages, which was nearly

1,000,000 tsh. I didn't have enough money for this and had to ask my relatives in England to send me some. It was so embarrassing.

I couldn't even manage to speak to Connor, who was very remorseful for his actions, but could give no explanation as to why! I felt like I was too angry to have a constructive or even decent conversation with him. When I have felt like that previously, I back away until I am calm enough to speak. I don't want my Son to feel my anger and take it onboard as a guilt thing. So I walk away, until I can talk about the problem.

This situation marked the end of my trip. The case was this; I was now nearly out of money. Manyatta had not happened, I couldn't stay for longer and find more stories because I wouldn't be able to afford the bus fares, let alone eat and pay my way. My chance at this story had come and gone. I felt absolutely devastated. Had I completely wasted my time, efforts and money?

We headed back from Kimba to Karatu, where Connor and I spent a few days packing and saying 'goodbye'. While I was there, I began to think about the trip, running a kind of overview and hindsight plan through my mind. One of the biggest problems we faced. Which if I could do it all again would be transport. If I had a car available, I could have got more pictures and more stories, and would not be running at a complete loss.

Manyatta had not taken place, which meant it was still due to. I could still have a chance! An idea kept coming to me, and would not leave me. The more I thought about it, the more logical it became. Did I have enough time to go back to Kenya, see my family, raise some more money and perhaps even come back with the Pajero?

I wrote Andy an e-mail asking him what he thought, he told me the car had some problems, but it could happen. With a raising excitement level, I told the Maasai what I was thinking of doing.

They felt just as excited as I did, but did warn me I could still miss Manyatta. I decided to take a chance.

The next step was finding a driver. There was a man I had met in Karatu called DC, though his real name was Alex. I knew he was looking for work and had a driving license and experience. I called him and spoke to him. He was comfortable with the idea of driving me back from Kisumu. It was arranged that Alex would travel back to Kenya with Connor, Samwel and I on the Akamba.

Doing things this way, there was a slim chance I would not have let go of my story. I knew it was slim, but I convinced myself with optimism. The truth was I so wanted the Manyatta. I wanted to experience it. I wanted to do it. I wanted to record it. Nothing like this had ever been presented to me before throughout my life, yet it was the kind of thing my subconscious knew I was always looking for. Covering items one would only ever see perhaps in the ' National Geographic' was so what I wanted to do. For once in my career and life I had almost formulated a plan, and I was not about to let it go!

Plans were made, decisions took, tickets booked. We were soon on our way back to Kisumu. Benja was not coming with us. He had some obligations to look after his family, had to go to Orpuul, and also be around for Manyatta, should it happen before we came back.

Orpuul is a time when Maasai go into the bush to eat meat and build their strength up. I didn't want to leave him, and almost begged him to come with us. He didn't, Samwel came with me instead, he had some other business to attend to in Kisumu, so was eager to get back there; someone owed him a lot of money and he wanted it back. Leaving Benja behind was not easy, but had to be done. I wanted to go ahead with this plan, I also needed to get back to my Church, and most of all my family in Kisumu. It had not been easy being apart from them for so long, and I was filled with excitement and anticipation just at the thought of giving hugs in abundance to my children.

At the Namanga crossing border, I felt this was the point I left Benja behind emotionally and headed towards my family. I had to become 'Sam the Mama and Wife' once more, I had to put on my masks and become who everyone thought I was. I felt tears well inside me just at the thought of this. I had spent so long of my life not knowing who I really was and hiding from myself. Despite all the problems I had faced in Tanzania, I had so enjoyed my time there, and was especially happy living with the Maasai. It was hard to let that go and get back to my large ex-colonial house.

The journey was long, boring and tiring. We left Arusha at 14:30 and arrived in Kisumu at 04:30. Gosh, my arse hurt! Standing in Kisumu bus terminal was Andy. I had sent him a text message informing him of what time I would be arriving, and he insisted on meeting us at the depot, no matter what time we got in. I got off the bus, greeted Andy, got our bags and climbed into the car. It was good to see him. We arrived back at the house, the children were still asleep, so I waited for them to wake up. I was so excited, it was very hard stopping myself from waking them up! Dawn came, they eventually woke up and we had a wonderful time of hugs and kisses. Gosh how I had missed them. A pain tore through my heart as I remembered the distance, then happiness engulfed me. I was with my babies once more and that was all that mattered. Oh the joy.

My first day back in Kisumu was spent visiting the church, the office and the computer school. I was busy and I did enjoy it. One of the most unexpected pleasures of my life in East Africa was the church/community work. I felt as if I was breaking new ground with the style of practical, no nonsense teaching I was capable of. I certainly had earned a reputation as either a Godsend or a heretic, which seemed quite valid and healthy opinions to me!

I loved the work of being on the ground with people, sitting with them and helping them work out their own decisions in life. I felt so fulfilled with that part of my life, and as I had only been ordained to teach 1 year previous, it was a completely unexpected area of my life that had come to play.

Some of my people were surprised to see me back in Kisumu. There had been rumours that I had left Kenya for good, which had disturbed Patrick and Francis, no end! I had never planned to leave Kenya for good, but that is the way gossip is, damaging and often untrue. The only choice we have to make regarding it is whether we should listen to it or not!

There was something wrong with Andy. He had not heard the rumours that were surrounding me. He also had had little chance to overhear something as he couldn't speak in Luo or Swahili. But, there was something definitely amiss. It felt as if, on that first day, we were tiptoeing around each other. We had both missed each other and were genuinely pleased to be back together. I had tried as much as possible to switch off my thoughts of Benja and my emotions. I tried hard to be just 'Sam'. It was so difficult, but out of respect and sanity, I had to do it. I could not ignore the fact that there was something playing around on Andy's mind.

I then realised what it was, jealousy. What he wanted was me. I had come back, and as soon as possible had checked up on everything else that was going on in my life here. In my defence I had seen him first and was able to spend my first few hours or so catching up with him, but it clearly wasn't enough.

I was unable to give him any more time that evening, as I had arranged to go to a showing of 'The Passion of The Christ' at the church. I would be free after 9 p.m., so I left it that he would get the children organised, I would go to the church, and then we would spend a nice night in together. I hastily unpacked my rucksack, gave Reesie, the maid, my smelly clothes together with a big apology for them, shoved the rest of my rucksack junk, such as notebooks and beads in my private drawer, then left for the church. In order to make it possible to show a film at the church, we had to loop electricity from a nearby hotel! The church was still just a tin hut with a mud floor; we had no power or water and were certainly no cinema! All we had was a desire to show this film, at no charge, to the local people.

'The Passion of The Christ' is one of those films that hit you hard. It doesn't matter that the language cannot be understood, or even what religion you are, because the actions speak far louder than any linguistic interpretation of them. It was ideal for us to show in the church, as not only was it a Christian film, it could relate to all people at all levels of education. The other thing we needed to give a showing of the film was a screen and a player of some description. We overcame this bridge by bringing our TV from home, and our Play station. When we left England we had opted to bring the Play station with us instead of a DVD player, as in addition to playing games you can also listen to music and watch DVDs on it.

So once a month we would take it down to the church, and show the film. Word had got around very quickly that I was back in Kisumu, and many people came to the church that night. I was so happy to be with my people again. The evening passed without incidence. When all was finished at the church, I went home, looking forward to a nice evening with Andy.

Chapter 9

I arrived at the house gate to find that no lights were on in the house. I wasn't late back, and couldn't understand why it would be like this. I then thought that perhaps Andy was being all romantic. It had sure been a long time since we had been intimate with each other. This idea pleased me a great deal, and I almost ran into the house thinking my luck was in! I dumped my bag, and went upstairs, half expecting Andy to be sprawled out on the bed. He wasn't, but then appeared at the balcony door. He had been outside, sitting taking in the night sky. I gave him a big hello hug, realising something was really wrong. He had not been up here awaiting intimacy or moments alone with me, he had been up here thinking on something serious. He didn't say it, but I saw it in his actions and lack of words. His whole feel towards me had changed since I went to the church that evening. What could have possibly happened? To change the mood this much? My mind raced as I tried to comprehend Andy and the frostiness omitting from him. What was there that could have done this?

I asked what was wrong, he said "nothing" and tried to put on a mask to how he was feeling. "Nothing doesn't bring these feelings," I told him. I remembered my notebooks and my blood felt cold. Could it be that he had found and read them? Contained in the pages of my notebooks were many notes, thoughts and even fantasy's regarding Benja. What if he had read them? I dismissed that thought though, as Andy would not violate my personal space. Even if he had seen them he wouldn't have read them. He knows that as a writer I play with my words and thoughts, so would have stayed well away from my notebooks. And well, I guess he just trusted me too much to go searching for something. Didn't he?

Still wondering what the shift in emotion was, I got ready for bed and climbed in next to Andy. This was the night I had been looking forward to. I was a young woman of 29, with a high sex drive and tonight I had the opportunity to enjoy myself for the first time in eight weeks or so! I knew Andy must be feeling the same, and whatever was bugging him, would be lost in the throws of passion. I started to come onto him, and let him touch me, but I knew half his heart was in it. We carried on regardless, finished the job, and went to sleep. I woke up a few hours later to find Andy crying and shaking next to me. He was saying "don't leave me, don't leave me." I was so confused. I tried to tell him to calm down and that I was here for him. What on earth was going on? I then managed to fall back to sleep. Andy woke me at around 8 a.m. with a coffee. Then the accusations and explanations of the previous day started to come. He had seen some of my notebooks. Seen them and read them. Page to page from the details he was giving me. Oh he said that he had only flicked through them, but he was able to draw details from one bit of it to the other. I felt sick. I was sorry he had seen them but I had nothing to apologise for. I am a writer. I have this world in my head where I live and create. It also gets written down on page. Why should I feel sorry for that? I gave him my explanation. He said he believed me, but why did I write those things on Benja.

It was then I decided that to tell the truth was the best and only thing I could do. I told Andy I was in love with Benja, but I had a level of morality I could not cross. Andy was hurt, I was hurt. Despite him saying he believed me, I knew he didn't truly. I felt as if I had been accused of doing all the things I had written, and nothing was going to change it. As the pain increased, I almost began wishing I had given in and done something about my feelings. At least then I would have a reason to have to go through all of this, but I hadn't.

Where most people would have jumped in dick-first, I wouldn't. Where I had commended myself for this, I now almost regretted it.

I began to feel very angry and violated that he had gone to find and looked through my notebooks. What was I meant to do? Comfort him? For what? It was the same as him reading a storybook, why should I have to feel guilt for that? Why should I have to feel remorse for something I hadn't done. Andy then began the inevitable questions about Benja. "How long have you loved him." "Why do you love him?"

I couldn't really reply. I didn't want to further his pain, he had already told me that the thought I was in love with Benja had insulted him so much, that I couldn't take the conversation further. The last thing I wanted was a slanging match. When I was younger, I grew up in a house where the parents had a lot of arguments. I lived the pain of hearing your parents rip each other apart verbally. It was something I would never do to my children. Today was one of the first times in my marriage that they really had the chance to hear derogatory things being said.

That was why I made the choice to walk away. I went to my office in Kisumu, and sat there. I wrote a little about how I was feeling. I then text Andy and asked if he could come there. He did. The feeling was surreal. He was acting like the betrayed husband while I felt like an insulted wife!

This situation had showed us that the trust had gone between us. In fact so much had gone. I knew I was no longer in love with Andy, I had known that for some time, but that had not forced me away. I also knew that we were very different people. The Andy I had set out on life with had become a very different person, and I guess so had I. How on Earth did this happen? Was it our fault? Where did we lose each other?

Over the next few days, Andy tried to be the person he is not. We spoke a lot, communicated in truth about our marriage, and even managed to self diagnose Andy with a possible dose of depression! It was almost O.K. and I thought that just perhaps we could work out a solution for the future.

Andy then he became sick with Malaria. When Malaria strikes, it often comes in such speed. This was the case with Andy. He was physically fine, then he was down and delirious. He needed treatment a.s.a.p. This case of malaria was so severe that he was nearly dying. He was seeing dead people and talking to his Dad, who had died some 28 years previous! It was just awful.

As I sat at his bedside, I knew I was meant to feel remorseful of anything bad I had said or done in our lives together, but all I could do was realise the truth, that I did no longer love him as a wife should love a husband. I wanted to. God, how I wanted to cling to my Andy. Was he was more like a Brother now? Realisation often strikes at the most intense of times. I sat and cried. I never wanted this. Where was my Andy?

Soon, Andy was over the worst of the malaria, which was a massive relief to us all. We began building up his immune system and soon he was back to normal and even refereeing football matches for the local teams of Kisumu.

With Andy's recovery came the resuming of the plans of heading back into Tanzania. However we had another problem to cross. Our Kenyan visas were due to expire in a few weeks. We had applications in the immigration office for our work visas, but nothing had come through yet. There were some decisions to make over location. Andy was tired, we were in different places mentally and emotionally.

Also, the projects needed some assistance with fundraising in the UK. So, therefore we decided to leave Kenya and go back to the UK to sort out the problems. Andy would drive to TZ with us, then fly back to London from Kilimanjaro, for a rest, while I finished off my work, keeping the children with me, so he could have some time to think. It was all terribly logical, and my heart pained at the thought of going to say ' goodbye ' to Kenya, but within my heart I knew I would return at some point. Probably alone. At this stage, all I wanted was to finish what I had started and not let people down.

On our second from last day in Kenya, we awoke to find a broken door. Initially we suspected the children of playing too rough, but then we looked further and discovered we had been robbed. All of the shoes, which were kept outside the front door on the porch, had gone. Some garden toys also had been taken, and more worrying, our lock had been damaged beyond repair. This was the most concerning. We thought it was possible someone was planning to rob us that night and by breaking the lock was making the way easier for them, so we left that day. No big goodbye, no cheerio, just getting in the car and driving. That was quite hurtful, we had done so much there, but we did not even get a thank you from the local people. Nothing. And, we left.

The drive from Kisumu to Arusha was very long and tiring. I was now used to long road trips. The children seemed to enjoy the ride, though sitting in the car for about 14 hours never did anyone much good! We arrived in Arusha, at around 4 am, and found a guest house to stay in, to get a few hours sleep.

Being back in TZ, was wonderful for Connor and I. We both have an illogical feeling of home in this land, neither of us can truly explain it, but both of us enjoy it. Xanthe, Zachary and Tabitha were equally excited to be somewhere new and eager to explore it.

Later that day, we went to a ticket office. Andy found a flight leaving in 2 days time. It was expensive, but needed. He got his ticket. We did have the plan to stay with him in Arusha until he left, but he was quite insistent we just went, tried to find Manyatta, get the work done and meet him in London. We went to get supplies from the store, then it was time to part.

So, on August 23rd, Andy and I said ' goodbye' to each other in the car park of ' Shoprite', in Arusha. I loaded up the car.
In theory we both knew this was a small ' goodbye'. We had been apart for longer times in recent months, but there was this ominous air of expectation hanging over us, almost smothering us. Alex got in the driver seat, started the car and we pulled out of the car park. I turned back to look at Andy, the tears began to roll down my face.

He looked so pained and so lost. He was not my Andy. I wanted to stop the car and run back to him, shake him or something and demand where this person who looked like Andy had taken the real Andy. He walked away. We drove the opposite direction towards Karatu. The sunglasses masking my tears, skin hiding my broken heart. I turned the radio on in the car, playing was the track

'Everybody Hurts' by REM. It couldn't have been more apt. Yet another soundtrack moment to my life.

This road was familiar to me. I looked around the scenery and felt a peace slowly enter my soul, taking away the pain of loss I was feeling.

We arrived in Karatu in darkness. I decided to head towards the house. Hoping someone would be there, and we could stay the night. If not, we would have to go to a guest house and work out the next move. Alex drove to the house, which is situated about 1 mile outside of Karatu town. It was in darkness. I banged on the door, just in case someone was there and either asleep or perhaps out of paraffin for the lamp, but there was no reply. It was empty. The old lady who lives next door to the Maasai house in Karatu heard the banging and came outside. She told me that nobody had been there for a few weeks but Pascalina, the housemaid, had left a key with her just in case we should return. I was relieved. We emptied the car and got in the house.

The first impression my children had of Karatu was awful! The house stank where it had been closed up, and it felt dirty. We couldn't actually see if it was dirty, but it sure felt like it!

The children and I said ' bye ' to Alex, asking him to return early in the morning. We then tried to find somewhere to sleep. As nobody else was here, the mattresses were all free. We put all of them in one room, laid some material on them as a sheet, and covered ourselves with blankets. Nobody had much of an urge to explore the house. Not only was it dark, we couldn't be sure what was in it! Xanthe had already managed to find cockroaches on the walls with our torch. But there were strange noises coming from the attic space, and while I thought it was just birds, there was a high-pitched sound I couldn't identify! The children all fell asleep, thankfully tired from the journeys. I watched them breathing, thanked life for getting us here, and let sleep take over my body.

Chapter 10

Our next morning was a crazy one. We awoke to see the house in the state it truly was. Oh my God! Nobody had cleaned it, for what looked like the duration of time we had been away! There were mouse droppings, cockroaches other bugs crawling around, some alive and some dead. It was absolutely disgusting! I quickly hurried the children awake. There was no running water in the house, and none from the well, so we decided to wash at a local guest house, grabbing our bags on the way out! This was not the first morning alone with my children in Tanzania I had wanted. They were thoroughly disgusted, though they did cheer up after we had washed and eaten.

The first task on our agenda was to find our people. I wasn't really sure what to do, but decided to head into the main street of Karatu and see if I recognised anybody. I wasn't sure who was where, what they were doing or anything. By the same token, they had no idea that I was back in Karatu. All I had was Alex.

In the main and only street that runs through Karatu, we found a bus which was heading towards Loliondo. This bus has to go through Piaya, so if anybody had any news, we would find it and them on this bus. As luck or chance would have it, a man I had met previously was there, ready to head home to Endullin on the bus. His name was Msima; Benja had introduced us one day, when I was in Karatu on the previous trip. I asked what the news and locations of my friends were.

He told me that Benja was in Piaya and had been sending messages to Karatu every time someone came this way, to see if I was around. I was thrilled to hear this. To me, it showed his care and concern. I also found out that Samwel was still in Olbalbal, and all my friends were still around Ngorongoro or Loliondo districts. What was even more exciting to hear was that Piaya had not had its Manyatta yet!

I was still in time to get the pictures and story I really wanted. My prayers had been answered! We arranged to get on the road to Piaya that very afternoon. Msima offered to come with us, especially when I told him we were going to take the alternative route into Piaya.

From looking at a map, I had discovered another road which led to Piaya. It out-skirted the conservation area, which meant not having to pay to get through the gate. Just as we were pondering over the map and route, Alex came back with some bad news. The car had a problem with its wheels and would have to be fixed before we could start out on such a journey. I felt saddened, but was assured it would take less than a day to fix, and we could set off tomorrow. This way was probably better as I could spend the afternoon stocking up on food and water to take with us, instead of leave in haste and perhaps regret missing something.

The children all seemed to be enjoying themselves. For Xanthe living in a house with cows and goats next door was such a thrill. I think she felt like Heidi of the mountains. Africa style!

While we had been in town, Pascalina, the housemaid who normally cleans up at the Maasai house turned up. She had heard someone was there and had gone to clean the house up for us, also to pick up her wages. When we returned to the house, it was like walking into a different place than the one we had left that morning. The floor was smooth and clean, not bumpy and crawling! I thanked her profusely, ended up paying her some wages. It was not my place to do so, but nobody had been around. The Maasai were all at their different bomas, so I paid her a small sum. We then settled down for the evening. Pascalina had cooked us some potatoes and rice. It was good to get some solid food down us before sleep, which came very soon after eating.

All of us had to wake up early. We anticipated it would take us a good 7 hours to get to Piaya. If we left by 5 we could be there by 12, and avoid the hottest part of the day.

The morning went to plan, and we left Karatu for Piaya. Everything was going great; the drive was through some wonderful scenery, we got a puncture. The tyre was easily changed, then just a few miles further on; we managed to get another flat tyre. At this rate we would never get to Piaya, because the further we drove towards the Piaya hills, the rockier the terrain became. Our anticipation of 7 hours had been low. Very low indeed. 10 hours into the journey we pulled into a little town village. Who told us we had another 3 hours to go!

Aaaaaagh!

Night was drawing in, we didn't know the road, and the location seemed to be becoming ever more remote. We hit a cross roads, which was not on the map. Great! Now what do we do! We are somewhere none of us had been before, in a car without a spare, on rocky cacti filled terrain, with night drawing in, and a bad map! Just bloody great! Then to cap it all, Msima, who up until now had been very quiet on this trip said to us all, in perfect English
"Good Morning"! Good morning? Hello? Not only was it evening, it was so completely the inappropriate time to say such a thing, that it broke the tense moment and we all burst out laughing. The funniest thing was that he totally meant to say it, and not in jest!

We noticed a Maasai standing on the edge of the road behind us, probably trying to work out what we were doing, sitting at a crossroads in a steamed up Pajero laughing our heads off!
When we had calmed down, Alex said "njoo" which means 'come' in Swahili. The Maasai came over and we asked him where we were. He told us we were near Wassaa. I could see that on the map, though I did of course wonder if our location was truly in existence at this point! The Maasai told us we were still over 3 hours away from Piaya! How so? Had we gone the wrong way or did everyone just say - 'hmmm about 3 hours away'. I hoped it was the latter. Apparently Wassaa had a few guest houses, and we were close to it. With this in mind, and our stomach's rumbling, we drove to Wassaa to find a bed for the night and some food for our belles.

Wassaa seemed OK. We got a room which staff told us was 3,500 tsh. The sleep was good, and we all woke up refreshed and ready for what we hoped would be the final part of our journey to Piaya.

When we came to leave the hotel though, the price had jumped from 3,500 to 10,000 tsh. I asked why and was blatantly told it was because I was Mzungu. I argued this and told them they were being racist. I was so sick of being treated different. I explained I was not a tourist; I work for a church and am poor. It took a lot of arguing, but eventually they agreed. I paid the 3,500.

Everybody piled in the car, relieved to be setting off again. My children have always been good travellers. Maybe it is in their blood, or maybe because they have always travelled, and had exposure to long trips from an early age? I didn't know why, but I did know that I was thankful to have such children, where we were not stopping for vomit sessions every so often!

We were on our way again, on hopefully what would be the last leg of our journey to Piaya. We passed the "Good Morning" crossroads from yesterday, and followed the different path.

The scenery was just spectacular to me. Not in a conventional way of breathtaking scenery, more in the absolute bliss of nothing-ness! For miles the terrain was just rocks and cacti. It was fabulous. It was a relief, when 1 hour into the journey I started to recognise the environment we were crossing. I wasn't sure of the way, but I knew the formation of our surroundings was starting to become familiar.

We saw a Maasai boma and stopped at it. I asked if we were close to Piaya. To which the occupants just poked out their tongues in the direction we should be heading! I had seen this action before with some of my Maasai friends, and always found it incredibly bizarre that they use their tongue as a digit! They point direction with it. I thanked the Esiankiki (young woman) for her help, and carried on the journey.

We started to descend, and I knew this was it. The final leg of our trip. I started to see the few structures which make up Piaya village. We had come in a different side to my previous trip here, and our approach was down a steep hill. At the bottom of the hill I could see a crowd of people sitting under the shade of some trees. Msima, who would now forever be known as 'Good Morning', told us that was the Morans of Piaya. If Benja was here, he should be somewhere under that tree. They were holding an Engigwana. A meeting.

A car arriving in Piaya is not a usual thing. So we instantly grabbed the attention of everybody. Some people from the group stood up, then I noticed 2 figures running over to the car. It was Benja and Laata! Oh how my heart and spirits rose. He was here. They were here, and what was more, they still had their hair! Manyatta had not been and gone. It was still to come. Elation and excitement overtook me, I was so ecstatic to see them again. We hugged, and talked, then hugged some more. It was so fantastic. Benja was so excited to see us all. He has always adored my children as much as he adores me, to see us all here was so thrilling for him.

We had to go to the chiefs' hut, where I did wonder what my reception would be. Would they remember their previous promises? They did. The children and I were welcomed into Piaya officially. It was a beautiful day, filled with much happiness and deep emotion.

I had been preparing Xanthe, Zachary and Tabitha for the mud huts. All throughout the journey from Kisumu, I had been trying to bring up in conversation what it was like inside one, how the Maasai live, and what would be expected of them culturally. It was now time to see what they thought. This time we had a car and drove to the boma from the village. We pulled up and Pilaso was waiting outside with a group of people ready to greet us. It was great to see her again, the children greeted her well, and all was going fine. We walked through the gap in the thorn bush fence, Pilaso beckoned us into her home. This was the time of truth, what would they say and do? I was actually quite nervous! My children are very Mzungu. They like their luxuries in life, and their thought of roughing it, was sleeping in a tent in the back garden of our old 3 bed semi in the suburbs! Connor knew what to expect and was happy to be there again, but the other 3 were my concern. I didn't want them to offend the Maasai, I also didn't want them to think we should be treated any different because we are Mzungu. I needn't have worried. All they did was walk in the hut, complain it was a bit dark and they couldn't see, and then sit down. It took them a few hours to venture back out though, but when they did, they just fit and with everyone else, enjoyed the freedom of the countryside, and the Maasai animals. I felt so proud of them and their acceptance of Maasai. I felt so pleased that the Maasai accepted my children. My Mzungu children staying in a house made of cow dung! Oh how the people back home would have freaked out at this! If mud huts still existed in England, I would probably have social services on my back for choosing to let them stay in one!

Life was good in Piaya, and we were all enjoying the area, except for one rather large problem. There was little food available here in this season. We were only offered small amounts of rice and milk for nourishment. This and the heat had led to us feeling more tired than usual. Even with our energy reserves being low, we had to climb a mountain! I think it would actually be classed as a hill, but to me, it was a mountain! Manyatta was due to take place in a location called Lololol, which just happened to be a long trek up and over a mountain!

Bloody hell, none of us were looking forward to this, but this was exactly what we were here for. A Manyatta.

We left the boma early in the morning, on foot to climb our hill. It was a hard climb, made more difficult by the fact we had little food. The Maasai streamed ahead, and we just trailed behind. Trying to catch up when we could. Connor had started to flare up with a cold the previous day. In the morning this was much worse, but he was insistent to come to Manyatta, so he did the climb. The scenery was fantastic. The higher we climbed, the more we saw.

There were paw prints of large cats around, so many birds, and such fresh air! It was very exhausting though.

Another thing that made it more unusual, was the clothes we were wearing. I had a simple cotton dress on, my children just light clothes. The worrying issue was our shoes. I had my Maasai tyre shoes on, so was OK. Zachary had walking sandals, Connor wore trainers, but Tabitha and Xanthe only had beach flip flops! Most of our shoes had got stolen in Kenya and I hadn't replaced them in Tanzania. I wasn't aware that Manyatta was actually in a completely different place to Piaya! I thought as it was the Morans of Piaya and district, it would take place in Piaya, where I knew the ground to be pretty much OK. I had never anticipated a mountain climb. Tabitha is a very clever little thing. At only 4 years old she managed to work out which Maasai to suck up to in order to get her carried over the mountain. For her it worked, and Samson turned into a suitable carry partner for her! I wasn't so concerned about Tabitha, Xanthe however, walked up and down the mountain in a cheap pair of flip flops from Bata, an African shoe shop!

The amazing thing was that whenever I had travelled previously, I had always gone prepared in hiking boots. In fact you look around any town centre in Europe; you will see shops selling things you absolutely must have in order to climb. All my Xanthe had was a pair of flip flops, and while I don't recommend it as the ideal climbing foot apparel, it certainly makes you question what you do actually need on such expeditions.

Arriving at Manyatta, we caused quite a stir. This was the first time a Mzungu had gone to the Piaya Manyatta. My children and I were stared at on entry, and then led to a hut where we could rest. The huts here, at this Manyatta were much bigger than the ones at the boma.

There was more air inside circulating, which was very welcome. The children all dozed off, all the Morans had gone to eat meat, and it seemed none of the women wanted to disturb me. I didn't want to be seen as a stuffy Mzungu, or to be treating their place as a hotel. I certainly didn't want to feel segregated. So I went outside for a walk.

Manyatta was big. A huge circle of huts, with a large animal pen in the middle. There were more Maasai here than I had ever seen before in one single place. I walked around the perimeter fence, greeting people as I went along. Inside I actually felt very nervous and even out of my depth. I longed to see someone I recognised, but as the majority of Maasai people I knew were Morans, there was little chance of that!

I spoke to a few Maasai women. They have this wonderful way of jingling as they walk. It is because of all the beads they wear as part of their culture and beautification. The women were interested to know who I was, what I was doing there, and most importantly who I was with. When I mentioned I was staying with Pilaso, they seemed to accept me. The name Pilaso carry's with it such respect in Maasai communities. I am not sure of the reasons why, but you can feel the respect from people just at the mention of the name.

The sun started to go down. Some Morans were returning from Orpuul. A horn sounded. Manyatta had begun. A single file procession of Morans started coming into the compound. They all wore stern looks on their faces and acknowledged the other Morans with nods. When all the Morans were in, another horn sounded. A voice shouted out above everybody else. The men responded to the shout. It was almost like a rallying battle cry. Then the singing started.

The sun was going down over the mountains, the Morans were singing in full voice, their sound of Osingolios seemingly filling the whole mountainside. It was simply fabulous. The children had woken up at the sound of the voices and had joined me outside. Watching this rarely seen spectacle.

Watching Manyatta was great, but we were all getting hungry. When Benja took a break from singing, I asked about food. We were made some rice in one of the huts. After eating, Connor and Zachary and Tabitha settled down to sleep. Xanthe and I went outside to watch some more. Pilaso beckoned me over and put her long line of beads round my neck. I already wore a few bits of Maasai jewellery which had been given to me mainly by Benja and Samwel, now in front of the female members of the tribe Pilaso had placed her beads on me. It was a symbolic sign of acceptance by her, and the other women loved me more for it. I was then invited to sing the women's songs and dance with them. I was honoured but a little nervous.

I had jumped as a joke before with my Morans in Kisumu, but never in front of other tribe members, including the 'big women'. It was a challenge, but once I got into the rhythm of singing, I found I was enjoying it. Then I was pushed into the middle of the circle to jump, I did, with my very proud daughter watching me! With every soar, I felt my spirits lift in happiness. I was here. Jumping with the Maasai tribe. It was the most fantastic night of my life. I was renamed with a Maasai name of 'Naduvoy'.

I couldn't stay for the whole of Manyatta. There was not enough food to sustain us and my children required more nutrition that what was available. When people heard I was leaving for a while they seemed genuinely sad. Benja and Meru (Kidri, but everyone called him Meru) said they had to go and pick up a cow from Endullin. They would come as far as that with us, then leave and go back to Manyatta. The cows were their contribution to Manyatta, so it was necessary to get them. I think if it had not been for cow, then the elders would not have let the men leave Manyatta. Benja was the leader of his Moran group, and, held a high position in the community. Also, this was his final Manyatta. After this he would be finished as a warrior and be a man. A Mzee.

We agreed that, after dropping them, I would go back to Karatu and stock up, then come back. If Manyatta was still on, I would return back to Lololol. If not he would meet me in Piaya. I found it difficult to leave Manyatta, but the need was present, so I had to.
The journey was not without problems. About 2 hours into the drive, the car broke down.

The whole power of it seemed to just die. It was getting late into the evening. We were on a familiar tourist road, but it was not the time of day for tourists. All we could do was sit and wait for morning and the next cars. Benja and Meru slept outside, there was not really enough room for laying out in the car, and they said this area was busy with the big cats, so they would sleep on guard. How good to have a couple of Morans around when you most need them! The night wasn't as bad as I thought it was going to be.

We all managed to get some sleep, dawn came, and before long a tourist car came, together with some jump leads. The car spluttered back into life. We carried on our way. The rest of the journey was long and dusty; we dropped the Maasai at Endullin, and then carried on our way, eventually arriving in Karatu at some late time of the night.

Chapter 11

We spent the night in Karatu, in the little Maasai house. The next morning was spent getting supplies, so we could eat. I didn't think we would need too much, but just to have something to cover the next few days. The car had suffered a bit on the trip, the petrol tank had a leak in it and needed attention, and also, I wanted to know why we had lost power. I couldn't go back on a journey through the wilderness, if the car as not right.

The children and I purchased what supplies were needed, while Alex saw to the car. He later came to tell me that the car would be ready in the morning, which was no big problem as we had been planning to spend night at the house in Karatu, and then set off the following day.

Some of the material I intended to gather here was photographic. I am not a fantastic photographer but I am able to take a reasonable picture. I wanted to try and capture some alternative views of the Serengeti. Something a bit different to the usual scenes portrayed. I studied the map and saw there were other routes we could take. Little tracks. I asked Alex his opinion, and he said he was happy to drive those routes, so off we went, taking the more remote track. I was assured by the fact that the car had just been serviced, we had water and supplies, and nothing could surely go wrong?

That is probably one of the worst things you can ever think, because as soon as the thought goes into your head, something is bound to go wrong. Never, say never. It is like a curse which comes down on you just to prove the words wrong in existence.

Something was disturbing the car. We felt as if we were going down on one side and the road handling was bad. There was no puncture, but something was very wrong. There was a loud bang. The left hand side of the car was slanting down, the engine was roaring. We were going nowhere.

From inside the car, Tabitha started crying a little, but was soon calmed down by me telling her we were OK. That we were fine? Which if course, we were not.

The whole of the left wheel had caved in. When the tyre was taken off, all you could see was snapped metal instead of the wheel brace. I looked at Alex and with a very scared but firm voice asked him why this had happened. If he had the car repaired like he had told me he had, then how could this have happened? Just a week ago he had told me that there was a problem with the wheels, I had paid money, it had been repaired, or so he said. How could this happen again? Alex then apologised. He had used the money for himself, the car repairs had never been done!

I was absolutely gob-smacked and mad. I could feel my blood boiling inside me. I had to calm down though and have my words another time. I know it was not the time for an argument. I was angry and scared, but I couldn't verbally rip into Alex right now. What would it achieve. With an amount of verbal resolve that I rarely have, I shut up. My children were looking to me for support. I had to get things in perspective, to work out a solution I couldn't find.

We were in the middle of the Serengeti plains, on a very remote path, with a broken car. We had no mechanic with us, and so far, no cars passing us. We did have some water, and some little food. In addition to this, night was beginning to draw in around us, and the nocturnal animals of the Serengeti making their existence in this place very much felt.

All we could do was pray and hope another vehicle came along. Night fell and we prepared our beds inside the car. Alex slept in he front, Xanthe in the passenger seat, Tabitha and I in the middle seat and Connor and Zachary in the back. All of the children managed to get to sleep. I couldn't. I was too worried about our situation. When we had broken down before the whole circumstance was different. Not in the least because we were with people who knew these plains.

In the distance I could see some headlights approaching. It was nearly 06:00, I woke Alex to flag the vehicle down, which he did. The driver and his mate were very helpful, they were mechanics! After inspecting the car, they said they would drive one of us to Karatu to get the parts needed and then they would come back with him to fix the car. It was such a relief. Of course I had to pay 100,000 for the help, but I was so grateful of it, I gladly paid half. Promising a further half when they had returned.

I said Alex should go with them, as there was no room for the children and I in their car, and I couldn't leave them here with just Alex to care for them. He agreed with this, picked up himself and a bag from the back of the car, and went. I would never see him again. I knew that this day was going to be a long one, but the end result would be good. We would get out from this spot, head for Piaya, do Manyatta, then I would get back home and write the story up.

It wasn't difficult keeping the children amused as they had so much freedom to roam and explore where we were. It was fun as we found snakes, lizards and stripped carcasses. I even managed to make a temporary washing line out of some string in the car and dry some of our washed clothes which had not been dried before we left. If I left them much longer they would just stink or get mouldy, so I tied the string and dried my clothes on my Pajero washing line! We managed to keep the fun element going, until the sun went down.

There was still no sign of Alex or the driver.

I wondered what was holding them up, and theorised that perhaps they had to go to Arusha for the car parts. It was completely plausible and likely to me, that this was the case, as the spare parts shops in Karatu mainly stocked bits for land cruisers. We settled down for the night.

As I prepared the back of the car for the boys to rest in, I noticed that some of my bags were missing.

I knew I had put them in the car, and during the day had just presumed that they had slipped under the seats. I searched the car as well as I could with it being dark outside, but couldn't find them. They were gone. In the missing bags were my clothes, some personal items, some papers, some notebooks, photos, negatives, some of our food supplies and all of my money.

The only logical person who could have took them was Alex. He was the only one who had been here and was not now. I ran through the scenario in my head. The vehicle driver and his mate and not gone to the back of the car, and as Alex had got his things I was speaking to the driver who had stopped to help us. A creeping fear began to run through my veins. If Alex had took the bags, and was so late back, was it possible he had stolen them with the intention of not coming back? I tried to brush it aside, but it was there. And it was ever increasingly real.

Thankfully the children drifted off to sleep, unaware of the thoughts rushing through my mind. I felt ill with nausea as I contemplated the scenario we were in. 1 adult, 4 children stranded with a broken car, no driver, no help, and no money. Some water and a little food. No phone or line of communication. No cars had passed this way at all today. Nobody would realise we were in trouble as we had told people we would be out of signal for at least a week, No friends. No nothing. What the hell was I going to do? I had no ideas, nothing to suggest to myself. All I could do was pray and hope I was wrong.

By morning there was still no sign of Alex, and I knew I was right. We had been abandoned.

The children were weary today and eager to move on. I had to sit with them outside the car and try my best to explain this situation. How on earth do you give hope to people when you feel a situation is hopeless? Still, I tried. I told them I didn't think Alex was coming back with the man to fix our car and we had to be very careful with the amount of water we drank and food we ate, or we could be in a bad situation. There was no pulling the wool over my children's eyes, they knew it was bad, but thankfully they have a wonderful naivety that comes with most children, and the ability to believe against the odds. If anyone was going to survive this situation it was going to be my children and I. Though quite how we were going to do it, I couldn't at that moment say.

Alex had been taken in as part of our family. In Kisumu, he had stayed in my family home. I had brought him there! The children really liked him and didn't believe he would do this. They thought he had just left and would be back. They even played games pretending he was with us.

We spent the day sitting outside the car, moving with the sun to sit in what little shade we could get. Everybody was terribly thirsty, but we managed to ration our water to a few sips every hour. However a few sips for 5 people soon eats into the supply.
Our food was nearly gone. All we had was a few biscuits left.

Somebody had left our remaining food bag outside the car on the previous night, in the morning it had gone and the scraps of plastic were around, torn by a very sharp claw or teeth or both. It was scary. I was scared, but I couldn't show it. I decided to try and make everything into an adventure for the children. Such as, if we saw bones we would try and guess what animal could have eaten the animal, while I prayed inwardly that the same beast wouldn't come and find us!

There had been no more vehicles come on this path since the one who took Alex. That was my strongest concern. If we had been on the normal tourist track, then this would not have been a problem. We could have easily got help and have been in Piaya with a fixed car by now, regardless of our driver abandoning us.

I started to fill with such anger at myself. I had brought my children to this place, and now, there was a possibility it was going to kill them. What kind of a Mother was I? Why was I like this? Why was it not enough to do these things yourself? Why inflict it on the children? Perhaps all of those people in England had been right. Perhaps I had been wrong?

I had to get off this thought path. Even if it was true, and I did certainly have reason to reproach myself, none of this was intended. I could not have predicted life and thinking in hindsight was not going to do anything for me right now. I hoped there would be time in the future for reflection and correction.

The children and I settled down for another night in the Serengeti. I marvelled at the stars, then my children. Most adults would be freaking out and going crazy in this situation, yet here they were, just coping with it mentally. Physically however, they were starting to suffer.

In particular Zachary. Zachary (nicknamed Manu) has never been the strongest of my children. Even in the womb, I nearly lost him and had to go on bed rest for 18 weeks!

Zachary is my thinker. My child who thinks a great deal about everything, before doing it. Zac was suffering the most out here. His level of dehydration was more severe than the rest of us; I could see his eyes becoming sunken, with lack of food. I was so worried for him.

Often, when I have been reading reports or watching documentaries on famine-hit countries, I think of the Mothers and wonder what it must feel like to be unable to feed your children. Normally this is in relation to a mother who would be breast-feeding her child but cannot because there is no milk, through lack of nutrition.

In the situation we were in, in the Serengeti, I found out what that feels like. To look at your hungry children and to be able to do nothing about it is the most awful feeling. You feel as if you have let down the very people who depend on you for their being. They look to you to solve it, you can do nothing and they start to starve.

My stomach rumbled to break my thoughts. Gosh it was loud! I then heard the children laughing at it. I thought they had gone to sleep, but they were still awake. Probably pondering just as I was.

We all laughed, which let out of a lot of pent up fear and emotion. As we were starting to calm down, there was another sound. This time it was outside the car.

It was a roar. I knew it instantly and also recognised it as a lion. We were in pure lion country here. During one of the nights we had previously spent in Piaya, Benja taught me some of the sounds of the different animals. I knew what was outside our car. The children asked what that noise was. As quick as a flash, I said, "that was my stomach rumbling ", and they all burst out laughing again!

Eventually they all fell asleep with hungry stomachs and a happy heart. For now. I sat thinking. On life. On love. On everything. Out of the window I could see the beautiful Serengeti sky. I couldn't see down, so was unaware if the lion/lions were still there. I hoped I would see more skies around this world. I prayed.

We had been stranded for 5 days. Zachary was by now seriously ill with what I could only guess was dehydration and lack of food. He was just staring into space, then just sitting up either asleep or his eyes shut. Xanthe was light headed and couldn't stand up. Tabitha seemed just as robust as ever, as did Connor. However, we all needed water. Desperately.

If I left the car, I could get lost, and I had little energy to move anywhere, but I had to DO something. I was not going to let my children or myself fade away here. Not here. Not ever.

I began to think of what I should do, and came up with the fact that in order to survive we would have to kill something to eat. There was nothing growing, and even if there was, I would not have known my poisonous leaves and berry's from my non-poisonous. Killing was the only option. I spent my day watching the land and trying to see what I could eat or do. There were birds flying overhead, but they were too high, Jackals walking around, but they were too quick, perhaps a reptile would be better. The rocks had plenty of lizards and snakes. I presumed that these reptiles must also be feeding on something.

As I sat and watched, I began to laugh at the situation I was in. Laughing at this stage was better than crying. Here I was, a committed vegetarian of 18 years having to work out a way to kill something. I then even felt proud of myself for sticking to a principle. I had always said, when questioned on my vegetarianism, that if it came down to survival, I would eat meat without a doubt. And I would now do it. Without a doubt. The only problems was going to be actually catching something to try and eat it!

After studying how the animals were behaving, I decided our best place to catch a reptile to eat would be at the rocks; I walked over to them cautiously to try and see what we could do. I had heard many sounds behind the rocks throughout the night and day; I wasn't too sure what was going to confront me. I heard something that jolted me from my thoughts, and caused me to turn round. Something was coming. Oh my God. It was a car of some kind!

It was still a long way off but I could hear the sound of the engine breaking the silence of the wilderness. I ran to my broken car, and told the children something was coming. Zachary was not with us now. He kept opening his eyes, then closing them again. Trying to speak but not being able to. Xanthe just laid there. My poor babies. What had I done to them?

Connor, Tabitha and I went to stand by the edge of the dirt track. I willed the car to come quicker and quicker, but like anything you are waiting for with a sense of urgency, it seemed to take forever.

Slowly, the car became clearer. I recognised it immediately. It was the driver who had taken Alex! Rage started to erupt in me when I saw him, but I knew I had to calm myself and speak to him. This was the only person we had seen since we last saw him and right now, we needed help. Connor flagged him down; he pulled over and got out of the car.

A look of recognition took over his face. The first things he said to me was "what are you doing here?" Gosh. Could it be he didn't know? I told him that he and Alex had never come back for me!

I had no way of moving. I had not been pretending that the car was broken. He said "so you have been here all this time?" The temptation to be sarcastic was great, but I couldn't. I replied with a "yes" and tears filled both his and mine eyes. According to the driver, what had happened was that when they got back to Karatu, there was no spare part available so Alex had to go to Arusha. He told the driver to not worry about coming back for me; he would get the part and make his own way there. He had paid the driver the money I would have given him on his return, and they went their separate ways. The driver said "so he never came back?" "No," I replied, "never, and now my children are sick and hungry and need medical help as soon as possible." The driver was heading for Loliondo, but would be driving through Piaya. I asked him to take me. At least there I knew we could get a little food and water. He agreed. We grabbed the few bags I had left, and squeezed into his Toyota Hilux which was full of maize and sugar sacks. I had no money to offer this man, and thankfully, after hearing of the predicament I was in, he didn't ask for any. We travelled in virtual silence. Relief spreading through the children and I. We were finally going somewhere.

Arriving in Piaya in the night isn't easy. There are no lights to guide you, just the stars and perhaps a lamp, if you are lucky. Tonight we had no lamp. The driver dropped us, wished us well, apologised and drove off. I stood in the middle of Piaya, looking for a familiar face. I remembered where one of the chiefs, who I got on well lived. It was now late, but this was an emergency. None of the little shops were open, and we were in dire need of water.

I walked to his hut. The door opened, revealing a very surprised looking Nkitok. She called her husband, who when he saw us and the state we were in, ushered us in to his hut. Somebody fetched water. We drank.

The chief started asking some details, and I explained that we had been stranded by our driver. He was horrified, then asked if our driver was a Maasai and was there anything he could do. Amazing, this was the man who I once thought had rejected my presence in his village. He was now my helper. In the face of his hospitality and care, I felt overwhelmed with the emotion of everything we had been through. I asked for news of my people. Samwel had left Piaya and gone back to his home for his Manyatta. Benja was now in the bush having Orpuul. The chief said he would send a Moran with a message to Orpuul to tell him I was back in Piaya.

Chapter 12

Zachary's health was worsening. His breathing was changing, he sounded rattly, and even with the water he had taken, he was not improving one bit. He was deteriorating. I knew I had to get him medical care. I may be first aid trained, but this was beyond me. I didn't really know what I was dealing with. Could dehydration really do this?

Time was of the essence, but I had no way to get out of Piaya. The only medical place I knew was right back in Karatu. A good 6 hour drive at least, but I had no car. What was I going to do? I spoke to the chief and showed him how ill Zachary was. He said the only possibility was to ask the lorry driver, but it would depend if he had fuel or not. I was shown to his hut. He came to the door and I asked for his help. First of all he said "no", then I told him I feared for the life of my Son.

He asked for money; I had none, but told him I could pay him when I got to Karatu. Reluctantly he agreed.

The passenger seats were no longer in the front of the cab, the lorry driver had been cleaning up the vehicle, and had not been expecting any late night emergencies. The only place we could sit was in the back. Which we did. The drive was awful. It was bumpy and painful. The other children thought it was a big adventure and laughed with delight at most of the bumps. Xanthe had picked up since eating a little and drinking. She was still not right. Zachary however, was ill. I clutched onto him, hearing his every breath and praying it wouldn't be his last. He wasn't breathing right, and kept slipping in and out of consciousness. I didn't know what to do.

We arrived in Karatu, and the driver took us straight to the Lutheran Mission Hospital. The DR. came and saw us. Xanthe and Zachary were both put on drips to combat the dehydration. Connor, Tabitha and I were given some special drinks to revive us. Hours crept by, and Zachary showed no signs of improving. The Dr's were worried and felt this was beyond them and suggested we transferred to

Arusha, where there were more specialists. We had to wait for the drip to finish before leaving, which gave us a little time to wait. I went to make the calls I had been dreading to make.

I called Andy and told him what had happened. His voice sounded a mixture of horrified and angry, then upset. We spoke for a long time, when the conversation ended, I couldn't make any more calls, I was so upset. I sent text messages to other members of my family telling them what had happened. Andy wasn't angry at me, he was frustrated that he wasn't here, and we had been in such danger without him being aware or able to help.

The truth is though, that if he had have been here he would have been no help. In his current state of mind, and with just how he is as a person, the stress he would have brought into the situation would have made everything worse. Andy cannot cope with changes in life, and having to face starvation and the possibility of death would have been too much for him to cope.

I was pleased he had not been around. It had allowed me to survive. After my initial call to Andy, he kept calling me to see if there was any more news. There wasn't, but it helped him feel better to hear us. I could understand that.

The children and I set off for Arusha. It was a 3 hour drive, and we had to hire a car to take us as the hospital had no ambulance. There was no money. I already owed the lorry driver 100,000, though he had said he could wait until I was next in Piaya. I negotiated with a taxi driver who I had chatted to a few times when I had been in Karatu previously. He agreed to take us to Arusha, and would wait for the money until I was next in Karatu. Gosh I was running up some debts, and only hoped I would be able to pay them back. In Arusha I could ask for some money to be sent over, but that would only work if the people who were able to send, had some available!

The hospital in Arusha we had been sent to was initially Mount Meru hospital. After an assessment of Zachary, the consultant here found he was physically OK, but mentally something was very wrong. We were then sent to a neurological unit.

Zachary wasn't with us. He wasn't moving. His eyes were not open. I was so scared. The consultant here looked at Zachary, and then spoke to us. He told us that Zachary was physically OK he had been suffering dehydration but the medication and drips would sort that out. He then went onto diagnose, either deep shock, or brain damage! Brain damage?

Inside I screamed. The only way to see what was going on in the brain would be with a CT scan. The doctor arranged for one, but we had to travel to Dar Es Salaam to get it done, in 2 days time.
I had to arrange somewhere for the children and I to sleep. There wasn't enough space at the hospital for us all, and I didn't think that would be healthy for the children. I so wanted to stay with Zachary, but I couldn't, and I did have 3 other children to be caring for. I had to prioritise and right now, even though Zac was sick, he had care. It was the others who really needed to know I was with them.

The only place I had known to stay in, in Arusha was at Katimakatano. The Maasai hotel. I also remembered where it was, which was a bonus! Knowing a hotel, which wouldn't cost much, and we could actually get to! The hospital was actually about 10 miles outside Arusha in Tegengero, so every day we would have to travel. Though I didn't think this would be too much of a problem, and the fares are very cheap.

The staff at Katimakatano remembered me from my stay here with Benja, there was a room available, so we took it. I explained to them my situation and also that my other child was in hospital. I also told them I couldn't pay yet, but I would have the money soon. This was fine with them. The maid who showed me to my room said "You are a Maasai, you are welcome." I smiled.

I now had to raise some money. I had literally nothing left. The only thing I could do was ask Andy and my parents and anyone to help. I was already in debt, and the hospital needed paying for booking Zachary in. I also had to feed my other children and pay for our living expenses here. I had no idea how to do it. I was already in debt. There was some money available on my credit card, but that was meant to be for my flights. I am not from well off people and I seriously needed help.

As I pondered my situation there was a knock on the door. I opened it to find Samwel outside! I grabbed him and hugged him so hard! The children were also so excited, throwing themselves on him. All of my family have held a special affection for Samwel.

Even Andy, who dislikes the Maasai, found him to be a nice man. To have him here with me was just wonderful. He had heard through the lorry driver what had happened to us and as soon as he could, came to find us. Samwel even helped us with a loan of 100,000 tsh, which for him was over a months wages!

The next 2 days, we spent mainly at the neurological clinic. Samwel stayed at the hotel and looked after the children. I didn't want them seeing Zachary all the time in such a condition, they had been through and done enough. I kept trying to make things light hearted for them, and now, with Samwel around, that would be far easier. Auntie Samwel was a tonic of laughter into our lives.

Zachary was doing nothing. It was as if my Son was just a carcass. He didn't show signs of recognition on his face. He showed nothing. He was just there, eyes shut, nothing going on inside. If I sat with him for too long, I cried. If I didn't sit with him, I felt I was failing him.

On the day we were meant to leave for Dar Es Salaam, Samwel asked if he could take the other children to Karatu while we were there. I agreed. They knew Karatu and had made some few friends there. This would be better than them sitting and worrying in a guest house room, wondering when Mama would be returning. I had complete trust of Samwel, and let them go. I didn't even mention to the other children where I was going, just in case they remembered it was by the sea! Zachary and I then got into the land rover defender ambulance and left on the long journey to Dar Es Salaam.

Families are very strange things. I had been trying to keep in as regular contact as I could with people, but when you have nothing new to tell them and are always told to "just get home," calling is not an easy thing to do. Just getting home was a great idea, but not right now. How could I just get home?

I had been asked if I wanted some members of my family to join me in Tanzania. I said "no." What I really needed was financial support. However, when I said that, very few people offered to help. I wondered. If people are able to come and be in Tanzania with me which would cost an airfare and a hotel fare before any living expenses, why could they not help me with the medical costs and my living costs here? Andy was going to send me regular money until either he could get here or we could get home, but it was nowhere near enough for what we needed. I couldn't tell him that. He was our only source of support, and I know what our financial situation is, there was no magic wand about to make any more for us. I had already shared with him about some of the bills that were accumulating, and he could do nothing about it, I couldn't see any point in worrying him further.

The day of the scan was very difficult. Zac had the procedure, we then had to wait for results. The results of this scan would basically define how I was going to live the rest of my life. It would see how my family was structured for the rest of our time together. Andy had called, he was anxiously waiting to hear something in the UK I had nothing new to tell him until nearly 6 p.m.! The day had been a long wait, but finally we had some news. His brain activity was normal, there were no signs of brain damage. Oh the relief! I cried with joy, and bubbled with happiness at the news and as soon as I could called Andy to tell him the news. I heard him flop back on a bed in relief as he exclaimed "Thank Christ for that." The Doctor is at the

Aga Khan diagnosed Zachary with having deep shock. Initially there was no medical treatment per se, just a format for trying to snap him out of it. We were due to see the specialist at the neuro clinic back in Arusha to work out a 'care plan' for our Zachary.

The journey back from Dar Es Salaam was OK. Obviously it was long, but at least I knew my Son wasn't brain damaged, the weight of that fear had been lifted from me. Zachary was still motionless. Despite this, I began to feel very positive. We would work it out. We would get our Zachary back with us. Somehow.

With all the time in the back of the land rover, I let my mind drift through my life. I wondered how Andy was doing. It must be awful to be so far away. The sense of being unable to do and see must be frustrating him greatly. There wasn't enough cash available for him to fly back out, especially as I needed everything he could send to be able to live out here. I had already used the credit card so we could eat. The Dr. had advised us to keep the children's nutrition level up. To let them eat food they were used to and enjoyed. Sadly, that didn't mean rice and maragwe every night, and a Mzungu meal for 5 easily came to 30,000 tsh. 3 meals a day was costing me at least 90,000tsh. Over a week that was going to be 630,000.

That was just meals, no extras, like water throughout the day or the roof above our heads. Just food. African meals would have been far cheaper, but the children had to be built up nutritionally.

All Andy could send me was about 400,000 tsh per week. I had asked for help from other people, but everyone was feeling a bit pushed, or I even got the impression, didn't want to help. I also had the medical bills to consider.

My thoughts turned to my work. It was blown. I didn't actually care too much as my priority here was my Son. However, I couldn't help acknowledge the fact that my career stood in tatters. I had promised the writing and photos to a media representative. I had no camera, memory card, or negatives.

I had a few previously taken photos, but not enough. I could salvage some of the writing. I still had my laptop, and a lot of saved work, which thankfully Alex had not taken.

I wondered where Benja was. If Samwel had heard what had occurred, then Benja must have. On the night we were in Piaya, the chief had said he would get a message to him, so he would have known before most other people. I guessed the full Manyatta was taking place, or he would have been here wouldn't he?

With thoughts of Benja I felt a desperate longing to see him sweep through me. I missed him so much and if I could have chosen anyone to help me through this time, I knew it would be him. Of course he is not Zachary's Dad, and if I only had 1 choice of someone to come, I would have been obliged to choose Andy, but hypothetically, if I was able to choose someone for me and the rest of the children, not Zac, I would have chosen Benja. The thought sent shivers of acknowledgement down my spine. I would choose my most loved friend instead of my husband of 10 years. It said so much, but the real reason was because I knew I could rely on Benja to help me. Not to go to pieces or blame me. But still, even with saying that, he wasn't here was he? He hadn't come had he? I let my emotions get the better of me and wondered if I had bigged up Benja in my life far too much? I didn't think I had, but there was a gap where I wanted him and right now, it hurt to have no one to hold on to.

The land rover carried on the lengthy road. I couldn't see much out of the frosted windows, so I tried to sleep. I couldn't. I tried to get comfortable, I couldn't. So, I just sat. Staring at my son, in the same way I had when he was a baby.

Zachary's life was what my Nan calls, a miracle. When I was 22 weeks pregnant with him, I suffered a severe placental abruption. We were told by the hospital in Taunton, Somerset that he was going to die, that I would miscarry the pregnancy. There wasn't much they could do, but advised me to rest for my own sake. I did, for both of ours. I never miscarried, but spent 18 weeks resting. At 40 weeks gestation Zachary Emmanuel was born. Zachary is a Hebrew name meaning 'God has remembered'. Emmanuel means 'God is with us'. The name seemed apt. The shortened version of Zac was cool in our other children's opinion. Ever since his birth I called him Manu. My little Manu.

We had made it and got him into the world. At 2 years old, Zac had the most beautiful curls crowning his head. He looked like a cherub. Manu grew up into a delightful little boy, with such an infectious dirty laugh! He charmed his nursery school; he had so many little friends before we left England. This boy was just adored by all. And now, here he was. Laying motionless. I lowered my body to feel his breath. Almost checking we still, at least had that. I wondered if I would ever hear that laugh again, and broke down in tears.

Eventually, Arusha was in sight. We pulled back into the hospital to find jubilant nurses, around us. They had already been told the results and were singing to God thanking him in a beautiful African song. Zachary was taken to his room. I followed. Then was presented with a hospital bill of 2,100,000tsh! Help!

After leaving Zachary at the hospital, I went to Katimakatano to freshen up and change my clothes. I didn't have a great deal of clothing with me, as most of my things had been in the bags which Alex had stolen. What I did have was being washed on a day-to-day basis with the help of the hotel staff. For a price of course! I let the water of the shower cascade down me. It was cold, a hot shower was such a rarity in this hotel, but with the heat of Tanzania, and the stickiness of the journey, it was just enough for the shower to be wet and cleansing. It did the job and that was fine! The relief of Zachary not being brain damaged had calmed me down somewhat, and I was letting myself think more on other subjects. I thought of Benja, wondering where he was, again. I thought of Andy presuming how he was. I wondered how everything was going to turn out between us all. What did I want to happen? What would be my best scenario?

At that moment in time I was scared to given an answer. Church ministers don't leave husbands, do they? I couldn't think too far ahead, as right now, all my strength had to go in to surviving day by day. That was more than enough to cope with.

I decided I would go to Karatu and get the children, a drive out there would be good for me and I could pick up some clothes from the house. I sat thinking about whether to risk my life in a matatu or a taxi, the public transport in Tanzania was slightly on the crazy side! White knuckle rides, speeding, corrupt traffic police, and being squashed into a vehicle carrying approximately 10 people more than it was legally allowed to were the ingredients of most journeys!

A knock on the door brought me back from my thoughts. On opening, I found a hairless Benja and Daudi facing me! Fantastic! My best friend was here together with one of the Maasai I was very close to. I hugged them hard and welcomed them into the small room. They explained that they had only just arrived in Arusha, and thought that Katimakatano would be the first place to try and find me, if I was still around. If I was still around? Did they think I would clear off and not try to say " goodbye" to them? Whatever! Right now they were here, and this thrilled me no end. I filled them in on what had happened with Alex in the Serengeti, with the chief in Piaya, the hospital in Karatu and what the latest news on Zachary was.

Benja felt so angry at himself that I had been in Piaya in such a mess and he didn't know about it until I had already left. He had followed after me 2 days later, when the lorry was next on it's way across the desert. The chief had kept his word and sent a message to Benja at Manyatta, but there was little he could do until the lorry was leaving again, as he didn't have enough money to hire it by himself. Daudi had come with Benja. News of what had happened to us was all around the Maasai communities of Ngorongoro and Loiliondo. Alex had gone into hiding.

Maasai are known by a fierce reputation, and if you cross one of theirs you can expect a retribution of some severe kind. I was accepted as one of their people, Alex knew this. I tried to imagine how he must be feeling, he must be scared. I even felt sorry for him, but if life is a sequence of action and consequence, then let him receive his in its fullness! I told Benja I didn't have time to think on Alex. I had to focus on my children.

Seeing Benja again was fabulous. Having someone to talk to, knowing that they truly wanted to hear what you were saying was so good. We were all going to share the room at Katimakatano. This wouldn't be so bad, as there were only the 3 of us. Samwel hadn't returned with the children, and as time was getting on, I presumed he would come tomorrow, if not I would go and get them.
Daudi and Benja went outside the room, into the small restaurant, to eat meat. I stayed in the room, and let sleep take over me. Feeling a lot calmer. It had been quite a positive day. Zachary was not in the worst case scenario and I had some of my friends with me once more.

I laid down, thanking God for bringing Daudi with Benja. At least, with him here also, I wouldn't have to find the strength to fight temptation this night. I wasn't sure if I would be able to. The thought of a feeling of intimate closeness with someone I loved was very tempting indeed, and it had been so long since I had been close to anyone.

I heard them return to the room, but kept my eyes closed. Daudi asked Benja where he was going to sleep. He didn't answer and just climbed in next to me. I felt him cover one of his arms over my stomach. He pulled me close to him and whispered in my ear "pole" in Swahili. I wondered why, but didn't want to let him know I was awake, so let the words swim in my head for a while. I had never had a problem with sleeping next to the Maasai.

Sleeping in close proximity to many others is so normal to Maasai. Of course, for us Mzungus it is a bit strange. I remembered a time that Andy saw Samwel laying on a reed mat next to me, in our house in Kisumu. We were watching the night sky together, while he was teaching me Ki-Maasai. Andy had come outside to tell me he was off to bed, when he saw us and jumped to the wrong conclusion!

He stormed off, I ran in after him. We spoke about it, but he never really understood that in this culture, and other cultures the way we do simple things are very different. In fact, when I had been feeling ill in Kisumu, the Maasai used to come and lay or sit all over our bed. This really pissed Andy off as for him it showed a lack of respect from both myself and the Maasai. To them it was just somewhere to sit.

For me it was somewhere for my friends to come and see me when I was sick. In fact, the jealousy of Andy had been one of the things that had excluded him from a late entry into our Maasai friendships. This saddened me so much. He should have been having the same friendships and cultural experiences that I had been allowed. He had chosen not to take them.

On my emotional edge, I felt the tears come streaming down my cheek. I missed my Andy so much. I had never wanted anyone else. My Andy had always been my one, and at one point I truly believed he was my soul-mate. Our 10 year marriage had not been easy at all. We have gone through so much together. If there was something that would break a normal marriage of today's standards, we would have been through it..... Infidelity on both sides, depression, anger, money trouble, unwanted pregnancy, lack of bonding with some children, indifference, too much work, not enough play. There was so much which had gone wrong already with our lives, but we had always carried on. The reason being that we were truly together and could face anything that life could throw at us. We had that indestructible sensation of being in a couple, where you feel it is just you two against the world, and somehow whatever happens, you are always winning. Even at the blackest moments, where I had mentioned divorce, we got over it and got on with it. However, once we lost the togetherness, we had broken up our marriage.

Now, when trouble came, as it always does in life, we stood alone, not as a couple. There is little you can do once that kind of break is there, as it goes straight to the very foundation of a marriage. I wasn't too sure how it had got there, but I remembered Heathrow.

Leaving London was when I had first seen the break. And the saddest thing was, that right at the time we should have been clinging on to each other, and enjoying the journey of life we were doing, we actually let go of each other. Andy, I believe was left back in London. I was here. We were on different a plain, that was for sure. We had become different people.

I had always believed in marriage and long-term commitment. From the day I sauntered into a church looking like a puffed up meringue until just before we left for Kenya, I held onto my vows as a mantra. We had both let go of them at one point or another, but those words of bonding together were something we held on to. I certainly didn't want to be feeling as I did, it was breaking my heart. I wanted to feel in love with Andy. I wanted to know I was with him. I wanted my marriage. Not this marriage. I was separated in marriage and in person from Andy. Yet as I lay in Benja's arms, I thought to myself, was there a future with Andy? Was it at all possible? Is my marriage worth saving? Please let it be so. I wanted my Andy back.

Chapter 13

Returning to the hospital in the morning, I wasn't sure what to expect. I had this hope that I would walk in the room and Zachary would look at me, smile at me and be himself. He wasn't. I don't know why I thought that, I guess I didn't really understand what was happening and had this theory that he would just open his eyes and be fine. The Dr. came to see us not long after our arrival. He suggested for is to be at the hospital as much as possible, to be in Zac's room and just act as normal as possible. Basically to live our lives in the hospital room. He also suggested listening to music that Zachary would be familiar with, watching movies, speaking to him as if he was part of the conversation. He was with us, we just needed to kind of wake him up and let him know he was with us! The Dr. wasn't happy to release him from hospital until he was mobile and communicating.

Nobody knew how long this was going to take. I was so thankful that even with all of the things Alex had taken, my laptop was not among them. Two years previous, Andy had brought me a gift of a new laptop. I was so thrilled to have it. It was the first thing in my life that I had never compromised on. My Apple G4 'PowerBook'. I had seen them in the shops, had read up on them and really wanted one. I couldn't justify the cost of one to myself, so I couldn't have it, and looked around at cheaper computers and processors. Then one day, Andy took me to PC World in Slough. I loved gadget hunting and looking, so it was not an unusual trip for me to take. We stopped by the Apple computer section, and he said "now, which one is it you wanted?" I showed him, he said "do you want it?" I replied with a "yes", I thought this was all a game, until he called the assistant over and we got it. My very first uncompromised purchase. Normally I would have to compromise because of price or need, this time I hadn't. It felt so good to me.

My laptop had become my life in some way. I had my writing on there, my personal writing, my book ideas, my music, it was a DVD player, I designed my thoughts on it. I loved it and it was normally with me wherever I went.

Now it was going to be used with us in the hospital. We could watch DVDs, listen to the familiar music, as I had saved all of my CD collection in the UK onto the Itunes programme. It was the most fantastic asset to have. All be it my only one!

I went to go to Karatu and pick up the other children. Benja and Daudi stayed with Zac. We returned the next morning.
And so it commenced. The living in the hospital room to bring back Zac. I went into Arusha town and hired many DVD's. We got a selection ranging from 'The Cat in the Hat' to 'Lord of the Rings'. We also managed to hire a Playstation 1. This would be familiar to Zachary who was a big Playstation fan. The hospital room was fast looking like a children's chill out room! It was lovely. There was always something happening. Some noises going on. Either music or movie or sometimes both at the same time!

We still couldn't sleep at the hospital, so had to journey to and from Arusha central every day. Some days the children would come, most days they wouldn't, choosing to stay with Samwel and Benja. They enjoyed their time spent with the Maasai. It gave them a time out from the hospital, because despite how chilled out the room felt, you couldn't get very far away from the fact it was a hospital and that was our Zachary laying there pretty much motionless.

Connor, Xanthe and Tabitha often went back to Karatu for the day with Samwel. They had friends there, and also enjoyed the journey. I had to consider their needs also. I was worried about them. They kept getting our trip and time in Africa confused and mixed up. Xanthe even started making some stories up and writing them down, I think, like me, writing is her way of coping and exploring her thoughts. I asked the Dr. about it. He told me to not push the children, to let them talk, let them think, but to not push them into talking. If we heard something way off mark, to not question it, but just to change the subjects and not let them go with it. The children had been through a lot and were trying to work it all out into a format they could cope with it. It seemed like a good strategy for all of us.

The Maasai were such a fantastic support to me. If I had no money they would loan me some, if I needed a shoulder they would let me have one, but they did have a slight problem with crying! When I first cried on Benja, he said to me "who's died?"

In Maasai culture, people are only meant to show tears when they have lost a loved one! With their help, we were getting through this time, they never left me alone, though I if I needed time out they would sit with Zac or take the other children. I had truly found good people to rely on in life. Once you are with the Maasai you are truly with them. Once you are part of their family, they treat you as part of them. I was considered family now. And I couldn't have asked for a better one.

I was struggling with my own family. I spoke to my parents most days, but I was still being constantly told to come home. I was trying to arrange tickets. I had booked some, but the dates kept changing. I also hadn't been able to book all of the tickets as I had used some of the credit card money on the hospital bills and food, though it still wasn't clearing it. When dates came for ones I had booked, they had to be changed, costing us a fortune and eventually losing us all the tickets.

I still had offers of people coming out. I tried to explain that with my Maasai I had people and support here, but they could send me the money as I owed a lot of cash and things were getting even more difficult. Nobody heard me. Still it didn't come. How on earth did these people think I was coping financially here? Was I meant to magic money into existence?

On one day, I just had Tabitha with me in the hospital room, which now was being called 'Zachary's different hotel'. I was sitting next to Zachary, and noticed eye movement. He was having R.E.M. which meant he was dreaming! It was something! We were getting somewhere!

Over the next hours, Zachary started coming round. By the time Connor and Xanthe had returned, he had his eyes open. He hadn't said anything but they were open and moving.

Following us around the room and seemingly recognising us! I was so joyful to see his beautiful eyes trace our movements. Every day, Zachary seemed to be getting more 'with it'. More with us. His state was improving greatly, and the daily relief as he become more like my little 'Manu' was wonderful. On one day, we had hired a film called 'Dodge ball'. It was such a funny movie.

The children and I were sitting at different places around Zachary's hospital room. There were so many laugh out loud moments during this film. Then we heard it. A laugh that came from a pit of a stomach into the mouth of its holder. A dirty laugh. My Zachary's laugh! He was laughing, and not just a little bit, he was laughing his head off! It was such a fantastic moment. His laughter, the emotion of the moment, and the film 'Dodgeball' set us all of laughing. We couldn't stop! If someone had looked through the window of the door, they would have thought they were in the psychiatric ward! It was such a fantastic defining moment for me.

I had thought, in one of the hardest moments I had recently gone through, that I would never hear that laugh again, and here it was. Flowing in abundance. I knew he was going to be fine.

And I laughed.

Zac went from strength to strength. We went from happiness to happiness. Finally the day came when we were told he could be discharged. We had done it. The doctor's, my family, my friends. We had got him through this time. I couldn't wait to get him out, and to get him back to England for everyone to see he was fine.
There was a rather large problem regarding getting my Zachary out. He had been discharged by the doctor, but the hospital manager couldn't let him go until we paid the whole bill.

This was standing at a whopping 4.3 million shillings! I simply didn't have the money, I had been paying off where and when I could, but I had also had to live on the small amount Andy could send. The hospital was insistent. They would need full payment before releasing him. The mood changed from a jubilant family, to a family facing yet another major problem.

I asked around, seeing if anybody could lend us the money. The people at Katimakatano had a whip round and managed to get us 500,000 and a cow! I was able to get another 300,000 together. There was still so much to go. I couldn't do it. Nobody could. Zachary was, in effect, a prisoner! Being held to the ransom of the hospital bill, which was increasing every day, because now we had to pay a rent for the bed he was being forced to stay in!

The doctor understood but the management would not be budged. They feared that I would leave the country without paying. No personal cheques or credit cards were allowed. Just cash or business cheque.

Zachary sat in the hospital a further 10 days; I was allowed to take him out for little trips. On the Dr's recommendation, we couldn't tell the family back home of this. He felt it would be better if Zachary only spoke with people he could see at the moment.
This was hard. I was happy to be able to take Zachary out, but I couldn't let others back home share the moment.

The children and I were still staying at Katimakatano. In the morning we would bring Zachary over here to meet the people who had become close to us. There was also a pool table, which my little man loved to play. It was usual for him to play pool. It was a game he loved and enjoyed very much, even at just 6 years old! One morning, the children and I were at the hotel. We had just finished our breakfast. While we had been eating breakfast the cleaning man came to me and asked for my room key so he could collect my washing. I was a little apprehensive, but this was a normal request from him. I handed it over, he brought it back. Hamuna Shida! (No Problem) The kids had asked if they could play pool. I agreed.

About 20 minutes later we went back to the room to grab bags and go to the hospital. I instantly noticed Benja's bag was missing. It had been placed on the bed, I knew Benja was not in Arusha this day, so he couldn't have come and taken it. He had been meeting another Maasai in a different town this morning. We looked around the poky room, trying to find it, but couldn't. Connor said "maybe it has been stolen." I almost laughed at the thought and even said to him "why on Earth would someone steal that horrible bag and leave my computer alone?" I could see my computer rucksack. It was on the side. After those words had left my mouth, I thought I'd better just check it was actually in the bag. It was not!

Oh my God! It had gone! Now I frantically searched my room, not that it was anywhere in there. I called the hotel manager to come to the room. He did and I explained what I thought had happened. I then remembered the cleaner and the key. I told the manager about it, he went to call the cleaner only to find he was not on the premises. Great. Well, at least we could assume who had taken it! I went to the police station and told them about the theft. They took me back to Katimakatano. The cleaner had turned up again, they promptly arrested him and we all had to go to the police station together.

The cleaner denied the charge of theft, but there was no other logical person who could have taken it. Not for the first time, I felt very sick. In Benja's bag were the passports of my children. In my bag was my laptop. My life, my work, my music, my everything was on that computer? How was I meant to work now? How could I support myself now? I was so angry and so upset. I felt like screaming but had to remain composed. I couldn't take much more of living on this constant emotional rollercoaster. Just as things seemed to be getting better, they then got a whole lot worse.

At the police station, I pleaded with the cleaner to give back my computer. I explained I was not a rich Mzungu, I was a working Mum of 4 children and without my notes, I had very little to work with. Without them, from a career perspective, my last 6 months would have been a waste of time and money! I told him I would drop all charges, but he refused. The police said that this was probably due to the case that the computer was more than likely stolen to fit an order.

Also, the police had been looking for me. When I explained who I was, they told me my car had been towed into their pound, and I had to pay to have it released. Alex, had tried to go and get it and had even had it towed to Karatu, where people recognised it as my car. The police had been called. Alex tried to say he was working for me, but the police didn't believe him, as gossip spreads very fast, and they had heard of our plight. Alex had then had to pay for the car to be towed to Arusha, where it had been held in the pound since. Nobody had known my phone number, and they couldn't find me, so it had just sat there and now I had to pay for it. Great, another bill! I paid up, then had it taken to a recommended garage.

Not only were we dealing with Zachary, the outstanding hospital bill, the credit card, the general living costs, the broken car, I now had a police case going on and had my most important work tool stolen. I felt like curling up and dying there and then, but I couldn't. I felt like walking away, but I couldn't. I had to cope, but inside I was beginning to crumble under the pressure.

Finally we had some sort of breakthrough. Andy's Brother in the UK had found a way to help us pay the hospital. It would take a few days to arrange but the money would come, also, he had also paid for Andy to come over and see us all! I had never got on very well with any of Andy's family, so was very shocked to hear the news that one of them was helping us, but so thankful. A cynical part of me wondered what the catch would be, but I let those thoughts drop, chastising myself for even having them.

Priscus, the owner of Katimakatano had told me that if I could get the money but needed some days to wait for transfer, he would write the cheque for the hospital. He did. Zachary was released. Of course it meant I would owe money to Priscus until I was able to receive funds from Andy's Brother and the amount of money we would receive would not be the amount owing, but it was something. Finally it was all falling into place. I had my Zachary back and Andy was coming back.

When Andy had told me he was coming, part of my heart leapt up, and part went down. I knew that the Maasai would not be near Andy, however, Benja and Samwel had been waiting for a chance to go and see their families. Pilaso was still sick, this gave them the chance to go, and also, not see Andy. I found myself wishing that they had a suitable friendship between them. I resented the fact that Andy coming sent my friends away. I resented my friends for being like this and both of them, for making the situation possible.

Would it always be like this? On the other hand, in theory, sharing some of this load with him would be good. I was weighed under, stressed, worried, and if he could offer me some of the support he had been promising, that would be fantastic. Another reason I was nervous of his arrival is that he didn't know the true picture about the state of finances or flights here. I wasn't even sure what I had said to him. I hadn't wanted to worry him further, I knew what money we were capable of, and now I couldn't even remember what I had said or had not said.

Zachary was released from hospital on the day Andy came back to Tanzania. It was a mad and crazy day. I got Zachary out in the morning, then went to Karatu with Benja and Samwel, then came back on the same day, ready to meet Andy off the evening flight. We waited in the arrivals hall of Kilimanjaro International Airport. All of us were so excited.

The plane landed, and some 30 minutes later, Andy walked through the gate. It was so emotional. He had tears in his eyes, had not been expecting to see Zachary there, or indeed any of us. But, I couldn't let him land without a welcome. It was just a huge bonus the welcome included our Zac! The kids spoke to him fast, trying to catch him up on things in the car, as we drove back to Arusha.

I didn't have time nor money to find a good hotel for us, but I knew I couldn't stay in Katimakatano anymore. Not only was it a predominately Maasai hotel, there was such a bad feeling between the staff and us, because we had called the police on one of their own.

Priscus was more than fine with us, it was his staff who were the problem, and made life very hostile for us there.

Also, the police had advised me to sue the hotel to get compensation for the computer. The whole situation was a bit awkward. So we had to leave. The hotel we ended up in was very basic. In fact the bed was just a mattress on the floor!

Andy's face was a picture when he saw my room! As he walked in and clocked the room, which was bare apart from a few bags, I think he started to realise how I had been living and struggling. I guess he never knew until he saw, and the last time we had been with each other, I had a car full up with bags and belongings accompanying me. There were a few items which had been left at the house in Karatu, but nothing big or major; just a few dresses and my ordination certificates.

We managed to calm the excited children down and settle them to sleep. In one day I had my son and my husband back. It was wonderful, but a little overwhelming.

The next day we changed to a different guest house. I was finding it difficult to talk to Andy, I guess because of nerves and anticipation. I didn't know what was coming or how we were going to deal with it. I had also moved on and gone through so much without him here, it was hard to let him in. Through our limited conversations, it became clear that Andy's agenda was to bring us back to the UK with him, and make sure we got home. That was his reason for being here.

From a practical sense, if we truly had to go, the first obstacle was the children's passports.

From an emotional sense, the hardest thing was going to be leaving my Maasai family. I tried to explain my pain to Andy at even the thought of leaving them, he didn't understand. Over the next few days, we kept talking, but it always ended in tears.

He was so eager to get the children back to 'normality'. To school and life in the UK, being incredibly intent that this was the only way things were going to be right again, he couldn't even truly hear me and my thoughts. Or even take on board what was in my heart. I sobbed my heart out at the thought of leaving. I had been through so much these past few months. So much pain and intense emotion. So much friendship and love. If I left, I couldn't guarantee my return.

I would have even less money in the UK than I would here. The thought of never seeing my people again, or even not being with them for a few months filled me with such pain. Andy would tell me "It will be OK. " But how? How will it be OK if you have to leave the things you love? How will it be OK if it hurts this much just at the thought of this? How will it be OK? These people had become my true family. I might not share their blood but I shared their heart. I was one of theirs and now I felt as if I was being forced to leave them. For the first time in my whole life I sobbed uncontrollably, covering my face with my pillow. Andy became angry at this and started to freak out on me. This was the moment we crossed from possibly having a repairable marriage, to completely breaking down. I knew my marriage was over. When your partner is crying inconsolably and all you can do is make it worse, there really is no hope.

The children were eager to get back to the UK at this point. Andy wanted us back there. I had no money to stay here and no energy to fight for what I wanted anyway, so I agreed to come back to the UK and settle the children down. At the time I did say I would return here to TZ, but I don't think he either heard or believed me.
The money from his Brother never turned up. I then found out that this relative did not believe the situations we were going through in Tanzania were true and the real reason he had paid for Andy's fare was to prove to Andy what was going on was wrong or a lie!

How dare he? The situations I had gone through and survived, the traumas, and all the time, Andy and his Brother had been sitting down working out if it was true or not!? What did that say about their opinions of me? Apparently he had told Andy that this was too much bad luck for one person, and something far more suspicious was going on. Other members of Andy's family had agreed on this point. Shit, I knew I was not ever their favourite person, but this showed me how low they thought of me. I was obviously being judged by the soap opera standards everybody seems to live by these days. Andy must have agreed with them at some level, because the children complained to me that Daddy was always questioning them. Just great. And the rot set in a bit further.

Chapter 14

A plan of action was formulated. Andy would go to Dar Es Salaam and get replacement passports for the children. I asked his permission if I could go and say "goodbye" to my people. I didn't want him to feel like he had any control but I guess in some way I thought it would show a little respect to ask if he minded. He agreed. 3 of the children would go with Andy. Connor would stay with me.

I tried to get back to Piaya, but neither funds nor transport would allow it. So I had to be content with getting as far as Ngorongoro and hoping Benja, Samwel, Daudi, Laata and so many other people were there. Some of my friends were there, but the 1 person I really wanted to see was not. Benja had gone to Karatu on the day I arrived in Ngorongoro. We must have passed on the road without realising.

I headed back to Karatu, and where I would normally have such excitement at seeing Benja, I searched familiar places with a sadness growing inside my heart. I then saw Daudi, who told me that Benja was taking some food in a local hotel. I found him in the Embassy hotel, which is a rather dodgy establishment in Karatu. It has a sign outside of it saying a 'V.I.P.' club member'. On my first trip to Karatu, Connor and I had come to the conclusion that 'V.I.P.' in Karatu couldn't possibly mean 'Very Important Person'. It must mean something else? Perhaps, 'Very Infectious Place'! I smiled as I remembered this. Longing it to be those times again, when happiness had been mine and my future looked good.

Benja saw me walk in and immediately came running over to greet me. He was outwardly shocked by my appearance and tired face, we left the Embassy and went for a walk. As we walked I spoke about what I had to do. Tears began falling; he once again turned to me and said "no- one is dead". If my control of Swahili was better, I would have gone into a lengthy version of how I was feeling, but I couldn't do it. I could only say a simplified version of how I was truly feeling "my heart is dying".

I had a few days spare, while Andy sorted out the passports. I spent all of them with Benja. We couldn't go to the place we really wanted to go, but we stayed in Karatu, together at the Maasai house. Samwel was with us, so were Mush, Laata, Julius, Daudi and Msima. All of my favourite people. My Maasai family.

Too soon, the last night I would see Benja came. It was the saddest night I had ever spent with them. An air of depression hung around ready to lay upon any of us. I tried to think of the positive things. One year ago I had never met these people, never felt this love, never felt this happiness. I was lucky to have experienced such depth of emotion and friendship. Some people go through life and never know these things, I was fortunate even to have tasted it. It was nearly working, I was nearly convincing myself that everything would be OK, and I could go the next morning, meet up with Andy, fly back to the U.K. and all would be fine.

Like I said, nearly convinced myself, because what it came to was the real acknowledgement that I didn't want to do what I was doing. I lay next to Benja that last night. Connor was sleeping on a mat on the floor next to us.

I willed Benja to touch me, hoping my telepathy skills were existent, he held me, but nothing more came. There is a saying, 'hopelessly in love'. It is often used in Western society, yet never often meant in its truest meaning. What Benja and I had felt like that. A hopeless love. Not in a romantic way, in a truthful way. It was absolutely hopeless and we had to let it go before it had even began. Morality had previously kept us apart, now distance would do the same. My eyes were stinging with the tears streaming through them.
I had to go back. I had to let go of Benja. If this was my last night of sleeping next to the man I was hopelessly in love with, could I leave it like this? A love felt only in the heart and not the body. A friendship that needed to be so much more and never would be.

I knew Benja was awake, neither of us was really capable of holding a conversation. Pain has the ability to take away words. Sometimes they seem so meaningless in the face of these powerful emotions.

Benja found some words to break the silence. He spoke to me about Manyatta. Had I enjoyed the time I had spent there? It seemed like a bizarre conversation, but I responded anyway. I replied in truth and had told him how much I loved Manyatta, the location, the fun, the people and the sense of belonging. He asked me to turn over, which I did. Then looking straight into my eyes, he said "Ayeu Iyei Nkitok". I want you to be my wife.

Tears fell and all I could do was hug him. I wanted so much to say "yes". I want to be a Maasai wife. I want my cows and goats to live with me and my family!

I want to be where my heart belongs. My yes had to come out as a "no". I knew I had hurt Benja with this. He could never admit that because he is a Maasai man, but I knew it had. I quickly explained to him my reasoning. I so wanted him, but I knew that right now, I couldn't give him what he needed. I told him I was out of money and had to go back to the U.K. to work, I also told him I was married and even though it is not a good marriage right now, I had to sort the mess out one way or another, I couldn't just switch husbands.

It hurt to say these things. I told him how much I love him and wanted him. I told him he was a good man, but it would be better for him to find someone else. My heart was breaking. Here I was telling the man I was in love with to go and love someone else. It is true that if you love someone you do have the ability to let them go. I only wanted what was best and didn't want to cause pain. I wouldn't make any promises I couldn't keep, so I had to say " no". My heart was screaming "yes".

We stopped talking, but neither of us slept well. It was the most awful night of my life. In the early morning, Benja woke me up. He asked me again to marry him. He said not to tell him now, but to go to London and see if I loved him there as much as here. I smiled. You had to admire his persistence!

The coach for Arusha left at mid-day. I had until then to say my "goodbyes" to everyone except for Daudi and Msima who would be coming with us to Arusha. Benja wouldn't come.

He didn't want to cause any trouble or have any scenes between Andy and him. I wanted him to come but respected his decision and was thankful for it. We arrived back in Arusha at around 3pm. Andy got there a few hours after us. I had booked us into a guest house at the top of the town. One with a good view of Mount Meru. I wanted the last morning I would spend in Africa to start with some of the glory of Africa's nature.

Mount Meru had always struck me as a very beautiful mountain. I had spent so long staying in the shadow of it, that it had become familiar to me, but it could still stun me with it's shape, size and aura.

Everything had gone fine in Dar Es. While Andy and the children had waited for the passports, they had basically just chilled out on the beach next to the Indian Ocean. They then got the passports and returned as planned to Arusha. The children had enjoyed their stay, which was a pleasure to hear, though they told me Daddy asking about you, where you slept, who you talked to and much more. I felt angry at this, but let it go. I couldn't cope with any more pain or accusations right now. My conscience was clear, and that was enough.

Between Andy and I there were these terrible silences. I knew he wanted to grill me so much, I also couldn't allow him too. It was taking all of my strength to remain composed. We slept, then awoke on my very last day in Africa. I was so sad. I tried to put a brave face on things, mainly for the children's sake. Daudi and Msima met up with us in the day. They were due to come to the airport with us, but they wouldn't have fit into the taxi so they couldn't come. I said goodbye to them in the car park of Shoprite. The same place where I had said bye to Andy before starting out on this adventure. I hugged Daudi so hard. Since March we had become such good friends. Then Msima. The man who had made us laugh so much and shared many times with us. How could I say "goodbye" to him?

I guess in the same way I had said " goodbye" to all of them. With regrets.

With a broken heart and tears in my eyes. I climbed into the taxi waiting to take us to the airport. The children were already in the car. Andy climbed into the front. We then left for Kilimanjaro.
The airport is such a small building and compound. An hour drive out of Arusha and you will find it. It has got to be my most favourite international airport in the whole world because of its small size. Yet seeing it, realising what was coming and dreading doing it, I wished I could run out of the car and up Mount Kilimanjaro, instead of airport Kilimanjaro!

The inevitable happened. We got on the flight and it took off. The seating arrangement wasn't great, but I was happy to get seated away from Andy. I could barely look at him. I was feeling broken and angry, and he had done nothing to acknowledge my pain or make it better or anything. One of my biggest fears with the situation between Andy and I was that one day, I would come to resent him. This started on board the KLM flight home. Perhaps illogically,
I thought of him as the person taking me away from where I wanted to be. He knew this was breaking my already broken heart and was doing or saying nothing about it.

The flight passed easily enough. On board, I ran over my memories of the past 11 months. There were so many. Lots of good ones and enough bad ones. The time in Kenya, the work we had been doing, the lives we had helped. I started to feel a sense of achievement. I didn't think I had done enough, but I was grateful for the work I had done. It was good. I felt good.

I thought of Tanzania. I had so enjoyed my life here. It was full of things going wrong and that was not easy, but it also showed me a lot about life. About friendships, about truth, and about whom I was.

I could now look at a mud hut on the discovery channel and know what they are like inside. I could read about Maasai anywhere, and know that my very best friends were part of that tribe, and so am I.

We had to change to a connecting flight at Amsterdam, then we arrived back in London Heathrow, at 08:30 on the 28th October. This was the first time in 11 months I had been here.

I was not the same Samantha who had left last December. I was now the real Samantha. I finally knew who she was.

Walking through the arrivals gate at T4, I had this amazing urge to run backwards! Was I ready to meet up with my parents again? I loved them dearly, but I didn't feel as if I could take them right now. I didn't want to hide my true self anymore. I didn't want to hear their abuse of Africa, and the inevitable 'bet you're glad you're home' conversations. I wanted to just go and sleep!

There wasn't anywhere to run to, so I had to carry on going. With every step I took closer out the gate, I could feel myself ache.
My Mum and Dad were at the barrier waiting for us.

The children ran up to them and gave them massive hugs. I followed. Even I couldn't have dissed this! I was genuinely happy to see them again.

We had arrived back in London as homeless people. We had nothing but the bags we were carrying and a few sentimental possessions scattered here and there, placed with kind people who had offered to take some of our boxes into their spare rooms.

The first few days felt surreal. I felt like a fish out of water. I would look around me and not understand what I was seeing. It was good to see my family and friends again, but nothing felt right. Nothing felt as wonderful as being with my other family. I was pining for them and had only been back here a few days! I was placed in a culture I had known for the first 28 years of my life, yet suddenly knew nothing about! I couldn't understand it.

I stood in the new 'Tesco Extra' in Slough and felt like screaming. Aisles and aisles of food. Heaps of money coming through the tills every second and I had seen hunger. I had felt hunger. How could I live like this again? Everything seemed so fake. I looked at people rushing around doing their lives and knew I didn't fit in. I was not a Mzungu. I was a Maazungu. I did not belong here.

There was plenty to do. Our priority was to find somewhere to stay and get the children into schools. The younger 3 children had been kept a place at their previous primary school. They started just 3 days after we got back in the country, with no problems. Connor, however, couldn't go there as he was now of the age for secondary school. Because he had not been transferred from the primary school, his name had been removed from the education lists in Slough, and we had to go right through the applications process with him, which meant he stayed home longer than anticipated.

We were staying in my parents 1 bedroom flat for the first 3 weeks of our arrival back home. A family of 6 in a 1 bed flat. Gosh. My parents had the sense to move out and stay with my
Nan until we found somewhere to stay. I couldn't blame them for that - and certainly thanked them for it!

We managed to get a rented house. It is a beautiful 1920's large 4/5 bedroom house. Just 1 year ago I would have been thrilled with the prospect of living in this house. But now, it just felt strange, and I felt removed from the whole moving process. It was as if the foundations of living a lie for the rest of my life were being laid. With every box that moved into the house, I felt a little more trapped and every day like I was going through the motions of a life I once knew. Nobody could understand me. Why was I not satisfied with this? Things were turning out O.K. We had a house, the kids had school, and Andy had found himself another job. If I was a normal kind of girl, wouldn't that be everything I would want? If I actually felt like I belonged to this materialistic society, wouldn't this be the ideal?

It was as if everything that had happened in Kenya and Tanzania was being swept away. The situation with Andy, was being forgot about and I was to be expected to do be what everyone else would consider as normal. I was meant to be pulling myself together and getting on with things. I was pretending to live my life and Samantha, the real Samantha became hidden in a cloud of Mzungus.

I had done this hiding game for long enough in my life, I knew how to play it, so there shouldn't really be a problem with it now. Should there?

I began to dread conversations with people, and felt myself start drawing into myself. All I would hear would be the 'oh, I bet you're glad to be back in civilization' lines. I wasn't, I tried to explain, but I was unheard.

I wasn't disrespecting my own country, I like the way we look after the poor and marginalised in society here. A lot more needs to be done, but we do have a good system here in the UK. That didn't mean I wanted to be here though! That didn't mean I didn't want to be part of the changes in developing countries.

So often I would hear people saying 'well it all comes down to money and it's all so corrupt out there'. Yes it does to some extent come to money, but it is also true that you do not solve a problem just by throwing money at it. Yes there is corruption, but it is not all corrupt.

People only take the bad, and sadly many come to the conclusion that it is Africa's problem and if they sorted themselves out, then we should help, not before. I had spent all the money I had in helping Africa. In trying to set up projects there, and trying to think ahead for new ones. I had given my life to Africa and in turn, I had discovered myself there. It is not all as bad as people make out. My problem was that I had to leave myself and my love behind there, not knowing if I would ever truly return.

30/11/05

I have done it. I have done what I came out to do. I have settled my children down into a new home. They are now attending their schools, and enjoying their Mzungu lives again. We often sit and talk about Africa. I asked today if any of them at a later time would like to go back.

They said for a holiday, but not to live. Connor is so much like me. He wants both. He wants to enjoy his school and friends here and be a Maasai in the holidays! When he is a few years older, he has been asked to join the Morans and be trained with them. If he does it he will be the world's first white Moran! I sit with an ache in my heart. I speak to Benja, Samwel and Msima frequently, but I know it is not enough. I walk around the town here and wonder why the hell I came back. I am desperately unhappy. I can feel myself slipping further down into a depression every day, each new morning I am fighting to keep myself up, because once I do get down, I am fearful I may never get up again. I suffered a dose of post-natal depression after having my last born. It took me 2 years to feel fine again. I don't want to go there again, but the path feels a little more slippery every day.

I find myself sitting and gazing out of the window, wishing I would open my eyes and find it to be my African landscape.
I have nothing to do except write. In some way's I wonder if I am writing for therapy, or to get my words out and make sense of everything. It is probably a mixture of both. I can't speak much because I seem to have nothing to say to people which doesn't end up upsetting or infuriating them, so I am trying to keep quiet. I know who I am; I know where I should be, but every day the dream gets a bit further away. I don't belong here. I do not belong in this culture. I am a Maazungu. I belong to a different tribe and place.

I regret coming back to England so much. If I had been stronger I don't think I would have. I should have stayed in Tanzania and perhaps gone back to Kenya.

I could have enrolled the children into an international school, that way they would have a good education and I would have my life and heart back. We would have worked something out. But now, because of money and social pressure I am feeling trapped. I would always have come back to the UK to visit, but right now I think coming back in what seems to have become a permanent basis was a huge mistake on my part.

I spend the days going through the motions. For the first time yesterday I even thought that this would all even be better if I wasn't here. If I was dead, then I would not have to cope with the pain. I am not sure if that means I am suicidal. I don't think so, because I don't actually think I would kill myself that would be an extreme waste of life. I just wish I didn't have to go through the pains of being separated from the ones I love and know I am hurting Andy so much. This is not nice for either of us.

With every passing day I spend in London, my pains for Africa increase. I do not feel alive here. I feel half of myself, half a person. I probably look normal enough. I think I have forgotten how to sparkle, the shine has been washed away with my tears, which fall most of the night. I waited a long time to know myself, and now I have gone. Regressed.

I found a notebook. It wasn't mine. It was Andy's. And in a 'what goes around comes around' kind of way, I got what I deserved, the shock of my life. It must have been awful for Andy finding my notebooks in Kenya, but at least I had the factual explanation of being a writer. He doesn't. I guess at least I really know what he feels. Andy never believed what we went through in Tanzania. He thought it was all some kind of 'plot' to have time with Benja. Even from my first trip in June, he suspected me of having an affair. I feel so angry at this.

The one point of support I thought I always had, and I never did, it was fake. He has accused me of so much and I did very little, apart from try and keep my children and I going. I had a feeling some months ago, when Andy found my notebooks that I almost wished I had done something, then I could at least account for the pain this has caused. Yet, it seems having a molecule of morality and actually giving a damn is never thought about. Andy has also been speaking his absurdities to my parents. I can feel such a distance between myself and them caused by the crap he has come out with. It is as if all of my main channels of support have gone.

I asked for a loan today from my parents. They actually owe me a lot of money, but I didn't ask for it back. I just asked for a loan. A friend of mine who has helped me greatly in Kenya has for some time been talking of investing. He wants me to come in on a coffee farm and a sugar plantation. I need £8000. I don't have it. When I asked my Mum if she could help, I almost saw her flinch, I guess such is the damage of hurt.

I hate feeling like this. Accused, when I have done nothing wrong. Everyone promised me support. My family said come home, you need to rest. The truth is, I can't. How can I rest when no one understands what I went through and am still going through? Even my own husband, the person who, even though he doesn't believe it, I have shown the most respect to, thinks I am some kind of mad woman.

Music has always been a huge part of my life, often when we go through strong emotions it can really help us to listen to music. The UK band Coldplay seem to either have the knack of writing such passionate songs about real issues which face people, or they have a map of our lives and are able to pen words which sum up everything. At every emotional time of my life over the past 6 years, a Coldplay song will come out which opens up the way I am feeling. I almost dread them bringing new albums out, it normally means something underlying is going on in my relationships! Currently there is a song in the charts called ' Talk'. It is everything I am feeling towards Andy contained in a musical note. When I looked through Andy's notebook I noticed how he had penned the lyrics to 'I love you- I'll kill you' by Enigma, down. Should I be worried?

DEC 1st

Today is the beginning of advent. I never actually realised until the end of the day, what day it was! Normally I would have had calendars ready and my Christmas cards written by this date. I feel angry at myself for not remembering. The children seemed OK about it. I apologised to them and promised to get them some tomorrow.

I feel so lonely. I am not communicating with Andy, there is too much hurt for both of us. We are living in some kind of shell like existence together. We are both encased in something so fragile that it cracks open at the slightest knock and exposes our lives for the mess they are. I try to talk but he does not hear. He asks me what's wrong and I will tell him how unhappy I am here. I know he is tired of my answers, and wishes they would change to the opposite feeling, but I don't know what he expects from me? I do love Andy. Very much. But it is different. This is not my Andy, I am not his Sam. Something has died between us.

If I was to die this very day, I would have gone with such regrets, living a life I had promised myself never to live again. When I was a child, I learned how to hide from myself and others. Coming out from that was difficult. Knowing and loving me was the most amazing revelation and life giving action. When I was 20, my Aunt died. Her early death has been another factor in how I live my life. Many people will say, if you want something in life, go for it, you only get one life. Not many people will actually do this, they will just say or hear the words.

I always wanted to make sure I did life. I sit here in England and feel as if I am letting myself down. I keep finding myself on the KLM website looking at the flights to Kilimanjaro or Nairobi. I should stop looking on the KLM page. It is only adding to my pain. There is a button that flashes at the bottom of the page, it says 'proceed to checkout'. Realistically speaking, if I was able to afford to go right now, would I? I would need to live and eat out there and departing from this land would mean I leave my children behind.

Could I honestly do that to them? Would it be right? I hugged them that little bit tighter tonight as I thought these things.

I went to bed tonight, an hour or so after Andy had gone. I laid next to him, and felt pains. Such emotional pain because all there was between us was a void of loneliness. I got back up and slept the night on the sofa. I would rather be in a single bed or sofa than in a double bed with such awful emotions. I hate this life and I rather fear it will kill me or leave me devoid of myself completely.

DEC 2nd
I felt somewhat stronger today. I had an update from Patrick on the church and spoke to Benja, though the main reason for the uplift is myself. I am refusing to get down about my situation. I will not ruin my children's Christmas time with my thoughts and depression.

I once had some terrible news on the 15th December 2000. It has since ruined every Christmas. Every time the trees come out, I remember the pain. Christmas is not a time for pain.

I cannot have my life right now, so I shall work towards it. Simple as that. I am not pretending it will be easy, because this pain is the most I have ever gone through, but one day I will live my life in truth again. It just might take me some time. I am thankful that I can sit with my memories. I will always have the shadow of my 'self'. Always my dreams and desires. I will always have the truth that I know who I am now. There will always be Africa and I will always be a Maazungu.

To be continued -

Transition
I did something I should probably regret. I have been having some job interviews for an international media company. I got the job. I found out I had to go to New York to do some training. I told Andy where I was going; he asked for how long, I replied with a false time

of "1 month". One month! I lied. I know I will be there for a few days maximum, but what I did, was give myself some time to go home, to see my people, to work out my future. I know I am trying to justify this action to myself, and it almost works, until the lie becomes a bigger lie, and I have to say it to more people, when they ask what I am doing. Before I knew it I had lied to all of my family. Is this me? I am in the pursuit of myself, and I have now become a liar.

I feel so terrible, yet I cannot stop it. How can I? Right now I have the opportunity of going home for a few weeks. I can't miss it. I booked the ticket for the day the children go back to school from Christmas break. Jan 4th. I have told my only true European friend the truth. I had to, because if something happened to me or the aircraft, I thought someone should know my real travel agenda. Half of me feels so excited, the other feels condemned. I spoke to Benja and Samwel today, I didn't tell them I was coming back. I just said "soon." I think I want to surprise them with my return.

I feel much more focused now I have a date for my return to Africa. I am scared because of what I have done here, but within me I feel a sense of direction, of doing what is right, but then how can something feeling so right actually be morally wrong?

Condemnation is something I feel like I have forever lived with. Feeling wrong is nothing new to me. As I examine myself and really get to know who I am and what I want, feeling and memories of years gone by surface, and just won't be pushed away. I tell myself that I have spent too long hiding and now, I know myself and what I want, it is time to be myself, but can I? Really? Can a woman ever really be herself, or must she always be subject to other people's expectation and role persuasion? Is it gender based, or are we all the same?

Do the majority of people just go through life never knowing who they are? Is anybody really ever somebody real? I hope so. I know I want to go further and really open myself, but I cannot.

Christmas is coming, the pretense needs to get fat, then I can go home and be Samantha. The real Samantha. The Maasai Mzungu. The Maazungu.

Chapter 16

The time and date came. January 4th. I said goodbye to my English family, leaving them in the knowledge that I was heading for New York. Which I am. Just not yet. As I checked into my flight heading for Kilimanjaro, the desk opened for the flight I should have been on heading for New York, and the guilt hit my stomach. What on Earth have I done? I have lied to get what I want. How can I do such a thing? Even to myself, I sound bad. Even to myself?

That is all I ever wanted to be, myself, but is my 'self' this person who lies? I spent the time at the airport in my head, hating my actions. But I guess not enough to stop the course I was taking and turn the other way.

I hadn't slept much over the last few days, and amazingly spent most of the flight to TZ asleep, or reproaching myself. I felt like nobody had heard me. I had tried to talk about how I was feeling, but nobody really heard or understood how important it was for me to know myself and be myself. It was as if I couldn't turn back now, I was open, alive and living.

When you spend so long hiding from yourself and keeping secrets, you don't live. I let my thoughts ponder onto my parents and my childhood. They don't understand or even like the adult me. They like the child, or the person they can relate to. The Samantha who fits in to everybody else. I learnt at a young age, that to look like you are fitting in and not causing a disturbance is actually what most people want.

My abuser had taught me that lesson. "You don't tell or you will cause trouble" were the words which walled me in. So I pretended to be whatever anyone else wanted me to be. I can't do that anymore. I can't regress. What I had done was wrong. To lie is wrong, but I felt I could reason my actions. Couldn't I?

We started to descend, and I felt almost nervous. I told Benja and Samwel I was coming, my plan of a surprise hadn't worked. I remembered that Kilimanjaro was a remote airport, and that it was a possibility I might not have a taxi on arrival. I couldn't find the number for a taxi driver I know in Arusha, so I was forced to tell them or arrive in the night, to nobody and being possibly stranded.

When I said to Benja on the phone I was coming, he kept saying "thank you Mum, thank you Mum". It was a beautiful moment.

The plane landed safely, and we went through to immigration then baggage. I was one of the last people off the plane, which made me one of the last people out of the airport. As I walked through the door I could see Samwel and Benja standing waiting with a piece of paper, upon which my name was written. My heart leapt, I nearly fainted with excitement. I ran to Benja and hugged him so hard, then gave my Sister, Samwel the same greeting. Seeing them again was fantastic. The simple piece of paper was also wonderful, for you see, Benja is illiterate. I had been trying to teach him to read and write, and to see his progress, where he could write my name was absolutely great.

There was a taxi waiting for us, we got in, and started on the 4 hour drive from KIA to Karatu. Benja and I sat in the back, Samwel was in the front. They both kept looking at me; they said it was to check I had really come back. They were as excited as I was. Benja took my hand and said over and over again, ' my wife, my wife'. I wasn't ready for that or to deal with it right now, so I just smiled back at him and looked out of the window. Maybe tomorrow I could tell him my feelings? Maybe tomorrow I would know what they were!

Arriving at Karatu in the dark reminded me of the time I had come here with the children. I wished it was that time again, or they at least were with me. Instead, I arrived to a dark house, which was then lit by a lamp to reveal three Maasai I was sure I had never met, but allegedly we had all crossed paths before.

We had dropped Samwel at Benja's shop on the way back to the house. Benja had been working hard on the shop and it now seemed to be working well for him and producing an income. I had put up the initial investment for this shop for him. It had not cost much, but it had fulfilled his ambition of owning a shop. Benja had spent a lot of his childhood hungry, and while young, had found an ambition to own a shop. I think he thought if he had a shop there would be no more hunger in his family. Of course, he didn't realise the amount of hard work that goes into running a shop, but he soon found out, the practical way. Samwel was working as the security guard at the shop in the night. I was pleased about this, because it meant Samwel would be around and also, I knew his family had a wage going back to them.

Benja got the bags in from the car, by now it was in the early hours of the morning, around 2 a.m. I went to the bedroom I had previously slept in, got changed, and laid down on the mattress, covering myself with the blanket. Benja knocked on the door, and came in without being told to. He sat on the end of my mattress and took my hand. I thought I could see wetness in his eyes, but was not sure. He told me how pleased he was I came back. Nearly all of our friends had told him I wouldn't come back to TZ. That whatever was between us was not real, and that when I had told him this was my home, I had lied. The reasoning for this was a kind of ' who would want you?' scenario.

Benja was told time and time again that a Mzungu wouldn't leave Europe or the ' luxury ' lifestyle to be with a Maasai who comes from a mud hut and struggles to make a living with a small grocery shop. I listened, but couldn't respond. I was tired but also still thinking in English, and was waiting for my Swahili mind to kick in, before I had anything like a deep conversation. I squeezed his hand and told him I was here now. He moved up the mattress and lay his body near mine, so we could face each other, as we lay side by side. All of the passions I felt for him came rushing back. I could feel myself moistening. I was tired, but I wanted him so much. I prayed for my sense of morality to kick in, but I guess that had gone out of me when the lie came in.

God, I wanted this man so much, and I knew he wanted me. His breathing had changed to a faster more nervous rhythm. This time there was no one else in the room. Nothing else to disturb us. He put his arm round my waist and pulled me closer. I could now feel how much he wanted me. His erection was obvious, his emotion was heavy. I allowed him to pull me in and I draped my arm over stomach. I started to touch him, exciting myself with the softness of his skin and the smell of his body. I had never desired anyone so much as this. I had never wanted to be as one with someone like this. My hands started to roam, and in a kind of ' student/teacher ' way, so did his. I got the impression I was teaching him something new, by touch. The caressing became more urgent, Benja then leaned over me. His hands went down my body to touch my, now wet and ready vagina. I gasped, and then he did also. Which then made me laugh, then he did also. I felt so relaxed to be sharing myself with him. Benja then touched my clitoris, he was amazed by it. I realised he had never seen or felt one before. His previous partner was a Maasai, and judging by age, she would have been circumcised.

It is only the young Maasai girls who do not always have the circumcision now. With the thoughts of circumcision, something clicked in my brain about what I was doing and where I was. Shit! I was here getting ready to have sex with Benja, ready to make love to him, but I had no contraception. Sure I couldn't get pregnant, but what about disease. I asked Benja if he had any condoms, he said "no," so I said "we can't." He laughed at me, thinking I was joking. I wasn't. He then got angry with me saying he had no problem so there was ' no problem '. Could he really be so naïve? I told Benja I was very serious, that if he wanted to have sex with me we have to use a condom.

He said "it is OK, I want to give you a baby"! I had never told him I couldn't have more children, and now was not really the right time for that. The passion of the moment was starting to die as, what was so beautiful and urgent between us, became logical and cold.

We stopped our actions and lay for a while. I broke the silence by telling him I wanted him but we have to be safe. He turned his back on me then accused me of being bad, saying he had a disease.

Exasperated, I replied with a ' whatever'. Tired and confused, I let it go. Just 10 minutes ago I had been ready to become one with the man I loved; now we lay back to back, frustrated and angry with each other. Not exactly what I had thought my first night back here would have been, but I didn't regret it. I feared AIDS enough to not be stupid about sex, I had previously made a mistake like this and the anxiety that caused me was enough to teach me. I had also seen so much of HIV and AIDS in Kenya, I knew the possible consequence of 'giving in'.

I wanted to speak to Benja about this and clear the air. I called his name. He responded. We spoke. I asked if he had ever been to the doctor for tests? He said "No." I asked him if he would. I would also, for his peace of mind. He said "No" again. I could hardly believe it, how could he not want to know? How did he know I was free from infection? How could a grown man be so immature? I said "fine, then we will go no further." It was his turn to be shocked. I knew I was coming into conflict with his culture here. Maasai women do not really speak about sex, let alone contraception or precautions and here we were, me refusing him sex until he was tested for HIV! It seemed Maasai women are meant to just have sex, with partners or their husbands, and not have an opinion on it or what happens to their bodies as a result of it.

Dawn was starting to break, and neither of us had slept. I got up and greeted the other people in the house, then made my way, to the town. Aware of the pain in my heart and aching of my loins. On the way to town you walk past the Marie Stopes clinic, I pondered on the fact that maybe if I showed Benja where you have it done he might go and do it. But what about the lack of respect he had shown to me and my body? Was this really just a culture clash, or now, was Benja showing me a whole new side to him?

I reached the shop and Samwel was still there. I ran to him and hugged him. My faithful Sister! Oh how I had missed him. We went to a small hotel nearby and got a coffee, then started to talk. I have always been so close to Samwel, and talking is so free between us.

Sure we have some language difficulties, but we manage to overcome them and have a fantastic time together. I told Samwel about the previous night, and he laughed. He then asked what HIV was! Oh my God! Perhaps that was the problem. Perhaps Benja did not even know what I was talking about last night? I thought I would wait and see how things were this day, then maybe speak to him?

Karatu hadn't changed much in the time I had been away. Everything seemed much the same as ever. Of course, I hadn't been away for long, but mentally, it felt like an eternity had passed from me and to me since I last stood on this land.

One of the major differences, was this time, it was just me. None of my children were here. On just my first day there, even with the excitement of seeing some of my Maasai family again, their absence was very much felt. More so because I felt within me, this was the time of reckoning. This was my time to make choices and decisions. Another of the reasons I had been so eager to return to East Africa, was to sort out the situation with the car and check on the church in Kenya. When I had left Arusha previously, the car had been broken in a garage, awaiting repair. I didn't have the money to get it done, so I left it.

On this trip I wanted to have the Pajero repaired, and then hopefully take it to Kenya, so I could clear some issues there. I also had a court case pending, relating to the case of my stolen computer. I wasn't prepared to just let this matter drop. So, a day after my arrival in Karatu, I went back to Arusha to start the process of sorting out the loose ends I had left behind. I only had a few days until it was time for me to go to New York, the place I was meant to be in, so I wanted to get on with what I had to do here. Samwel joined me in my trip to Arusha, and I welcomed spending some time with him.

Since the first night with Benja, we hadn't managed to break the air which hung over us. He felt insulted, I felt a big lack of respect. We were spending time together and it was wonderful to be near him again, but we couldn't get any time alone together to actually talk about what had happened, and what we both expected. Some more people had come to stay at the Maasai house, and Benja was busy in the shop, and speaking about such things in front of all those people was not really something I wanted to do. I also knew speaking openly about sex was not something Maasai often do, and I didn't want to cause offence. I hoped the time would come we could speak on it. I had waited so long to be here, and I didn't want it to be like this.

From the moment I entered the police station in Arusha, a realisation of how much of a struggle this trip was going to be hit me. The police had ' lost ' the case, and the case number was in fact assigned to a completely different case altogether! Gosh, how convenient. I wondered how much ' kitu kidogo ' that had took the cleaner at Katimakatano! Kitu Kidogo is the term given in Swahili for a small corrupt act. It literally means 'something small'. However the consequences of ' something small ' are actually something large. It seemed to me that in some parts of East Africa, there is a whole way of life based on Kitu Kidogo. I wondered if this was what I was dealing with now. I hoped not, because I don't do Kitu Kidogo. I left the police station with a promise that I would return, and truly wanted my case to be found by the time I did, or I was going straight to the regional police commissioner.

My next stop was the garage where the car was. It was strange coming back here, almost like walking through a time tunnel because despite the insistence that the garage had done something in my absence, they had not. In fact, the position of the wheels of the Pajero had not moved, and there were bloody cobwebs in my car! I could hardly believe my eyes or how lazy the fundi was! While I had been in London I had sent him regular e-mails, and he had told me he was slowly working on the car, doing everything he could do without sourcing the major parts, which would cost a lot of money. Now I was back, I could see he had done nothing and had lied to me. I was very angry, but I managed to compose myself and calm down. Allowing myself and the fundi to go to the garage and get the parts needed.

Next was the hotel. The owner of Katimakatano gave me a warm welcome on my arrival there. I liked to think it was through genuine pleasure at greeting me again, but I knew it was really due to the fact that I owed him some money, and he thought he was getting it back! I hoped he would, but I had to sort the car out first. Priscus offered me a room for the night. I declined. I didn't want to stay there, and the thought of staying overnight in Arusha made me sad. I knew living in the city would cost me more money, and it was not where I wanted to be.

I decided to leave Arusha and commute between there and Karatu when needed. It would soon be time for me to go to New York, and I had some unfinished business with Benja to try and clear up, and also, I hoped I would have time to touch base in the wilderness before setting off again.

Samwel and I arrived back in Karatu, and headed for the house. It was already dark, and the way was not easy to find. I have never felt scared when walking at night in Africa with my friends, though in a logical sense, perhaps I should have. We arrived at the little house. I went to my bedroom, shut the door then flopped on the mattress, exhausted.

Benja was not here, which was not nice. I knew I had no reason to demand or expect him home, but I missed him. We had spent long enough apart, and now, we were in the same town, where we could supposedly spend time with each other and either lack of communication, understanding or pure pig headedness was keeping us apart. I wondered if this was worth it.

Benja arrived back during the night at some point. Presuming it was OK for him to come and sleep in my bedroom, he walked in then lay on the mattress next to me, and whispered ' pole' in my ear. I did my usual trick of pretending to be asleep. However, this time he was insistent to wake me, speaking my name softly into my ear. I moved my body to face him, he took me by my hips and pulled me close.

His touch was rough and insistent, he knew he wanted me to lay next to him and nothing was going to stop him! He then said over and over again, "sorry, don't go back to London." I told him I hadn't planned to right now, but we did need to talk.

He hushed me with his mouth, then proceeded to kiss me with a tenderness I had not felt before. I melted next to him. I was so damn angry at him, but with every tender caress, he warmed my iciness until I was completely defrosting in his arms. I wanted him, he wanted me, but he knew my rules. Would it be the same this time? I started to speak, he hushed me again, putting his finger to my lips. He then said "I know, not now. When we are married!"

Oh my God! I was so shocked that this was his conclusion, but also felt kind of respected. Benja then went on to tell me that he had been speaking to people about Mzungus. Apparently he had been told that we need to be married. Quite an outdated view of course, but this was now what he was thinking. I smiled, he kissed me, and held onto me so tight. Scared I would go.

Happy we were there. I could feel his erection, and I wanted it. I reached down to touch him, feeling my way in the darkness, tracing my hands over his skin, then he got up and left the room! Aaaaggghh!!!

Frustrated but understanding his action, I lay in the dark room thinking. What a strange evening. I had gone from angry to turned on to frustrated and now relieved. I hadn't gone too far with Benja, he had shown me the utmost respect, and even though saving myself for our marriage was not my initial thought or intention I appreciated what he had done. Relieved that we were now communicating again, I fell easily into sleep, where my dreams and nightmares all mingled into one.

Chapter 17

I awoke the next morning, haunted by the familiar dreams I could neither remember nor explain. Benja was next to me; he had not slept in the same room. He had come to wake me up by stroking my long hair. It was wonderful to wake up next to him. I knew I loved him, but was beginning to wonder in what context we were meant to be together. If we were meant to have a marriage style relationship, wouldn't we have been more than this? I felt him as a protector; someone who I knew would always look after me. In fact, I now understood that one of the parts off me that the Maasai had subconsciously tapped into was my need to be looked after. I had always acted so tough and pretended to be strong, and in some ways I am. I can survive and get life done. But, I think subconsciously I had always wanted someone to care for me. To look after me and make things better. Laying next to Benja, on our crap smelly mattress felt like the most comfortable and safe place in the world. Home?

It was a Sunday, so we got up and went to church, as most good Africans do! As I sat in church, guilt consumed me. I felt so awful for being in Tanzania the way I was, with the lies I had told. I tried to reason to myself that nobody back home was listening to me, and I even got to the point where I could blame them for my actions, then I stopped it with childish recognition. I alone was responsible for the lie I had told. I would have to live with the guilt and eventual confession of it. Thoughts of my children filled my mind as I listened to the preacher speak. I resolved to myself that I would call them after church had finished. Moses, the preacher carried on speaking for some time. On what the subject was, I cannot quite recall as I was away in my own thoughts. I have always admired the teachings of Moses, but it would probably help me a lot more if I could remember more of what he speaks on!

Church finished and we made our way out of the building, heading towards the little house in Karatu. Benja was staying in town, but Samwel came with me back to the house.

We arrived at home, it was quiet, so I thought I would take the opportunity to call England and speak to the children. I found my phone, which was in my handbag. There was little battery life on it and no electricity to charge it in the house. I thought I could get away with a quick call, after I had received the barrage of messages which always arrives when I switch my phone on after some time without it. The first texts were nice, all pleasant greetings enquiring how I was and what I was up to. Then it happened. I started realising the shit was truly hitting the fan. There were some very angry messages from Andy, who had found out where I was. Then worried messages from my friend who Andy had tried to contact in his angry state. Then more messages from Andy, telling me how awful I was. I felt myself dragged down with every derogatory word that was directed my way, of which there were so very many. I eventually managed to hear all the messages, and call Andy. He was absolutely fuming with me and told me he would be contacting his solicitor for a divorce. So this was it. We were over.

Tears streamed down my face as the absolute gulf of guilt hit me. I was responsible for this pain. I had caused this. I had made Andy suffer his anger and I deserved his wrath. This much was true. I wished within me that he would understand, but I knew, he would never truly take on board who I really am. I loved Andy so much, and despite not being in love with him, we had shared a lot together.

The grief of loss opened up my soul, and in my weakness, in my vulnerable state, it was as if the floodgates of guilt, shame and pain I had carried over the years erupted.

Samwel came to the bedroom. He had heard me on the phone to Andy and the crying that followed. He opened the door, and came in. I was slumped in the corner of the room, curled up crying in the feotal position. He lifted me slightly and just took me in his arms. I sobbed like I have never sobbed before. Every breath releasing pain, from years gone by, right up to the present time.

I had never expressed the pain my childhood had scarred me with. Nobody really knew about it. And here I was, with my crumbled marriage, wrecked life, in the arms of my Sister, who happened to be a man, letting out absolutely everything. I felt as if I didn't have any control, the grief permeated my every vein and pumped out through my heart, flooding my being.

Benja came back. He found Samwel cradling me and did the usual Maasai question when faced with a crying person, of "who's died?" Samwel explained to him what had happened, as he understood it. Benja came to sit the other side of me. And there we were. I was at my most broken ever, but also my most supported. I was letting out everything I had in me, because there was no space for anything else, and even though the way I had done things was not right, as I sat in the small bedroom, on the mattress, flanked by Benja on one side and Samwel on the other, I knew that now, it was time to let it out.

Now I was loved without condition or pretense. Now I did not fear those around me. Now I was able to just be myself. Nothing more. Nothing less. It was the most painful and freeing experience ever.

For what seemed like an eternity, the three of us just sat there, holding each other. By the time we were starting to move out of the bedroom, it was getting dark. Benja and Samwel were hungry, but my appetite had gone. I told them to go to town and get something to eat, that I would be fine, but they refused. Benja went to get food, Samwel stayed with me.

I knew I should try and communicate with Andy again, but I had also heard his tone on the phone. I was thankful of the physical distance between us. I thought I would e mail him tomorrow and try to explain. I have always been able to express myself with words in a far more detailed and open way, so this seemed like the best option.

The tears had dried up, and the relief of the outburst of emotions was immense. I felt tired but rejuvenated. Like a massive weight was being lifted from me. I no longer had the guilt of the lies I had told, the pains had been released and in the exposure had helped to start a healing process.

Benja came back with meat, which was a wonderful choice for a carnivore. I was thankful my appetite had ran from me. I just drank milk instead. After eating, Benja asked how I was feeling. I said the truth of, "awful but fine." Another contradiction in terms? Or perhaps a way of saying I am OK, but feel like shit right now. He then proceeded to say that he thought I should go home!

I could hardly believe my ears. I had come here, lying to my family about my location, so I could see my Maasai family and tidy up the loose ends I had left before, and here he was, telling me I should go home? My soon to be ex-husband had just told me that divorce was our only option, I was worried over the pain I had caused, I had just let out all the shit I had carried around in me since the age of 5 years old, and here was the supposed love of my life telling me to go home? How could I have made such a terrible judge of character? If he loved me, how could he say this? Confusion reigned and tears rained. I ran from the house, into the darkness. Across the land towards the maize fields at the back of the house. I didn't care that it was night; I just wanted to get out. Anger was beginning to seep through me. How dare he reject me when I had given so much? How dare he fool me then push me away when the going got tough. This life that he had wanted with me was never going to be easy. This much was always true and he had seemed to understand that. So what now? It was all a lie? I ran as fast as I could, thanking God for the night and the cloud covering the moon, which should give enough shadow to make up for my lack of speed and ability to actually run very far at all.

Benja had run out of the house after me, and I thought he had gone the opposite way. I should have known, with him being a Maasai, that being out in the dark looking for someone or something was not actually hard, for he found me quite easily sitting in the maize field. He edged towards me, asking why I ran. In a raised voice, I told him I hated him, that he had used me and made up things to try and please me, but he was a fake and I wanted nothing to do with him.

Wind blew through the maize, creating a chill around us. He stepped towards me; I could now see his features. The clouds had moved, allowing the moon to spread its light over the field. He was crying and looked bewildered. Then Benja said to me "fine". You want to go, it is fine". Exasperated, I replied with "but you want me to go"! He shook his head and said "no " many times. He explained that he had said what he did because he thought I needed to go home, and before I said it, he wanted to let me know it was OK with him. He wasn't sending me home, he didn't want me to go home, he just wanted me to be happy, and if that was not here with him then I should go. Shame now came to me. In my heightened state of emotion, I had absolutely lost it. I had believed the worst case scenario, and not any other possibilities. This day was so awful; I was in such a mess. Tears fell; Benja came next to me and took me in his arms. The wind was still whistling through the maize.

He kissed me on the cheek, mopping up some of my tears with his mouth. I moved my mouth to meet his, we kissed. The emotion and passion in both of us began to rise. We began exploring each other with urgency. The emotional stress of the day had burst from both of us. Leaving holes that needed filling. Leaving pain that needed to be hugged. We kissed frantically, and then slowed down as we lowered ourselves to the floor, fallen stalks of maize becoming our mattress. And we did it. Safely. Benja and I finally became one that night. In the open air, surrounded by stalks of maize, feeling nature, feeling free. Feeling loved. It was the most perfect sensation in the midst of such awful trauma.

When sense and reason had come back to us, we got up and headed back to the house. Nothing was said between us as we trekked back across the maize field. I think a feeling of disbelief was with Benja and I. For months now we had battled our urges, and now we had given in, in a way neither of us had expected. It was awful but there were no regrets, just immense shock on my part.

Arriving back at the home, Samwel came to see if we were OK. Both Benja and I said fine, then went to the bedroom. We lay together on the mattress, talking for a while, then giving in to the sleep that was waiting for us. I held Benja in my arms, with his head resting on my breasts, he sleepily looked up at me and said with full heart and intention mirrored in his eyes, " I love you my wife". And I loved him. We were one.

Every so often, in life, many of us will wake up with that ' morning after the night before ' feeling. Where you either have a hazy memory of what took place, or have full recollection and possible embarrassment to live with. Sometimes, some people do not even remember what they have done in heightened state of emotion and stress. As I lay on the mattress, recalling the day before, I wished for a bout of amnesia to come and get me. What the bloody hell had I done? I should have been mourning the loss of my marriage, not nearly getting together another one with Benja, shouldn't I? He moaned next to me and I looked at him.

Everything I felt was a contradiction in term and actions. I dressed and headed into town. I wanted to e-mail Andy as soon as possible, which I did, trying my best to explain what was happening, where I was, what I was doing and why I was doing this. All I could do was open up my whole truth, and leave it there. I had nothing else to offer.

I seemed to pass this day in a haze, I knew I was here, but my head and heart were away with guilt and self-questioning. I had to leave for NY the following day. This was crazy, but had to be done for work reasons and to have the chance of providing, eating and living. Everything was happening so fast, but I either had the option of getting on with it or getting down.

I had to get on with life, even though the alternative did seem to beckon me somewhat. I bid farewell to Benja, again. It was difficult, but I knew I wouldn't be away for long.

The trip to NY was absolutely awful. It seemed just fine, nothing went drastically wrong or bad, but with the mess I had left in 2 continents, and the emotional trauma everyone was going through, I felt absolutely drained. I also know that I do not belong in Western life. So here, where it is the epitome and centre of everything commercially Mzungu, I felt sick. Like a fish out of my water, pining for home. The UK was more bearable, not through any sense of home, but through the fact that my children are there. NY had nothing for me, and I could not wait to get to my real home. As soon as was possible, I left the States, and headed back to Tanzania, to my people and my home.

By the time I had returned, there was a reply to my ' warts and all ' e mail I had sent Andy. He in fact was very supportive in it, saying he now understood a lot more about me, who I am and why I am. I hoped it was true. I told him I would be back as soon as I got done here, and had been to Kenya. With a lighter sense of mind, and a stronger sense of direction, I carried on sorting out the car and the police case. Commuting between Arusha and Karatu most days.

Everything seemed to take so long, there was always paperwork pending, or parts to be sourced. I was enjoying the work I was doing. I felt right to be clearing up the mess I had left behind. It was also good to spend a few weeks of ' normal ' life with my Maasai family. Eventually I was able to move on to Kenya, the car was ready, the court case was done. Benja could not come with me to Kenya. He had his shop to run, so Samwel said he would come. Benja found someone to cover the work of Samwel, and allowed him. He trusted Samwel to look after me.

Yet again, I was having to say "goodbye" to Benja. I didn't know when I would be back, as my plan was to go to Kenya, sort out FFI, give the car back, then leave for the UK. On my last night in Karatu, we spent the evening sitting outside the house, listening to the 'World Service' on the radio. Talking, laughing, and just simply enjoying each others company. I sat there, knowing this was my life.

The missing element of my children pained me so much, but the found element of myself helped with that pain. Even though I had no plans made for my return, I felt much more peaceful than the last time I had gone back to the UK. So did Benja, because I had proven to him I would return if I said I would.

Sitting under the small trees, listening to the evening animals come out, Benja turned to me and told me again, he wanted me to be his wife. Before I could answer, he told me that his elders at one of the bomas he grew up in were telling him they would find him a wife. He had told them "no" and that he had found his wife. They asked who it was, and were disappointed when he had told them it was me, his Mzungu. I sat silently, listening. I always knew there was going to be a problem with some of the Maasai, who viewed me with much suspicion. The elders of Piaya had accepted me, but there were other people who held a generational influence over Benja and his life. Benja went on, explaining that he had told them he did not want to marry a Maasai woman, and again stated he had found the woman he wanted as his wife.

This was initially unacceptable to the elder, who then came up with the suggestion that Benja could marry me, as long as he took a 2nd wife who was Maasai. My stomach turned to knots. Why had Benja even bothered to tell me? He knew how I felt on the subject of polygamy. For me, I couldn't accept a second wife. If Benja and I were ever to marry it had to be monogamous or nothing. I braced myself for being dumped. I know how the Maasai culture was important to Benja, and also being the eldest child of a family, he had to be an example to the other siblings. He had responsibilities, which I could not expect him to compromise. I respect who he is too much to expect a compromise on such a huge issue as marriage.

Also, I reasoned to myself that if this is a problem now, it would bring further troubles into our later lives. Benja sat with his head hung low. I knew his pressure. It was time to let him go.
I could feel my tears well, as I looked at him, aware that what I was saying was indeed the opposite of what I felt. I started to speak, telling Benja how much I loved him, and wanted to be his wife in the future. But I would not, I could not, I loved him too much to cause such pain in his life and divisions in his people. I would leave, come back to visit my Maasai family sometimes if this was acceptable, but would leave him free to take a Maasai wife in accordance with his culture. I got up and walked away. Leaving him in the evening twilight, under the light of the rising moon, contemplating the words

I had just said. I don't know how I walked, I felt like falling. I hated what I had just done; I went in the house and started to pack my bag. I kept expecting Benja to come into the bedroom and speak to me, he didn't. I glimpsed out of the window a few times, he was still sitting under the tree. It didn't take me long to pack my bag, I hadn't even unpacked the bag completely from my previous trips. All I had to do was add my few other possessions to it. I took off my silver cross holding it in my hand. I had been given this on my 18th birthday; it was so precious to me and had been worn most days over the past 11 years. I wanted to give it to Benja; I didn't have much in the way of precious possessions, but what was most precious I wanted to give to him, probably in some hopeful attempt that he will always remember me and the life we nearly had.

I called a taxi friend of mine, arranging to go to a nearby hotel, until morning when I would leave for Kenya. Benja then came in to the house, he said nothing. Just came and held me. I bid him farewell, placing my cross in his hand, then went on my way. Somehow controlling the pain I was feeling inside. I had let go of my love and my protector.

I got the taxi to stop at Benja's shop, to tell Samwel where I was staying the night and where to meet me in the morning. Samwel wasn't there, so I resolved to come early in the morning, and then went to the guest house, into a night where both sleep and dream escaped me, which at least meant I did manage to get to see Samwel in the early morning.

The drive to Namanga takes around 5 hours from Karatu. The car was running well, and the journey was enjoyable. A Maasai called Raphael was driving. He had been introduced to me through Benja, and had been great company over the past weeks. He held a valid and legal driving license, and was looking for work, so I employed him to drive me to Kisumu.

We approached the Namanga border between Kenya and Tanzania, then got out our papers and passports. Going into the immigration office, I was confident that I knew the procedures here. My visa for

Kenya had expired back in August. So I had to get a new one, it is possible to get this at Namanga for the cost of around $50. I filled in the forms, gave over the money, only to be told that I could not enter Kenya!

My Visa application was not successful. This was absurd. There were no legal reasons that I should not enter this country, I am not a criminal, had done nothing wrong or bad there, but immigration would not be budged. Saying that the decision was with their superiors. I had to put in an appeal and as it was a Friday, we had to wait until Monday for the result of the appeal.

Bloody great. What was I meant to do now? I didn't want to stay in Namanga for the whole weekend, so between us we decided to stay in Arusha and come back to immigration on Monday, which we did. Only to be told the same thing. This time there was a bit more elaboration. The immigration officer told me that there was an open file regarding me, and until the immigration office had satisfied their enquiries I was not allowed to enter Kenya. What? The words were going in and registering, causing an amazing amount of anger to rise in me. There was nothing I could do to change this decision, just keep appealing, which would also cost me a further $50 each time! I was gutted. I had sacrificed myself in so many ways helping Kenya. I had come to Kisumu, assisted in setting up a community project, supported many of the people, used my own money until there was very little left, and all I have got back in return from the majority, but not all, of the people was stress, problems, deceit, and now a denial to enter the country. I could hardly believe it. It hurt so much. I questioned myself over and over again, had I done something to cause this? I found myself pondering on the enemies I had made there. I wondered if there was a link and some ' kitu kidogo ' in use.

Something I could never prove of course, but it seemed kind of logical. I contacted Patrick and told him what was happening. I had not been planning to tell him of my arrival in Kisumu, so he was shocked to learn I was only in the next country. I had wanted to see how things were, when I was not around or expected to be around.

He also came to the same conclusion, that there was foul play afoot. We decided between us to file a report to the anti corruption committee in Kenya in the hope something could be done.

Samwel, Raphael and I headed back to Arusha. I was unsure of what to do or where to turn next. I felt such a mixture of sad and angry. If I stayed in Arusha, what would it be for? My work there was done. I couldn't get back into Kenya. Benja was in Karatu, which would be difficult situation to return to, so soon after leaving. But, also, so were my other Maasai people. The only other alternative I had was to go back to the UK.

Chapter 18

I received a call from the regional police commissioner. He asked me to stop by his office to pick up some paperwork relating to my case. I had stayed in Arusha the previous night, after my disastrous trip to Namanga, so it was not too much trouble for me to go to the police station. I climbed into a land rover taxi which was heading towards Usa River, passing the place I needed to be. In a moment of mind recognition, as I climbed in I noticed the door catch was broken. Damaged cars used as taxis were nothing unusual here, but the way I saw this gave me a very spooky feeling. Sometimes you can feel the significance of something before you know what it is. This sensation often happened to me, for example, I always knew that the name Andrew was going to be important to me. As a child, when I heard that name I could feel shivers down my spine. Even with more recent events, like crossing the Serengeti for the first time and feeling the pull of it in my soul and mind. I shuddered to myself, said a quick prayer, then got in the car.

Throughout Arusha, there are many open drains that line the streets. I was looking out of the window, people watching, when the vehicle started turning over. There were some screams from inside, we were going to crash, everything was going so fast, and very wrong. I then fell out of the car. The broken door flew open and I tumbled out into one of the open drains. Impacting my body on the concrete and sewage as I landed. The car scraped along a bit further, then completely crashed on its side. The windows caved in and people were screaming to get out. I tried to get up, but fell back down again. My knees caused me so much pain. Bystanders came running over to assist us. My head felt heavy, I was feeling ready to vomit, I couldn't keep my eyes open any longer.

I must have drifted away into unconsciousness, because the next thing I can recall is laying in a hospital bed. Somebody had brought me here. I tried to think, but every thought seemed clouded. I couldn't answer myself with the details of what had happened, I just knew that we had crashed. Nothing else. I tried to remember. It hurt. Something was missing in my recollection of the chain of events, but what was it? The door opened and a Dr. came in. he introduced himself as Dr. Mbogo, and went onto diagnose me with some concussion and medium scale injuries. I needed further X Rays and he asked me if I was able to stay in for observation. I agreed. He left, leaving me with some strong painkillers, I took them, then struggled to remember again, before falling into a deep drug induced sleep.

When I awoke, the room was in darkness. I felt a little better, probably thanks to the sleep. My knees felt awful, and the pain from them as I bent my leg was strong. Despite sleeping, I felt very tired. Then I remembered. Samwel! That's what I was missing, my Sister. Where was he? He had been in the car with me when we crashed. I forced myself out of the bed, to try and find a light. I must have made a noise because the nurse came in to see if I was OK. I explained that I had lost the Maasai man I was travelling with at the time of the crash; she smiled at my concern, then told me that all of the people who were in the accident were brought here for assessment. She would look for him.

Somewhat relieved, I went back to the bed and lay down, waiting for news. Everything was such a mess. I had come here to try and sort things out and progress, and I felt as if I had actually got nowhere. Sure the court case was done, the car was now repaired, but for what? I couldn't take it to Kenya just yet, until my ' open case ' was closed. Then there was Benja, my darling Benja, I had let go of him, hoping I was doing the right thing for both of us, even though inside I was crippled with the pain of knowing I would never be with him. And now, to top it all, I had been in a crash. I reached the point where I knew I could go no further. I was drained of energy and feeling an absolute wreck. I wondered if nothing had gone right because I had been so wrong in my actions. It was a thought that didn't sweep away easily.

A knock on the door brought with it the entrance of the nurse, and Raphael. He had been told of the crash, and the fact there was a Mzungu involved. Bad news against Mzungus seems to always spread very fast in East Africa. Raphael had tried to tell himself there were many Mzungus in Arusha, and the likelihood of the one in the crash being me was so low. However he couldn't shake it from his mind that it might have been, so he came to ask at the hospital, where he was told his feelings had been correct. I was here. I told Raphael I was doing fine, and was only in for concussion and observation. I asked again about Samwel. The nurse had found him, but couldn't bring him to me. He was too sick. Samwel had suffered more than I in the crash, he had some severe internal bleeding, and they didn't know if he was going to pull through. Only time would tell.

I tried to register the information I was receiving. My head hurt, and waves of nausea hit me. No! Not my Samwel. Not my Sister. I asked to go to where he was, but the nurse didn't think it was advisable. Raphael piped into the conversation that he would push me in a wheelchair, and if I felt any worse or passed out he would bring me straight back. The nurse agreed, and took us to where Samwel was. The room was bare, save for the bed and a side table. Samwel lay sleeping. His dark skin very bruised, and cuts all over him. I gasped inwardly in shock.

Then somehow managed to get the strength to talk to him, as if nothing was wrong. Something clicked in me, and the inner resource that had got me through the time I had suffered with my Zac, kicked in. I could do this, and if it was true that my Samwel was going to die here, then I wanted his last thoughts to be of our happy times. Recalling the tears and the large amount of laughter we had shared.

I proceeded to talk to him, sharing our memories with whoever was in the room, but to me they didn't matter. Samwel mattered. With hindsight it was so funny, I was sitting there with

Raphael laughing his head off, Samwel sleeping, I was talking and a gobsmacked nurse kept crossing the sign of the crucifix on her as she heard about the things we had said and done. The nurse was especially shocked to hear about the banana and condom lessons!

Samwel woke up to find us all in his room, I knew he would not really understand what his condition was, but we tried to explain what was happening to him, and the seriousness of it.
The next day, after many X rays, I was discharged. There was nothing wrong with me, and the concussion had not caused any further problems. I was only bruised and aching. However, I didn't leave the hospital. I wanted to be with my Samwel.

Over the next few days he started to improve, which was a relief for us all. He then had to be discharged. Not because he was ready to but because we had used all the money available to us, we couldn't afford any more of the hospital bills. I wished there was another way, but there was not.

We discharged Samwel from hospital, and booked him in to the charitable hospital, where the bill would be cheaper. I only hoped that the level of care would be good.

With this change of location, I decided I should head back towards Karatu and tell some people where Samwel was. Raphael had left for Moshi a few days previously, on the promise of some work. There was no other person around who I knew that was a friend of Samwel, so I felt obliged to go.

At this point, I was so drained and devoid of energy. So much had happened over the past few weeks, I was tired out. My mind was in a whirl, and my body felt like just resting all the time, and my emotions were all over the place, facing the constant battle between morality and what I really wanted to do with my life. Every contact I had with back home, made me fear reading my e mails. I would sometimes even reject calls, because I could not face my own sense of failure and their sense of judgement. I was living a constant guilt trip that I had put myself on. I would look at a calendar, and know it was coming to my son's 7th birthday, would I make it home for his celebration? I certainly had intended to when I left the UK, but would I? There was so much going on. I also felt so sick and nauseous all the time, and food just wasn't going down. I had become weak and everything just ached.

It was at this stage I realised I could not carry on. I needed to get back to the UK. I needed rest, and to sort out the problems with Andy and my family. I booked my flight.

Booking the flight was such a sad event. I wanted to do it, but leaving Africa was always traumatic. Leaving my Maasai family was always difficult, but such is life, and sometimes we have to face our issues, deal with them and then move forward.

I had a few days to get to Karatu, and try to arrange some people to care for Samwel, before I went back to London. I did wonder how I would be received in Karatu, especially after how things had been left between Benja and I.

I seriously hoped Benja understood why I had felt the need to finish everything with him, not that we had ever really started. Oh how I wished things could have been different. I loved Benja so much.

On the matatu, heading towards Karatu, I sat running over all the recent events in my head. Everything had happened so quickly. The emotional rollercoaster seemed to never get on to a straight section. It was always a massive high or a massive low, and right now, a very nauseous corkscrew. I couldn't shake this nausea from my body, and as I sat on the badly sprung and uncomfortable seat of the kamikaze matatu, watching the plains rush by through the window, a bizarre thought came to me. I quickly tried to push it aside as illogical or impossible, but the more I thought, and ran past the checklist of what I was feeling, the more I recognised my symptoms. I realised it might not be completely improbable. There was the chance, that right now, I could be pregnant. Shit!

The thought of it made me feel more nauseous than the sickness I was already feeling. I hit a kind of panic mode in my brain, then managed to get onto a more logical thought path. I would arrive in Karatu, go to the 'Marie Stopes' clinic and do a pregnancy test before anything else.

As with many of my best plans, the trip to the clinic did not happen. When I arrived in Karatu, the nurse who does the testing had left. She would be back in the morning. So, I had to wait. I went to book into a guest house. The only path which headed the way I intended to go, went straight past Benja's shop.

I did plan to go and see Benja, but right now, I felt as if I wanted to just sleep and worry by myself. Not share what I was thinking, or even pretend I was OK, when I wasn't. I also didn't want to take on board any more pain and seeing Benja again might just remind me of how much I wanted him. With a sense of dread in my mind as I walked, I had the hope that Benja would have closed up for the night, but that was soon dashed, when I turned the corner into the path which runs by his shop. He was sitting outside, on the little wall, talking to a group of Maasai. It seemed as if nobody had noticed me, but then, with my every step approaching closer to their group, somebody turned to look at me.

They then looked at Benja, and said something. Benja looked up. Shock and surprise were evident in his facial expression. I smiled, he returned my smile, and then leapt up from where he was sitting, and literally ran over to me. He embraced me so tight, enveloping me in his arms. I felt my resolve melt as he had his arms round me.
He had so many questions, and I found a new strength and ability to speak about everything which had happened in Arusha. He asked where I was staying, and I said the guest house. He asked me not to, to come and stay at the house. I agreed. I had missed all of my family so much, and to separate myself from them for this one night, when I was in the same town would have been stupid. So we left for home. My family and I. My Maasai.

I was not sure how the sleeping arrangements were going to be, but as we were a large group at the house that night, there would have been little chance of Benja and I being left alone. A thought which both saddened and elated me.

Everybody seemed to go to sleep early that night, except Benja and I. There was a heavy air of expectation between us, but I knew that

if we were going to have any chance of knowing each other in the ' friend ' capacity, I couldn't cross the boundary I had set. He held my hand and we spoke about so many things. I couldn't tell him about my pregnancy fears, I wanted to have the test and collect my own thoughts on whatever the result was. Feeling my tiredness
finally get the better of me, I lay down next to Benja, he put his arms around me, and we drifted off to sleep together, as we had done so many times before. And it felt perfect. Like the most natural thing in the world.

Chapter 19

I woke up to find Benja had already left the mattress where we had slept. Waves of nausea ran over me as I came to and remembered my plans for the day. I could hear some people speaking outside the house, so I decided to get dressed and join them. This was likely to be the last time I would spend time just ' being ' with my people for some time, I wanted to enjoy it. Benja was also outside. He smiled at me as I left the house and came to join the group of Maasai who were sitting in a circle, speaking, sharing, and hairdressing! I sat with them, which was an absolute conversation killer. A silence seemed to fall upon the group, I presumed it was obvious they had been speaking about me, so I just started a new conversation, which broke the iciness and allowed for some good communication. I told them about Samwel, they were thankful I had returned to alert them to his needs and condition.

Laata told me I was such a real Maasai and asked why I could not be with them all the time now. It was at this point I said to them I was leaving for London in a few days time. Benja had been busy making somebody's rasta on his head, my previous statement had stopped his fingers in the braid. He asked me "ukweli?" Meaning, is it true? I replied with a "yes." All of the people who were in this group almost begged me not to return, except Benja. He just stared at me. The silence fell again.

I stood up, to leave for the clinic. Laata and Daudi said they would walk into town with me, Benja asked if I would be around today, I said I would, and would meet him at his shop in an hour or so, then left. I didn't really want Daudi and Laata to come to the clinic with me, but I was thankful of their light hearted company and laughter as we walked towards the town. The 'Marie Stopes' clinic was soon in my sight, and I tried to ditch my two companions, but they insisted on staying with me. Many people come to this clinic for a variety of reasons, so I was not concerned they would find out what I was there for.

I was called in to the Dr, and told him I wanted to have a pregnancy and an HIV test done. He sent me to the nurse, where she took blood then did the standard 3 minute urine test, which just looked like the same thing you can buy in 'Boots' back home. I couldn't see the test stick, the nurse had placed it out of my view, then left the room. So for 3 minutes I sat there remembering when I had done these tests with my previous pregnancies. I hated the anticipation of them, the feeling of dread then joy. Or even further dread, which would be true in this case.

I then managed to talk myself out of it. I had been sterilised at 24! The likelihood of a failure was very remote, wasn't it? The words of the obstetrician who delivered my last born rang in my head "a sterilisation failure is more common if the 'snip' is done at the time of a caesarean delivery, you should perhaps reconsider your approach." I didn't. I wanted it all over and done with at the same time.

The nurse walked back in, went to where she had hid the test, picked it up, took it with her, and told me to go and wait for the Dr. again. Bloody hell! Why couldn't she just tell me?

The Dr. called me in, and let me know the 'good news', I was expecting a child. I felt sick. It was true. 1 night of craziness in a maize field and some high jumping sperm and this was the result. In my weakened state, I also felt the weight of the possible consequences. We had used protection. How had it gone wrong? I thought back to the night, and realised I only saw the packet and had felt the condom on him. I hadn't checked if it had slipped off or broke or had a hole or anything like that. The HIV test would take around 6/7 days for the result, but it probably wouldn't show anything just yet anyway, even if there was an infection.

I left the clinic, going straight to Benja's shop. Laata and Daudi kept asking if I was ok, I of course said "yes". There was a little time before I was due to meet with Benja, so I went to get a coffee. My escorts were heading into the little town, and left me at the hotel. I then proceeded to move to another hotel, where they would not

know I was. I needed to drink and think alone and in peace. Pregnant. I kept running the word through my head. I was so shocked with the confirmation of my symptoms. What was I going to do? I have always been very pro life, but now, here I
was, not in a real relationship and with child, Maazungu child. Not English, not African. I knew that in the UK I would be the absolute shame of my racist family, I also knew that by staying here, I was upsetting Benja's elders. But, this was Benja's responsibility also. He should know what was happening and that, if all progressed according to plan, he would be a Father. Though quite where his child would be, I couldn't say.

I resolved to go and get it over with. I went to Benja's shop to tell him my news. He was waiting for me inside the shop, and then insisted we go and take a walk together. We walked to 'Paradise Garden', a small hotel with a beautiful garden to sit and enjoy. I thought it would be better to just say what I had to say and try to sort this mess out somehow, but before I could get there, Benja had started talking in a fast and very deep way. He told me that while I had been away, he had thought he would never see me again. And that was far too much to handle. He went on to say, he knew he would be upsetting his elders, but he wanted to marry me, and refuse a 2nd wife. My arrival in Karatu yesterday had confirmed a lot of his feelings, and how he truly wanted me as his wife. I wasn't sure what to say. Again I knew what I should say, I should say "No." I should say "just go and be a normal Maasai, I am not right for you." This time, unlike the answers to his previous proposals, my reply came out as a "yes." "Yes, I will marry you. If you stick to the monogamy rules, and know that at the hint of a 2nd wife I will leave, then I will marry you."

Benja was so happy; he leant over the table and promised me he would be good to me." It was then I decided to tell him about the baby. It was either going to completely ruin the moment or add to it. On receiving my news, Benja asked if it was true, then told me he was so happy today. He had a wife and a child. Ever the realist, I told him that both of those titles needed some work on them, I need to be divorced first, and the child needs to grow, before it is here. But that didn't seem to dampen his enthusiasm.

I spent the next 2 days just being with my people in Karatu. Then Daudi, Julius, Laata Benja and I all went to Arusha. Daudi and Julius were going to go and be with Samwel. Laata and Benja were coming to see me off at the airport.

Goodbye's are never easy, but I didn't have any doubts this time over my return, so did not feel as anxious or lost as on my previous trip back to the UK. I bid them farewell, and headed through to the air side of Kilimanjaro airport. Aware, that on my arrival in the UK, I should be ready to face the inquisition of a lifetime. It almost made me run back through to land side.

I touched down in Heathrow, after a smooth flight. I went to visit my friend for a little rest and moral support, before heading back to home. Andy knew I was returning, but I turned up earlier than expected.

Our reunion was hardly intense or passion filled. I wasn't sure how to take him; he wasn't sure what to do with me. There had been too much damage. Even holding a basic conversation was difficult. I had wondered if he would be angry or even potentially violent towards me, however I soon realised that this was not something which was going to happen.

Despite the hurt between us, and the pain I in particular had caused him, Andy was still very much in love with me, and only wanted me to be OK.

Part of me wished I could return the sentiment. Thoughts of the days gone by where all we had was each other and a heap of love between us sprung into my mind. I loved this man so much, but I was not in love with him. He was such a part of me, but not the ' heart pinging ' part anymore. I think I wanted to be in love with him.

It would sure make life easier. But for how long do you lie to yourself? I do love Andy. I know that. I want to ping. I want to ignite with him.

We spoke about some things, then the conversation turned to the e mail I had sent a few weeks back. The one where I had just opened my soul on everything. Andy had shown this to my parents. I was a little taken back. Because in it was details of the sexual abuse I had suffered as a child. I had never been able to tell them about this, so for someone else to have done it for me was rather bizarre. Andy held my hand tightly, and said to me "they don't believe a word of it." The words rang in my ears and pain struck right into my heart. I broke in tears.

I had never spoken about the abuse to them because of fear. My abuser had scared me enough to stop me, and by the time I got older, I guess I had just learned how to survive. My biggest fear from the age of 5, when it happened, to my present age of 29, was that nobody would believe me. When I met Andy and our relationship became more serious, I did manage to open up a little to him. I was aware of how the trauma had affected my life, for example, even little things of how I lived stemmed back to that time, like only having very hot baths. At a young age I had trained myself to tolerate very hot water. For some reason I will never know, I thought that if I washed in hot water I would feel clean again. I wanted Andy to try and understand me, so I told him, 12 years ago, what had happened. He had been great, initially. Very supportive and ready to listen.

So now my parents also knew. As a child I had reasoned them not being able to help me with the fact they did not know. As an adult, I had used the same format of reasoning, but now they did know, and what did they say? It was as if they couldn't believe me. I tried to put myself in their shoes, of course it must have been a shock, and perhaps initial denial might have been acceptable. But this was a few weeks back. They had now had time to think back and work it out. Yet they were still in denial.

The very thought that my parents now knew the trauma I suffered and would not accept my truth, crushed me. I felt like the little girl, just crying out for someone to notice her pain, all over again. I had learned how to survive child abuse, but this was like experiencing the same sense of shame and pain all over again. If my daughter in 20 years time said the same thing to me, I know I would believe her. Even if I had some doubts, I would believe her. How could a parent not?

My mother had left a message with Andy, that if I wanted to speak to them I knew where they were, but it was up to me to make the first move and apologise to them! It is a step I will not take. I had spent the first years of my life never knowing who I really was, what I wanted, where I was going. I had spent most of my time on Earth hiding from myself and feeling trapped. I was not going to let go of myself now. I was open, exposed, vulnerable, and most of all free, ready and able to truly live as Samantha. If people cannot accept me as me, then the problem must lie with them and their conscience. Not me or mine.

Over the next few days, Andy and I spent a lot of time talking, crying, and trying to work things out. I had never felt so close to him, perhaps because he finally knew all of me. Amazing, some 12 years after we had first met, he felt he finally knew me. I don't think he would ever really understand me. We seem to be coming from different places mentally. He is happy with the routine of what is seen as a normal English life, and I seem to run from it.

Being back in the UK felt surreal. I knew I was here, but it was in body only. I enjoyed my time with the children, I adore them. Though. I must admit I kept wishing I was enjoying time with them all in Africa. I wake up feeling like I want to cry, when my dreams of my African landscape are shattered with the morning view of Slough in my eyes.

I know that I constantly face a battle between what I want and what I should do. In some ways, I now understand that is just life, we all have to find a balance between desire and reality. Also, when your decisions affect other people's lives, you cannot just go for what you want.

If I do go back to Africa, I cannot take my children. I want to, but in doing so I have to consider if I can provide all they need. I want what is best for them. There are no good English schools in Karatu, and Arusha would be a 3 hour commute every day. I don't want them to go to boarding school. Also, when would they see their Dad? Just a short trip home would come close to £3000 a time. It is something I cannot afford. Despite whatever my problems have been with Andy, he is a very good father. He can also give them the kind of routine and stability they need, I guess? I don't know.

If I stay here, I will lose myself. This much I do know. If only 2 weeks here can make me feel like I am constantly battling against depression, then what would living here full time do to me? I know that sometimes we have to just accept our lot in life and get on with things, but I don't know if I could do this to myself or the children. If I am here, I will be living a life in a location I don't want to be. I will be forever thinking on my people, my Maasai family, my home. I will go back into hiding, just after I managed to emerge. Can I do this to myself?

Then what about my unborn child? If I stay here, I will be on my own with the child. If I go there, the child will have it's cultural identity and it's Father.

I believe in action and consequence. I believe in everything happening for a reason. I can't help but notice that right now, I have lost my blood family. But in what is taken, something is also given. I know that I have an alternative family. We may not share blood, but we share soul. My soul is a Maasai, my body Mzungu. I am a true Maazungu. Maybe the first of my kind!

I will return to my home, with some sort of compromise of living between the UK and there. It is not great, but right now it is the best I can do, without letting my children, Andy, Benja and myself down. I booked my flight home.

March

It is now March. I have been back in the U.K. for a month. So much seems to have settled down between Andy and I. We are getting somewhere; I am trying to open myself to him. I know I cannot empty overnight and also that I have to train myself to live without hiding everything from him. It is hard. For both of us. I have lived my life hiding, it was how I coped. I don't want to be like this, it would be far better for everyone if I could stop it. If I could have the freedom of Samantha that I experience in Africa, here, I wonder where I would want to be. Is freedom just a state of mind? If it is, then theoretically it would be possible to be free anywhere. Though physical distance of over 4000 miles from your past and the people who disturbed you is of massive benefit I must say!

Benja and I communicate often. We suffered a miscarriage, which was perhaps a blessing in disguise. We do not have a future. I have got my feelings for that man into context and understanding. I love him. I will not have a future with him. He needs his culture and someone who can give him more of life than I can.

I want to try and salvage my marriage. I want to learn how to ping again if that is possible.

One of the hardest issues I am facing here is my Parents. I have such intense feelings of anger towards them. I don't want to see them. Ever. Yet I do every morning. I cannot drive legally. Illegally I am pretty good at it, but legally in this country, it is not an option! Andy is working, starting very early in the morning. We live a few miles from the school and off the bus route. Getting the children to school is near impossible for me, so I would have to rely on a taxi, which would cost £24 per day, to and fro, or my mother. In an ideal world I would choose the taxi. My head and my heart want the taxi. My pocket cannot allow the taxi. A family of 6 is not cheap, and an extra £120 on taxi rides a week is not something we can run to. This hurts so much, but at times logic has to prevail I guess. So, every morning, I get the children ready for school, at 8 a.m. My mother turns up to take them to school in her car.

There has been an attempt of communication from her part, and absolutely none from mine. It is awful. I stand at the window with tears of hurt and anger in my eyes, canting that she will not come closer to the house with me in it. Oh I know what people might think. It would be better to communicate? Communicate?? Right now, I cannot. I feel as if they had their chance, and they ruined me with it.

Andy has been great. It is very difficult for the children to understand as I haven't gone into great details with them. They love their Grandparents and do have a good relationship with them. I am not sure how that makes me feel. In some ways hurt? In some way, perhaps a little jealous, because that is something I did not and will not ever have.

I am not sure what I am doing here. I am with my babies I guess. Despite the pains, life is getting better. I feel connected to Africa, I don't think I will ever feel at home in the UK, but I am prepared to compromise and find a balance if it is possible. I speak to somebody from either Kenya or Tanzania most days. The business plans regarding a tourism company seem to be coming into some part of fruition, which is exciting. I feel as if I am actually going to be part of something, a team? A plan, a growth, a future as myself? I feel very positive about the future.

The Maasai seem to be doing OK. I don't know who is where right now. Raphael keeps calling and telling me Benja is in Endullin not Karatu. I don't know why he is doing that. Raphael has always been a very strange Maasai man to me. I can't quite put my finger on what is wrong, I think it is perhaps some jealousy issues, but who am I to know?

Jealousy is actually very common among the Maasai people. Finding this tribal detail surprised me. I had always thought of them as a community tribe, which they very much are, but there is also a hell of a lot of jealousy among the same age set groups.

For example, a Moran can have respect for his elder on owning 100 cows. However if someone from his own age set is owning 100 cows it is very likely that he will be jealous of him. The degree of jealousy also seems to be relating to the location.

The Maasai from the more arid areas of Tanzania seem to hold a lot more envy towards the counterparts from the more fertile land. I am no anthropologist, these are just my personal studies based on what I have seen and lived.

I do miss my Maasai family, but I am also enjoying my life here once more. Trying to find my feet and way in life here. In some ways I feel as if I am faking it, because of the pains I feel from my un-family, yet I do also see glimpses of a reality in my life, which is reassuring.

I look at Andy and feel the pinging of my heart once more. It is beautiful. I do think that in the future I am going to find a good balance between my different lives and locations, I just don't quite know how I am going to get to that point yet. Or exactly what it will involve!

Every day is becoming more and more painful when my Mother turns up in the morning. I am grateful for the assistance on the behalf of my children, but it makes me sick because I know that for me, I am just using her as a taxi, and if there was an alternative I would bloody well use it. A painful truth, but a truth none the less.

I noticed something about myself which is scaring me. I am a great thinker. Oh don't get me wrong, I do not mean great as in 'brilliant ', I mean great as in large. In depth. And very critical. Every time I see that woman in the morning, I go into a massive low. Just looking at her seems to push me into thoughts of my past pain, of my childhood abuse, rejection, and the current distance.

I then seem to pull myself back from these thoughts, but instead of going into a region of 'normal' thinking. I get into a very happy phase, I don't just mean happy. It is a kind of over the top happiness, which is shallow, fake and more often than not results in a shopping trip into town either by myself or with my friends Delphine and Isabelle. Even though that sounds fun, I don't really enjoy it. I buy rubbish that I do not need. I have enough financial trouble as it is, I don't need to add to it. I am scared of the way I cannot find a middle ground for myself. I am either elated, in a state of near delirium, or low. When I do hit a low, it is not just a feeling bad, it is a real downer. The issue which is giving me the most concern is this; I can feel what is happening, yet I feel powerless to stop it. How can I know what is happening and not be able to control it? What is happening to me?

It is Mothers Day soon. How beautiful and awful. Why is everything in my life both good and bad? One day I long for just good, or is it just reality that we must take the good and the bad. The whole ying and yang of life I guess. I won't be buying a card. I am trying to not be hypocritical as much as I can help it. I already feel like a big enough shit with using my Mother for a taxi ride for my children every day. Buying a card with flowers and pretty things for the person I feel has let me down the most is not something I can do. Happy Mothers' Day? I would rather forget it. The bittersweet taste of receiving from my children but not giving to my Mother will haunt me every March I fear. The circle of family has well and truly been broken, and I am to blame. I cry. If I could forget who I am, my past, and live in the same role as 'good Samantha', then everything would be O.K. If I could just be amiable, then I would have a family. If I could stop the accusations against them, then I would be allowed my parents. I can't. I spent long enough running from myself, to try not to go that place again.

The temptation to run is always on me. I feel as if everybody here would be better off without me. I don't feel as if I have a place. My place is in Africa, not least because of its physical distance from *Good Samantha*! I am starting to understand a bit more about my desire to leave and be far from my past. I now understand I ran to Africa because subconsciously I simply could not cope with life anymore. I couldn't cope with myself and the daily ritual of lying that everything is OK, when it has never been.

At 5 years old, I was sexually abused by a family member. My cousin. My mother was working a night shift, at the local nursing home. I don't recall where my Father was, my teenage cousin was baby-sitting my brother and I. In the night, he came and woke me up, and told me to come with him. He was my family, I trusted him. I was 5 years old and he was big, so I just did as I was told. The house we were living in had stairs which turned round a corner, separating the staircase into 2 sections. 3 large steps broke the straight stairs into a corner before proceeding on to the landing area. My cousin put me on the second corner stair, which would have hid me from the view of my brother should he wake up, and also conceal me from the downstairs environment.

He gave me a pen, a small bottle, and other objects telling me to put them into my 'little lady'. I didn't understand what he meant, so I just stared at him. He opened my legs and showed me what he meant by my little lady. He stuck his fingers into my vagina, I couldn't move. He then started putting the objects in me, showing me what he wanted me to do. It hurt. The pain was so intense, I can remember crying. He told me to shut up and enjoy it because this was what good girls did. Did they? I didn't know. Maybe I was not such a good girl. The phone rang. He went to answer it. I think it was my Mum, he was telling her we were being very good for him and everything was OK I could feel a cry inside me screaming "No it isn't. It is not O.K. I think something is really wrong," but I couldn't even speak. I wanted to run back to my room, my legs would not move. I was stuck to the brown patterned carpet in fear. Such fear. My cousin came back to the stairs. He touched my vagina again. Sticking his fingers inside, he had some Vaseline in his hand and was putting it in me. I felt all slippery. Hearing a sound, I looked up. He had unzipped his trousers and was rubbing his penis. It was very big. He opened my legs further and pushed me back on the stair, he tried to put his penis in me, it was too big and hard and wouldn't fit. I cried in pain.

He hit my vagina and told me I was bad, that I was to be quiet and enjoy. He made me touch his penis then told me to start putting the objects back in my vagina. I did as I was told. He stood over me touching himself, rubbing his penis, while I was putting these things inside me. Tears were streaming down my hot and confused head, I thought to myself "why does he look so happy for me to be so sad?" Then he let out a groan and came over me. Putting his poison all over my face.

My cousin took me back to my typical girls bedroom. My bed was covered with dolls, teddies, I guess the average things and possessions for a 5 year old girl. He put me in my bed and threatened me. He said if I ever told anyone, nobody would believe me, and it would hurt my Nan so much she would die. I have always been close to my Nan, I was scared. So frightened by what had happened and what he had said. I lay crying. Terrified. At Sunday School they had told us if we have problems we can tell God and he would help us. Would he? Would he tell my Mum for me? I tried. Nobody knew. Nobody came to help. Nothing. Life carried on, but I don't think I did.

Something happened to my head that night. Fear controlled me. I never felt like I was truly part of anything. If I was part of my family then I would have felt it wouldn't I? If I was part of my family then why did a member of my family do this to me? Why did no one stop him?

I understood that my parents did not know because I had said nothing to them. I couldn't. I wanted to. I tried to. The abuse continued. Not in any degree like the first night. Touching and object penetration became our 'game'. Any chance that man got, he would take. If my family visited his home, he would take me to his room and make me touch him, and he would touch me. Soon it just became normal. I understood how it worked. If he was there, this was going to happen.

When I was 7 years old, a family friend was staying at my house. I don't remember why he was there, but it was not an unusual event to have somebody staying the night. He had been given my bed for the night, and I was to share with my brother. In the night, I wanted to get something from my room. I had forgotten my favourite teddy, my cookie monster, the character from 'Sesame Street'. This teddy was my comfort and companion for sleep.

Clive, the guest, was still awake. He saw me come in and asked if I wanted a hug. I didn't. Men in the dark scared me. Men full stop scared me. I wanted to say no, the word wouldn't come. He grabbed my arm and took me into bed with him. He held me so tight it hurt me. I said nothing. His hands started running all over my body. He then said to me, "pretend I am a horse, sit on me and bounce up and down ". I sat on him, I didn't bounce, he made me bounce. I starting crying silently. I could feel his penis was hard. He kept pushing it against me. He then took me off, I thought it was over, until I realised he was taking off the underpants he had been wearing. Clive lay me down, and climbed on top of me, pulling my legs apart with his body. He put his fingers up me. Opening me up wide. It was hurting. Then came the most unbearable pain I had ever felt. I opened my mouth to scream, but it was silent. I was screaming with no sound. I wanted sound. God. This was awful. He moved in me and as he moved I felt my whole body move with him. He was so big and was hurting me so much. His penis was in me and he was moving very fast on top of me. He grunted then let out a big groan. I remembered that sound, it was similar to the sound my cousin made.

That liquid stuff had come out. But now it was in me making me dirty. I felt dizzy and sick and wanted to run. I found the strength and got out of the bed. He grabbed my arm, spinning me round to face him. Then came the warning. Just like the previous ones. I was not to tell anybody, if I did nobody would believe me. I understood. I knew the drill by now. I ran out of the room.
I went to the toilet. There was blood coming from me. I felt so scared. I wondered if I was going to die, and realised that to die might be nice. It would stop people doing this to me. I

could just sleep and play in heaven. That thought now shocks me. I was 7 years old and having my first suicidal thought. It was not going to be the last. Of course in the morning following the rape, it was like nothing had happened. Everyone looked normal. Even I looked normal. It was inside which was not or was it ever going to be again.

Time went on. Everyday was awful. I wanted to speak. I wanted to scream. I looked like a normal child. I may have even acted like one, but I was not normal.

Normality is something which other people had. Life is something other people could do, not me. I didn't belong. I started hurting myself. One night, in my room, I began rubbing my skin. I don't know why. I don't know how I thought of this, I just did. I rubbed the skin on my face so hard that the skin opened and was weeping. I didn't understand what I was doing, but I felt I was trying to talk through my actions. I couldn't verbally speak my pain, but maybe if I could show them something was wrong it would stop? I carried on for months. I was stopped from school, because nobody knew what these strange marks were. I can remember going to the doctors and hospital. Then it stopped.

The last time I hurt myself in this way was just before going to see a specialist, though quite what he was a specialist in I don't remember. Was it a skin Dr? Or a mental health doctor? I don't know, all I was told was that I had an appointment at a hospital in London. My Mum had told me it was a big important place. I remember making the marks come. My GP hadn't stopped my pain. The local hospital hadn't. Maybe this time someone will know what is happening. I spent the night before the appointment rubbing my skin, making sure they would see. The following day I went to London on the tube, accompanied by my Mum. I was nearly happy. I thought the doctor there must know what to do. They will stop my life hurting. I thought it was all over. It wasn't. There was some kind of argument between my mum and the doctor. I often wonder what it was about. Perhaps he told her that I was doing it to myself? I can only speculate as I will never know. We marched out of the hospital. Never to see another person about the problem. So I stopped attacking myself. I now know that I was self harming in an attempt to get heard. Nobody listened.

I shudder at the thoughts and pain of my past. It has controlled so much of who I am now, and even has resulted in this terrible split from my family because they cannot believe it as true. I haven't even gone into too many details with them. They only know the surface of what happened. The anger and hatred burn inside me every day. I know it is negative and unhealthy for me and them, but what is the option? I cannot go back into the person they all want me to be. She was only ever a fake. Someone pretending at living. Now I can only try to be me. Broken Sam. Africa Sam. Running Sam?
Happy Mothers Day? I think not.

Chapter 20

The tourism company I am setting up with a Tanzanian businessman seems to be coming up well. He calls and e-mails me most days checking on my progress and when I am returning to Tanzania. He likes my ideas and concepts, and with this, I feel so respected, like I am finally going to be a valid part of something real. Working in tourism, with people and exotic animals feel so exciting to me. So different and fun. Everything I am saying is being taken on board and even if it is not quite what David and John are thinking, they tell me. I even like that. A little bit of criticism in a positive way.

Amazingly instead of taking it to heart and feeling negative about myself, my work my life and so on, I am able to listen and try to grow and construct from their comments. There is a lot of mutual respect between us. I so need a relationship like this in my life. A working, profitable, respectful and true one.

The steps of progress I am making seem so good. I am a long way to being alive fully, and I have a lot of balance to find but I am in progress, and one of the most positive things is the new business and the challenge it presents.

I need to get back to Tanzania. I have been asked to get some photos of rural and traditional Maasai. Because of my connection to the Maasai, the acceptance of myself in their community, and also the fact that I can speak well in Ki-Maasai, it was felt I was the best person for the job. I am in no way the best photographer. I can take a reasonable picture, but I have such poor equipment, I wonder if I can really do it? My boss for this job is someone I owe a lot of both money and favours to. He is helping me to get published, has let me borrow money, so I feel very indebted to him. I am not the best person for this, but he kind of has me by the short and curly's, so I should do it. Also, John, my business partner, would like me to assist in setting up the main tourist office in Karatu before the high tourist season starts.

I am a bit fearful to tell Andy what I am thinking and where I want to go. I know I hurt him very much with my previous lies. I don't want to hurt him again, so honesty is meant to be my only option. You know, one of the most awful things about being a secretive person?

You often don't know what secrets you keep, what truths you have, or what has spilled out.

Some severe financial issues are troubling me. I cannot even tell Andy about the problem. If I tell him, I will feel like such a failure. I am trying desperately to get us back on track. I, by myself have created most of the financial mess. I have credit cards that are mounting, personal contacts I owe money to, bank debts and so on. If I have created this mess, then surely it is my responsibility to try and clear it? I feel so bad.

The person who has asked me to get the Maasai photos is somebody I owe money to. Mr. Wilson. I've known him a while, he owns a media company. I did have a great deal of respect for him, though right now it is more like I have a lot of obligation to him. I do like Wilson, but I feel the pressure he is putting me under, together with the control he has over me is something he both likes and uses to the best his best advantage. This man has made an offer to me that he can get my book published, which is something I want so much. He is a well known journalist and trainer, so has the right contacts.

Of course there is a charge for it, but he virtually guarantees I will have it published. I am so thrilled at this. One of my only ambitions in life was to write. To have my book published would give me such an affirmation of self, for many reasons, the main one being; I am a writer. I write. It is actually the only thing I can do well. I can ' pass ' in the rest of life, but to actually do something with an amazing ability is something which evades me, it is only writing where I can hold my own. Oh, and fucking up; I have an outstanding talent at that!

I did it. I asked Andy's permission to go back to Tanzania. I managed to explain what I wanted and needed to do. I felt it was only right to ask his blessing, out of respect and practicality. He said he would think. I don't know if it will be forthcoming. I am trying. Leaving my children again will be so difficult, but I know it is for the best. This business is perhaps the only opportunity I have right now to make something of my life and try to sort out my mess.

However, I have to also admit that the thought of not seeing my Mother every morning is something which is a huge fuel to my desire to leave. Every morning it breaks me into little pieces, plummeting my mind into such low and desperate thinking. The pain is too much to bear, it is like an open wound that will never heal and gets exposed every single day. I cannot cope. The lows are getting lower, the happy times fewer and fewer. I feel so useless here, and I am finding it hard to express myself or change the situation. If only I had learned how to drive and had a legal license for this country. If only, so many things.

Andy agreed! He gave me his blessing to go back and get this work done. I feel the happiest I have felt in a long time. Is that wicked? That I only get happy at the thought of leaving? God, I must be bad. I know that my real happiness is coming from the idea of 4 weeks of freedom without the constant pressure and pain of every day here.

I will see my Maasai people for a short time only, as I have to get on with the work that John has. I guess the only time will be when I go to get the photos? We'll see. But I am returning to my home. My beloved Africa for 1 month. The ticket is booked for 31st March.
Of course I will meet up with Benja and see how his life is now. So much has happened and not happened between us that I am confused as to what the situation is right now! The last time I saw him he proposed again and my heart was in pieces. He knows that is not the case now, but still? What is the case? Where do we both stand? Raphael keeps calling me and telling me Benja is in different locations from where he has said he is.

I feel very distant emotionally from Benja right now. Perhaps because Andy and I are getting on much better, or perhaps because I have come to see the attraction for what it is and was. Escapism. The need to be looked after. I do love Benja, but I have that into a good context now. I know he loves me, but I don't think it is the same as my Mzungu perception of love. Any marriage between us would have been crazy! Wouldn't it?

Packing and leaving my London home was such a positive experience for me. I had done this small action in a correct way. I had asked Andy his permission, and I had it. No stories. No lies. It felt very refreshing. I had to leave to get my flight early in the morning, it left Heathrow Terminal 2 at 06:30. I got into the taxi, while the house was still sleeping.

As I stepped in I had a very ominous feeling wave over me, which shook me. It was just like the feelings I have experienced at numerous times in my life. In my happiness and desire to run, I ignored it.

Nobody knew I was due to arrive in Tanzania. Except for John the taxi driver, who I figured was not in the place or even phone number enabled to tell anybody. I have known John since my first trip to Tanzania, when Connor stole a cassette from his car! Somehow we manage to laugh at that experience now, and have remained friends.

I didn't tell anyone of my impending arrival, I guess to surprise my friends and to see how things really are when I am away. I wondered what was happening with the calls from Raphael and Benja. One such call from Raphael told me Benja had not been working in his shop, but running off and leaving other people. I am very interested to see what the situation really is.

Chapter 21

I arrived in the evening of March 31st. Taking the decision to head straight to Karatu. It was night, I was exhausted from the flight, but I didn't want to run the risk of anyone seeing me. I know from experience that Arusha to Karatu has one of the hottest and most active grapevines possible. The point of a surprise arrival was simply that. Not to allow others a chance to spread news of my arrival before I got there. So, tired as I was, I did the journey from Kilimanjaro International Airport to Karatu. I didn't have a place to stay organised, but managed to find a guest house who would accept weary travellers when we finally arrived at 3:30 am! I dumped my bag, and got a taxi to the Maasai house.

Raphael had told me prior to my departure from London that Benja was in Endullin. Benja had told me prior to my departure from London that he was in Karatu. There was no reason to lie to me like this, but who was lying?

The little Maasai house was in darkness, the headlights of the taxi shone through the windows, alerting the Maasai inside to someone's arrival. My head and heart were both excited and nervous. One by one a stream of 6 Maasai came out of the house. I recognised 4 of them, could only name one; Meroro from Olbalbal. No Benja. No Samwel. No Raphael.

Not one of the Maasai who were staying in the house were relevant in my life. I went back to the guest house, alone and feeling even more confused than when I first arrived. Getting ready for bed I felt tears falling. I was exhausted, but my mind was racing. I got into bed. My first night back in Africa, should have been far more joyous than this. O.K. I didn't want an arrival committee, but as I drifted into a few hours of fitful sleep it seemed that everything was wrong. The onimosity that had swept over me when I had left London came crashing onto my soul. Everything really WAS wrong.

The morning brought with it the gossip that 'that' Mzungu really had returned to Karatu!

Word soon got around and I was tracked down to the 'Mzmbazi' B guest house where I was staying, by a welcoming group consisting of Samwel, Raphael, Meroro and Laata. Samwel had been working as a guard in the shop last night, Raphael had spent the night with him there. Probably because he was too drunk to walk to the Maasai house judging from the smell emitting from him and his bloodshot eyes! Laata had gone to the house this morning and had received the news from Meroro that I was indeed back from UK He had then raced to the shop to tell Samwel.

I asked after Benja, they all looked at each other, before Samwel told me he was in Endullin. A look of smug satisfaction spread over the face of Raphael. I proceeded to question why Benja kept going to Endullin. I knew he had some form of family there, but I felt confused as to why Endullin had become his latest hotspot. Benja had family in most of the villages of Ngorongoro and Serengeti.

The Maasai didn't seem willing to answer me, even though it was obvious in their body language they had something they wanted to say. I shut up and called Benja. The conversation went well. I asked him how he was, what he was doing, and erm, where he was.
To which he replied Karatu! Karatu? Really? I asked where he had stayed last night. He said the Maasai house, which of course I knew to be a very huge lie. I then told him I was in Karatu. He didn't believe me. I passed the phone to Meroro who then told him in Ki-Maasai that I had turned up in the middle of the night.

My stomach reminded me with some volume that I had not taken anything to eat since yesterday evening, and that was plane food so couldn't really be classed as a meal could it? I asked the group of people in my room to leave and give me some space to wash and change. They seemed reluctant to leave me, was it the novelty of seeing me or did they want to watch me undress? I hurried them out and locked my door behind me! I was so happy to see them. Especially Samwel. Hurt was in me from Benja, but I guess I had some forewarning of what was happening, because it was either Raph or Benja who was up to no good. I wished it had been Raphael.

After getting dressed, I went with Samwel to take some coffee and food at a local hotel. People stared at me on the street. Remembering me, talking to me, questioning me. I was inundated with people wanting to greet me, which was kind of nice. In the U.K. I seem to hide from people, yet here I have the freedom to be alive, to speak and live. Between Samwel filling me in on the situation with Benja, as he saw it, and others coming to greet me, it took nearly 3 hours just to get some coffee down. I had to leave this hotel and find somewhere to chill! I thought I would head back to the guest house, so started to walk down the main and only real street in Karatu. Then I saw him. Benja. Walking up the same street that I was walking down. I wanted to run to him. I had such excitement at seeing him again, but somehow the hurt of the morning revelations calmed me down. It was time to be cool Sam.

Benja greeted me in the same cool way I greeted him. We both expected so much more, but nothing would come. Then I couldn't help it. Cool Sam doesn't actually exist for very long. She is a really poor act I attempt to do, because I am more Kali Sam! Hothead Sam, especially in this kind of circumstance. So, I asked him outright what was going on. I was aware that I didn't really have the right to question him like this. Neither of us was ever sure if there was a relationship or not, but I did anyway. He said he lied to me about where he was because he didn't want to worry me? What? How on earth could that make sense? It didn't!

Worry me about what? This guy can fight lions, was raised in very harsh conditions, and can survive. Unless he had some raging disease, what the hell was I going to worry about? As he tried to talk to me further, I realised what was really going on. Samwel had told me he thought he had a Esiankiki (young girl/girlfriend) in Endullin. Raphael had also said this. Perhaps it was true. Perhaps he really did? If so, it would be better to just tell me, so we could actually start to put some boundaries into our friendship/relationship. I asked him.

He denied it vehemently. He then asked to speak to me in a more private location. We walked to my guest house. Once inside, we were able to speak. He told me clearly he had no girlfriend, that this was all lies against him. I started to believe him, I don't really know why. Perhaps I just wanted to. I accepted his story, even though in my heart I knew it was just that, a story.

I did feel very sad at this, I guess because of past desire and the eternal ' possibility' status that would always hang over Benja and I. For myself, I thought I had him in perspective now. He was someone who had tapped into my childish and very real need to be looked after, he had showed me attention and a different life. I loved him, but the feelings were now in control. Weren't they? Still, the news that he was with somebody else hurt.

Benja never admitted it, though in my soul I knew it was true. Remembering part of the job I had come to do, I asked Benja if he would take me to Piaya, or another such remote Maasai village. If it was up to me, I would choose Piaya, mainly so I could greet Pilaso and my other friends from up there before I started work with John.

It was important for me to get started on the work as soon as possible, in order to be able to get back home after the month, as promised to my children. Benja agreed to take me to Piaya.
There was a lorry in Karatu that day, which was due to leave the following day at 05:30.

Excitement ran through me. Everything was clicking into place in the work capacity. Maybe for once I was going to not be a failure.
It was obvious that night, as we spoke of our plans and lives, that Benja still wanted me. He even asked if he could stay at my guest house. I said that it would not be right to do so. The girlfriend being the major reason why not! He denied her existence again, but I had to try and keep some resolve.

If we were just going to be friends, then we should try to start on the right step. This was not an action Benja agreed with. Rather sadly, he left me at the guest house and went to stay, I believe at the Maasai house, arranging to meet me at 5 am so we could get the lorry together.

Getting into the big blue lorry heading for Piaya is always an adventure in itself. Many many tour companies travel through Karatu on their way to the Serengeti and Ngorongoro Crater.
Most of them in good 4x4 vehicles. People coming, the majority of them wanting an adventure. Yet they sit in luxurious cars! Imagine if the Mzungu tourists who come had a real experience of life in Africa. Of travel in Africa! Maybe this is something John and I should market? For example, you could be picked up from the airport in one of the remarkable 'dala dala's.' Remarkable in the sense that the fact they are actually moving along the road, picking up passengers, used as a business tool, despite the very real possibility there could be a door hanging off, no windscreen, no brakes, or a combination of all 3 ailments!

Literally, the Tanzanian 'dala dala' is amazing. There was one time in Arusha, I was walking along the road with my children. A dala dala was driving on the opposite side of the road. It pulled over to pick up a passenger and there was a loud crashing sound. Turning to see what had happened, my Son Connor shouted out " the bloody door just fell off!" It had! The door of the little bus was on the floor! We could not stop laughing for a long time. It was so very funny. The conductor of the dala dala then proceeded to pick up the fallen door and slide it into some kind of place, with the assistance of a passenger. Absolutely amazing Tanzania!

So, after being picked up from the airport in a dala dala, one could also experience 'plain' travel in a big blue Bedford which should have died a long time ago, a choice of seats are of course available consisting of ' no spring' seat. 'Very springed seat'. Or 'no fucking seat '!

Travel in African style is such an uplifting experience, mainly because you are very lifted as you try to hold on for your dear life, crossing the rocky and deserted plains!

After a bumpy and arse aching 6 hour drive across the Serengeti and Loliondo plains, we arrived in Piaya. It was around mid-day. Piaya looked so different from the last time I was here. There had been rain. Instead of the arid dry place I had seen some months before, this land was green and productive. I was surprised by the transformation. Many Maasai recognised me and came to greet me, which was so nice. I was not just greeted as Benja's friend, they wanted to speak to me. They knew me as Naduvoy, their half Maasai!

It was a truly beautiful moment. Standing among the few mud buildings which make Piaya village, swarmed with Maasai men and women, enjoying conversation and story. My heart rose. Forgetting what I was feeling with Benja and the news of his Esiankiki. With these people I felt a valid sense of being something which had evaded me for perhaps my whole life. In some ways, the sensation was dangerous, because it was so good. So refreshing and very addictive.

Here I could be me. Could I become addicted to that freedom? Did I need or deserve that freedom? Thoughts like these, and similar ones kept coming until I found the strength to push them away and just enjoy the moment, and enjoy it I did.

As we were in Piaya, and I was a guest of Benja, Maasai law and custom dictates that I should stay in his boma with his Mother. This was not a problem to me as I was used to sleeping in Maasai bomas, and appreciated the family of Benja and their company. We began to walk up the hill from Piaya village to the boma, absorbing the fantastic views of the Lololol hills.

I was spotted long before we got to the boma. The children of the place ran out to greet me, laughing and shouting. I was so welcomed. Even Mutarra (Take my Hand) seemed to run, or was it a honeybeer induced fast stupor? I didn't care, I felt so happy and lifted up to be received in such honest pleasure.

My bags were put in Pilaso's hut. Where we sat and drank milk from the Calabash. I was really back. Maasai Sam. Naduvoy. Why does my soul ignite at these thoughts? After the kule (milk), Benja and the Morans of the boma went to eat meat, as is the culture. I always think that Maasai men get a much better deal than the women. They get the best meat because their culture states the warrior needs the strength. What about the women? Who also need strength as they are responsible for so much more, such as building houses, looking after the whole group's children, making beads, looking after cows, and running the place! I wondered about promoting the Soya TVP packets in my bag? I mean Soya would be good because of the protein, and the fact it is far cheaper to produce and use than cows.

Of course, culturally, Soya and Maasai are not really a compatible combination, but on the other hand, many Maasai are now eating ugali. A dish made from ground maize and water mixed together, so would a little TVP really be so bad?

I sat pondering these thoughts on my favourite rock, watching the sun go down over my beloved wilder lands. I heard the night animals coming, then the Morans returning from their meat feast. The wonderful Serengeti night sky was about to erupt before my eyes, soon this place would be a hunting ground for animals. It was now time to go back into the boma.

I was tired out from the long trip and overwhelmed by my welcome. I asked for permission to sleep as I was so exhausted. Pilaso wanted to cook in her hut, on her cooker consisting of
3 stones and firewood. I didn't really mind. I laid back on the bed made of sticks and cow hide, listening to the Maasai speaking, sharing, and eating. I relaxed, letting the sleep come and take me.

In the morning, I woke up to find Benja next to me. Even though I was surprised, it felt so nice and comfortable. Benja stirred, then placed his arm round my hips. The air was heavy with some sort of expectation neither of us knew how to word. Then Pilaso, his Mother walked in with the morning's firewood! Saved by the smoke! We both said nothing to each other.

Pilaso spoke to Benja in Ki-Maasai asking if he was awake and was I OK. I wondered why wouldn't I be, but wasn't really ready to talk to her yet, so lay silently listening to what was being said.

There was some kind of party being arranged, a Soukokou. Maasai have Soukokou for the celebrations of life. They are where the whole clan come together to celebrate as a family. I smiled and my heart jumped at the thought of this. How fabulous that I was going to be here for the Soukokou and I would be able to get pictures of it! Great! When I let everyone know I was awake I would ask some more details on it. Just what I needed. A good story and fantastic photo opportunity. Things are falling well. Serendipity?

Chapter 22

Sometimes we find ourselves in situations where we don't know what the hell to do. I am now in that position. After the morning's talks of a Soukokou, Pilaso started going around her daily business, and looking for people to come. It seemed that this was a big event. An air of excitement was through the boma and it was certainly buzzing when I finally emerged from the mud hut to take my morning pee in the dried up riverbed. I presumed there must not have been a party for sometime, and people were just happy. I walked back from my 'short call', thinking I must find Benja and ask what the Sokoukou was all about. I didn't want to cock things up from a cultural point of view, so it would be better for me and all concerned if I had a level of understanding as to what was going on and what I was meant to do!

I caught a glimpse of him standing with the other Morans, and stopped in my tracks to see what was happening. In everyday Tanzanian society Benja never really looks too good, or does very well. However, watching him in his Moran group, I could see how he had become their leader. Not the tallest Maasai, but able to jump very well, he had applied his knowledge of Maasai law, family history, and sense of humour to get him a good position in the community. Many people were already tipping him to become a village chief when the age set would allow it of course. He was speaking to his own group as if he were an elder, with authority and understanding. I was a bit too far to hear what they were saying, but the way the interaction of the group was being presented through body language, you could see the respect placed upon Benja. I smiled to myself. He truly belonged in this land. Not in Karatu, not Arusha, not Kenya, but here, in Maasai land. This was where he was himself and could just be Benja. A freedom I both craved and understood so very well.

The Moran group started to disperse. I called to Benja and started moving towards him. I wanted to find out what my role was for this Sokokou and also what it was for, what I should wear e.t.c. Though I knew from previous Maasai ceremonies that nobody wore anything different. Maybe a new enkarash if they could afford it, or a change of colour if they had just moved up an age set. I caught up with Benja, he took me in his arms, which both surprised me and pleased me. I was taken by surprise as the Moran group was still around, not together, but in different locations around the boma. Public displays of affection with the Maasai don't happen, it seemed that Benja couldn't hide his genuine pleasure at seeing me, here in his homeland.

We spoke on the day coming, but nothing about the morning, and the physical affection which had nearly happened. Something appeared to be weighing on Benja's mind. It was as if he was trying to speak an issue but the words were not coming out right either in Ki-Maasai or Swahili. I wondered what it was, I guessed it was important, but the light heartedness and excitement of the coming day was in my mind, it surely wouldn't be too heavy, would it?

Benja led me by my hand to my favourite rock, we climbed it and sat down ready to have a chat. The things which Benja said, shook me. Physically, mentally, emotionally, anything- ally! The Sokoukou that the Maasai were running around preparing for today was in fact my wedding! My what? My fucking what? Shock could not describe effectively what I was feeling. My wedding? To Benja? Like when was this arranged? When? Who had agreed?

The last proposal I received from him I turned down. I am very fluent in Ki-Maasai and Ki-Swahili, there was no chance of a mistranslation, and the word 'no' is pretty much understood everywhere! Oh my God! What the hell was going on here? Benja hurriedly tried to explain before my emotions became volcanic. I was certainly close to eruption, and in my current mood the result would have been a pyroclastic flow. I mean? For Fuck's sake! Here was my friend telling me we are about to be married in a Maasai cultural ceremony. The whole fucking community knew about this before I did, I did not have a clue what was going on. I thought I was a guest, not the bloody celebrant!

Benja's explanation was pathetic. He told me that he had told his Mother and community, a long time ago, that when his Mzungu returned to Piaya they would marry, and this was what was being arranged around us as we sat on the rock. I was fuming. Why didn't he just say we were not getting married instead of arranging the ceremony without my knowledge or even my acceptance!

Now he would face further embarrassment because there was no way this could happen. I am already married! He turned to look at me, pleading with his words to not shame him. He was a Moran leader, a respected Maasai in these lands; his family were of good reputation. If I walk out on the ceremony he would lose that. The 1st wife of a Maasai is the chosen for good standing in the community, he would lose all of that respect if I walked. What a selfish bastard!

He was not thinking about me, the fact that up until 10 minutes ago I did not have a clue what was happening, the past pain and experiences. He was not considering anything except himself and his standing in the community. I was furious with both myself and Benja. I had to get out of here and this situation. My heart wanted to walk, no, run over the Lololol hills. My head quickly realised I could not. The lorry was not going anywhere today. I did not have the supplies for walking across the desert, I did not have the capability of surviving the harsh conditions and potential animal attacks by myself. I was stuck in Piaya until the lorry next left for Karatu. What was I going to do?

Benja asked me to just go through the ceremony. Let people think we were married and then when I leave Piaya I can just go about my business. No one will know. He will marry again, a Maasai wife as expected of him, and I can just live my life, but to please not disrespect him and shatter his future hopes for his life and promotion. I could hardly believe my ears! How could he ask such a thing of me? For starters, I am married! How can I marry someone else? I spoke to him about this. He said, "no one will ever know." I considered my options. Of which there were few. I could say No. With this option, I would stay legal. Benja would lose his respect, but was that really my problem? I did not ask him to prepare a wedding ceremony! If I refused, I would have to leave Piaya, because it might not be safe for me here, however it would be impossible to leave the village until the lorry next moved, and Lazaro, the owner of the lorry and village elder was busy killing goats for the Enkiyama, my wedding ceremony! Ecstatic that a Mzungu was going to be marrying a Maasai in his village!

I could agree. I could say yes. I would not be legal, Benja would not lose his respect from the community, though he had certainly lost it from me. I would also be safe in the village until the lorry next moved. I have seen enough of the Maasai culture to fear angry Maasai, and angry Morans from the rural areas are perhaps the most dangerous.

In Maasai culture, if you are against one of the age set, you are against all of the age set. If you are for one of the age set, you are for all of them. If I did a mistake against Benja, it would be the same as doing a mistake against all of the Moran warriors in his age group. What was I to do? This dilemma was awful. I spoke to Benja, my disappointment clear in my voice and emotional distance from him.

I decided to do it. For my own self-preservation. However there were rules. This was not a legal ceremony, it is a cultural one and has no legal standing. There would be no 'marriage '. It would only be a sham to get Benja out of the shit with his people. There was no rights over me, I was not his wife, and at the first opportunity I would leave Piaya, go and see a lawyer and get an oath signed stating that this cultural marriage was not really a marriage, but a piece of journalism.

Benja agreed. Happy that his status in life was not going to be let down. I smiled tearfully, thankful I had managed to come to a sensible decision, but so angry at the circumstances.

How the hell did I get myself into this situation? I was now about to take part in a Maasai Enkiyama, which, if I was Tanzanian would have sealed my fate as a Maasai wife! I felt so sad, but decided to put on the act and go through this for the sake of myself, and hey, I guess it would be a good piece of journalism, but the fact that I could never tell anybody about it might be a bit of a stumbling block!

So, it was my wedding day. I had nothing to wear. Was in a village in the middle of nowhere with only cargo pants, vests, and one Maasai Esiankiki skirt to adorn. The ceremony was due to take place in the late afternoon, after the sun had crossed a certain point in the sky. I didn't want to wear my clothes. For two reasons - one being that I didn't want to wear my clothes and associate them with my wedding day. The other was that if I was going to pretend to do this farce then I needed some Maasai clothes to wear and not just an Esiankiki skirt, I did have an African dress with me, which might have to do. I had left my Esouce beads in London. I never thought for a minute I was going to be attending a Maasai ceremony while here, let alone my own Enkiyama, so I hadn't seen a point in bringing them with me and opted for packing my knee high leather boots in their place!

I knew of a few Iraqw ladies in the Piaya village who might be able to lend me something to wear. The majority of Piaya is Maasai, however there are a few immigrants and inter marriages between other tribes. In Piaya there are under 10 immigrants, most of them women. I have always got on very well with pretty much everyone in Piaya, so thought it was possible the ladies might be able to help me on this day. I walked to the village centre to ask.

I was in luck. One of the Iraqw ladies had her wedding veil and skirt from her special day with her. She was a good size, reasonably similar to me but with slightly bigger breasts and a more African arse. My soon to be 'Sister in Law' was going to lend me her Esouce beads. I would at least look the part I guess? I took their clothes and went headed back to the boma. As I walked up the hill, Meroro one of Benja's Moran group and the guy who had been staying at the Maasai house in Karatu came down the hill towards me, shouting something at me. He was giving me some instructions as to what to do and right now, according to their culture, I was not allowed to be any closer to the boma until we are married.

I needed to get changed and to find out what I had to do for the Enkiyama. We moved to the riverbed for privacy. My own personal toilet and changing room in Piaya! So there I was. In my dried up riverbed, in scorching heat, lizards and Meroro watching me adorn a red satin dress and ghastly veil for the wedding I only found out was taking place in the morning, and felt obligated and forced to take part in. The iraqw clothes hadn't fit, so I had to wear my African dress.

Meroro was giving me instructions. I had to walk up the hill towards the boma with a Calabash of fresh milk on my back. An old Koko would come with Benja to find me. We would all walk together then Benja would take the Calabash from my back, pour me some milk, when he had seen me drink it, he will walk ahead to the boma, with a Moran. Koko and I would proceed to walk together stopping some metres from the compound entrance, where the family and friends of Benja would be waiting for my arrival. They would then shout gifts to me.

For every gift I accept, I should move forward a few steps, for the next gift, a few more steps, until I reach the entrance to the boma. Where Pilaso would come and greet me, giving me a gift. If I accept her gift I give her my hand. She walks me in to the door of her hut, where one of Benja's Moran group is waiting. He gives me a gift. If I accept, I can walk into the hut, but I must not touch any of the wood beams or the marriage would not be allowed. Benja will be waiting for me inside the hut. His Mother will join us, she will then take my shoes, Calabash and walking stick the old Koko has given me. Benja will speak his gift to me and I will speak my gift to him. If we both accept, we drink milk together and are then married. Benja will then leave the hut, and go to eat meat with his Moran group, leaving me with his Mother, Grandmother and Sisters, until he is ready. He will then come and call me to join the celebrations outside.

It sounded straight forward enough, and I was relieved I didn't have to make any verbal promises or commitments to Benja. Just a gift? What gift could I give to a man who had put me in this position? An audience with my real husband? A slap in the face? I knew from culture I would have to give him a cow, but I wasn't bloody going to. I would say it but I knew I would never do it. This was not a real marriage, so no real gifts, right?

The Koko and Benja came to join us in the riverbed. Benja was wearing full Moran beads and the usual 3 enkarashes. He looked very beautiful, and even in my anger I started to feel a little excitement about the things we were doing. I mean how unusual could you get. Getting married but unmarried to a Maasai on a hill in the middle of rural Tanzania!

Koko tied the Calabash full of milk to my back. I was surprised how heavy the simple milk container felt. This was it. The day I fake a marriage. I felt awful, my head and heart in the worst possible turmoil. We stopped as per the given instructions. Benja untied the Calabash and gave me a little milk to drink. He then left me with the Koko. We carried on up the hill, stopping a short way, where my gifts of goats, cows and sheep were hollered at me. I accepted every one of them, not knowing what the hell I was going to do with my growing collection of livestock. I was received into the boma by Pilaso, the Moran guarding the hut door let me in, and I went inside. Blinded by the change of brilliant sunshine into complete darkness, I stumbled through the door, and out of reaction and instinct not to fall down I held out my hands to support myself. The only thing to grab inside a Maasai hut are the wooden beams, which if course I was not meant to touch. It was either that or fall down on the floor, so I grabbed it. Dooming the marriage. Benja had seen it and laughed, telling me not to worry. Of course I was not worried. The marriage was already doomed because there was no bloody marriage! Touching the wood of the hut was not actually going to anything that was not done already!

Benja promised to give me cows. I promised to give him a cow. His Mum nicked my shoes and stick. We drank milk. And that was it.

Married. Benja left the hut and I sat watching and listening with some amusement and sadness at the situation. If I had really just got married to Benja I think I would have felt a massive disappointment in how everything was conducted, however, because this ceremony was in my head firmly as a fake, I felt able to study what was going on and was able to take an objectional view! I felt sad for the guests who were clearly delighted at the days events, but could see how they would have felt if there had been nothing to do today. I guess Benja and I were like the village show at that time. It sucked.

I needed a pee, and asked for my shoes. Pilaso said "no." No? Why not? I explained I needed to go to pee, and being inside a mud hut, there was no available toilet, so could I please leave the hut. She refused me again until Benja had given his permission to leave. I was his wife now and had to wait until he said I could leave the house and be viewed by the community as his wife. What? I knew Benja had gone to eat meat. An event which can take anything from an hour to several, depending on the amount of
Morans that turned up. This was a Sokoukou. There were already many Morans around. I had seen them as I walked my walk of Enkiyama. I pleaded. I said I would be quick and discreet, which was of course impossible being the only white woman in the village, especially today as I was wearing a large red satin dress and a white veil trimmed with said satin! Discreet was not going to happen today at all! My only options were to wait like a good Maasai wife, or piss myself.

In Maasai culture urinating inside the hut for the humans is a strict no no. Of course the animals that stay inside might be able to just let it out, but the humans have to go outside. Feeling my full bladder, I wished I was one of the goats residing in the animal pen!

A constant stream of female Maasai visitors come to the hut to greet me. Each bringing with them a Calabash of milk, which I am encouraged to drink! I couldn't possibly drink anymore, my bladder is set to sprinkle at any moment, so I pretend with some of them, and make excuses with others. I realise that when I make excuses for not drinking milk, Pilaso looks happy. I guess because it means there is more milk at a later date for the family to consume.

Two hours later, Benja turns up. By which time my stomach is hurting with need. I am extremely fed up. I just want my shoes so I can run over the hill to my riverbed and pee! No conversations, no more gifts, no more bloody milk! Just my shoes, which he promises to find for me. Benja calls Pilaso to ask where they are, she turns to find them, but can only find one! No! By now I am absolutely desperate to go. I am at the point where reason and respect for culture are going and I just have to piss! Then they are found, under the pile of milk Calabashes. I hurry to put them on, touching the wood beams for support then run the fastest I have ever run to the riverbed. After relieving myself, and my God it was such a relief, I sat in my private place thinking and looking, I then started laughing at the days events so far.

Was it a laugh of desperation, relief or madness? I wondered. It sure let out a lot of tension though, and seemed to strengthen me to go back and join the celebrations I was now free to
be part of.

The Enkiyama celebration seemed pretty much like all of the other Maasai Sokoukous. After the food, which is eaten separately according to the age set and gender of the people, there is singing. The Morans come and form their group, each holding their spear and adorned in full beads. They cover their faces in blood dye and sing their songs of togetherness and blessings. The women then join in, first of all Esiankikis and Ntitos come, followed later, when the house and food work is done, by the Entasats. The singing and jumping goes on until late in the evening. It is always wonderful to be part of such events, especially in such natural and beautiful surroundings, under the Serengeti sky. This sky which has seen so much of my life recently. The tears, the fears, the pain the joy, the hope and desperation. These stars have seen it all.

The Morans sing songs of protection for me. Accepting me as a Moran wife to be watched and looked after. The Maasai women of different ages sing to me about being an Nkitok and being blessed with children and cows. The old Maasai men sit around listening, drinking honeybeer and reminiscing. The young children seem to just roam around and join any of the age sets, except the Morans, who everyone watches with respect and admiration. It was a truly beautiful night and celebration.

I retired to the hut of Pilaso, happy and exhausted. I had done it. We had got away with it. A very bizarre day in my life had just taken place. Of reality and unreality, all existing together. I drifted into sleep, thankful that Benja had to sing the whole night with his Morans, and full of gratitude this day had now passed. The day I became Maasai wife.

Chapter 23

The morning after the night before sensations flooded to my head as soon as I opened my eyes and allowed the thoughts of the previous day to come. Was it real? Or some bizarre dream? Had I really got married to a Maasai man? To Benja? The veil hanging from the roof of the hut confirmed to me the truth! I really had allowed this to happen? What the hell was I thinking? Oh, I understood the reasoning, and if I was faced with the same choice again today, I would probably do the same thing, but it was wrong. My soul knew it was wrong, my heart and head definitely knew it was wrong.

I could hear people outside, no doubt going around the everyday business of a Maasai boma. I sat up, realising I was alone in the hut. For a good half an hour I sat thinking and pondering until it was time to hit the riverbed. Walking across the plain to my personal loo I laughed to myself, remembering the time the previous day when I had not been allowed to come here. What a crazy day. Thankfully it was over!

Benja was coming out of the wooded area near the riverbed when I caught my first glimpse of my 'husband'. It made me feel sick to my stomach. He had deceived his villagers because of his own respectability and I had gone along with it because I couldn't see a way out. Who was worse? I was nothing but a bigamist.

Greeting Benja was difficult, I just told him I was tired, but the truth is that to look at this man in the eye was hard to do. With the reality of the cold light of day, or hot sweat of morning which is perhaps more appropriate for the area we were in, I thought to myself the best thing I can do is get out of Piaya and carry on with my work. I asked Benja when the lorry would next be leaving. He replied in 2 days. So I had to stick it out for 2 days. 2 days pretending to me a newly wed Maasai bride. In many ways I was thankful to the culture I was in. Maasai are not like Mzungu. A wife is not so much of a lover; she is more of a cow carer, so at least there were no visual expectations or presumptions of the ' just married' being loved up people being placed on Benja and I!

I kept myself busy for the next few days. Benja knew how pissed off I was with him. I think he also realised that these actions had turned our friendship that always had a possibility hanging over it, into a sharp decline of respect and love. I managed to avoid any expected advances or sexual contact. I tried to avoid anything physical whatsoever, it was not hard to do. He was busy with cows and goats, I just walked around absorbing the beauty of Piaya and making plans for the business. The two days passed with amazing and unexpected ease.

We were soon heading back to Karatu. Where I was Samantha the Mzungu, he was Benja, and nothing else was known or expected of us. Fantastic!

In Karatu, I went straight to take coffee at ' Paradise Garden'. The local hotel I favoured, which was also run by John, the man I was going to be working on the tourism company with. I had spent the last few days thinking on ideas, I now wanted to get the work done, and get away! Fuelled and I disgusted by the previous days events, I just wanted to get on with the work I came to do.
Over the next few weeks, we managed to turn an old office space into a ' Visitor Information Centre', with a section for the safari business. It was a very exciting time for all involved. John and David saw their initial ideas coming into some sort of fruition, I was finally feeling involved and part of something. Needed as myself. Not as a persona I had created or lied about. Needed, wanted, valued as Samantha. Nothing else. Freedom entered me and ignited me in such vibrant ways. I was alive, in context, working, earning a little money, and respect. I was me. All I had ever wanted.

I didn't see much of Benja during my weeks in Karatu. Initially, after we returned from Piaya he wanted to come near me. I let it known through my actions and avoidance of him I was simply not interested to know him further at this stage. I felt very hurt and exploited by what had taken place in Piaya, the further the distance the better it was for both of us.

Time was hurtling along at a frightening speed. The 'Visitor Information Centre' was running well with only a few teething problems, however the tourism company had a major problem.
We had not been granted an interview date to get a license from the relevant tourist authority. It was getting close to the time I was due home in London. The licensing board wanted to see me, interview me and check I was not an investor into Tanzania before they would issue a license. The tourism company could not operate without the license. I had promised I would be back in London after 1 month, yet here I was, nearly 1 month into the trip, painstakingly aware that I was going to have to take some extra time, but also aware that I would be breaking a promise to my family by taking the extra time. If I stayed, we would hopefully get the license and I could leave full in the knowledge that I had done what I came out to do. I wouldn't have to fly back out for the interview, costing more money and time.

I was stuck in my dilemma, I e mailed Andy and asked for his advice, telling him I would do what he said. I couldn't hear him well on the phone and had little money for credit. I waited for his e-mail response. Thanks to the dodgy electricity supply in Tanzania, some severe rains, I couldn't receive my e-mails the day I needed to. Sitting in the Karatu fortune internet cafe, I felt alone and realised I would have to make this decision by myself. I chose to stay in Tanzania. Finish what I came to do, and for once in my life not fail those around me, or myself. It was the worst decision I ever made.

I called KLM, the main airline provider for Kilimanjaro, and who my flight was booked for. I gave them my reference and told them I wanted to change my date of travel. I was advised by customer service it would not be a problem, I had up to 2 weeks left for changes, according to the ticket rules. It would cost me $50, but there was no other problem. Great.

I was disappointed with myself that I had broke my promise to my family, I thought Andy would understand. I knew my children wouldn't, but I could explain it to them couldn't I?

10 days later, the work was all done. The interview had taken place, the license was on it's way, I could go home. I left for Arusha, to get my ticket all excited and satisfied. A sensation which was not going to last, for on my arrival at the KLM office, I was told my ticket was cancelled as it had had no changes left! Gobsmacked, I tried to make sense of what was being said and compare it to the facts given to me by e-mail and verbal conversation by the customer service staff. KLM apologised, but their staff had made a mistake in what they told me. Fine, but what about my ticket? KLM said they would gladly re-issue the ticket, for the price of a new one! I disagreed. This was their mistake, surely it was upon them to resolve the situation? I argued until I was blue in the face and no more tears could come. They would not be budged. Placing the blame on me for not double-checking. I would not be moved from my position, which was that KLM had told me everything was fine. There was nothing to do except complain to customer services, which got me absolutely nowhere. A written apology does naff all when you are stranded 4000 miles or so from where you should be. I had no ticket, and was stuck in Arusha again, for not the first time in my life. I told Andy. He was angry with me. I told him I would get home somehow, but right now I didn't know how. The only people I knew didn't have a huge amount of money. As I thought I realised I had to get back to Karatu. I didn't really want to stay in Arusha, and if anyone was going to help me, I guess I would find them in Karatu as I know more people there. I got in the dala dala, and headed back to the town I had only earlier that day left with a big farewell.

People were surprised to see me back so soon. I didn't explain to everybody what had happened. I wanted to weigh up the situation and try to work out who to ask. My obvious choice seemed to be John. He had an income, was my business colleague, we had trust and respect between us. However, John was out of town and in the rural area until the next week. I tried to call him, but I couldn't get a signal from his line.

My other option was to ask Maasai. Which I did. I had helped these people tremendously, it was now time for some sort of reciprocation.

Maasai are generally not rich in finances, but the ones blessed with money convert it all into cows. If I was in a need, I should ask the Maasai with a good amount of cows to take some to market for me. I did. Some said they would help. Some said they could not. Some lied and said they would but never did.

After weeks of markets and waiting for cows, I only had 400,000 towards my ticket. John was late back from the rural area, and I was getting desperate. Andy was angry with me, I suffered a bout of Malaria, and most of all I missed my children.

Before I knew it, it was June. Over a month had passed since the problem with the ticket had occurred and I was only a third of the way towards getting home. The only positive thing in my life was the work. It was getting to high tourist season, and the 'Visitor Information Centre' was proving to be a resounding success, with the nationals and visitors alike. Many tourists would come. I felt challenged and useful in this role. Some days I would be in Karatu in the office, but as often as possible I would go out with the visitors, staying in Manyara or the beautiful Endallah nature camp. Endallah was truly a natural and enchanting place. Situated on the boundary of Manyara National Park, and blessed with meadow and natural grasslands, it overlooks the soda waters of Lake Manyara. Here, at this wonderful place, you can truly feel part of the natural world and observe a wide array of animals. Of all the places I had ever stayed in, in Tanzania, this was my favourite. I was able to learn new animal observing skills. Had close encounters with tree climbing lions, leopards, various snakes and insects, elephants. It was an absolute haven.

8th June came. My birthday. My 30th birthday. The worst birthday I have ever had. For the past 12 years or so, I have always had my children with me on this day. Even if there was no money for gifts or parties, my celebrations have been with them and Andy. Those very special people who give some sort of meaning into my life. Today, I had nothing or nobody.

I woke up to a text message from Andy, which did nothing but remind me of how far I was from where I wanted to be. 30 is meant to a big celebration. I could do nothing. I cried and cried. The ever-increasing waves of depression attacking me with such power and intensity. I knew I should try and mark my birthday in some way. There were no cards, no nothing. Nobody cared.

Esther, a Karatu resident Mzungu from Germany who runs a safari lodge had called me to see how I was doing with getting home, I told her how things were, the fact I was feeling shit and the reason why.

She told me to come up to the lodge. I didn't really want to, but she was insistent, and I had nothing else to do. When I got to Kifaru, the lodge she owned, there were 2 horses waiting outside. Esther, the lodge owner, is an accomplished horsewoman, so seeing her and horses together was not unusual. I walked into reception, and asked for her. The lodge manager called for her, and she appeared in the doorway adjoining the reception to her quarters, wearing her riding clothes and holding a cowboy hat. I was warmly greeted, we spoke a little on life and being. Esther than asked me if I wanted to go on a horse ride. A birthday gift from her. I was a little taken back, but hastily agreed.

I have never been horse riding. It was one of the things I had always asked to do as a child, but had never done. Either due to finances or forgetfulness. Esther proceeded to put the cowboy hat she was holding onto my head, and off we went to the horses which were waiting outside.

So on my 30th birthday, suffering from a massive depression and separation, I experienced something that I had first wanted to do from around the age of 5. It was actually a very exhilarating day. A day when I thought what my future might be like. As I sat on the horse, walking through the Ngorongoro highlands, I longed for my daughter Xanthe to be with me.

It was great, but no amount of horses or new experiences were going to pull me from my thoughts and longing. I wanted my family more than ever. 30 years old. Broken, depressed, and slipping further away. I then had a thought which seemed to both shake me and comfort me. If the 1st 30 years of my life had brought me to this point, did I really want the next 30?

With some clarity of mind I knew that I did not.

Chapter 24

John arrived back from the rural lands. It was now mid-June. My eldest Daughter's birthday was on the 1st July, I really wanted to be home for her special day, especially after remembering the horrors and depression of my lonely birthday!

I asked John for help, he immediately agreed. I was thrilled somebody trusted me enough to help me this way. I had made so many financial mistakes. I began looking for flights, everything was so expensive, and I knew John probably couldn't run to the $1700 being asked for. He may be a businessman but he is in no way a rich man. $1700 by Tanzanian standards is, for some, a lifetime's wages. I started looking at other options. Different dates, different airlines, routes etc. Et Voila! I found a fantastic flight, flying with Emirates from Nairobi for just under $600. It was even a return flight and I could book to come back and check on the work within a 3 month time period. It was absolutely perfect, as if God had finally heard my prayers. I told John, who quickly arranged the amount needed, I then travelled to Arusha, to 'Rickshaw Travels' and paid for the ticket. We had done it! I was going home to my babies.

The only catch was that it was leaving the following day! It was now the evening of June 19th. The flight was for June 21st from Jomo Kenyatta airport in Nairobi. I only had tomorrow to get there. Arusha to Nairobi is not as far as it sounds. Perhaps about 6.5 hours on the coach, on a good day. Traffic and potholes permitting. June 20th. I didn't have much to pack, I had left a bag in Endallah at the campsite office. I never needed too much to travel with and I had clothes in London I could wear. Also, I did not have the time to go back to Endallah and pick up my bag. I was Nairobi bound. No detours, no nothing. I didn't want to leave any window for a mistake or other problem to happen.

I hadn't told anyone in the U.K. about my impending arrival. I didn't want to get hopes up, just in case I let them down again. I guess there was also a part of me that wanted the surprise and joy, or perhaps the recognition that I could really do something and was not such a screw up.

I took the Impala Shuttle from Arusha. Passed Namanga border without hitch or shida, and arrived in Nairobi in the early evening. I don't know Nairobi very well, and in the night time I didn't really want to explore the city's streets. I got a taxi from the bus stand to the 'Greton Hotel'. A guest house I had stayed in with Andy nearly 2 years previous to this time. It was nothing grand, in fact it was a dump, but I didn't know anywhere else that would not charge me either a fortune or Mzungu tax. Sometimes it is better the devil you know. Isn't it?

I was exhausted from the travelling and speed in which I had made the arrangements to get here, but very satisfied I was on my way. I climbed into the bed, trying not to count the cockroaches climbing the wall. Despite my tiredness, sleep eluded me. I got up several times in the night for the bathroom, or to watch out of the window. When dawn rose at approximately 6 a.m. I took the opportunity to go downstairs and look for my breakfast. Surprisingly the loosely termed restaurant of the said hotel already had some customers. I greeted them as is normal and polite in East Africa, then took my seat.

Excitement was running through me. Also, a kind of sense of mischievousness! Nobody knew what I was doing today! O.K. John in Karatu did, but nobody in the U.K. knew where I was heading and that by tomorrow afternoon I would be back in London, hugging up my babies. Tears of joy came to my eyes at the mere thought of it. So long without them. I made some resolves about what to do when I got back. They were rest, have fun, hug, and get help. The creeping sense of depression was constantly through me. Part of me wanted to shut down, the other to run home. I was glad to be doing the latter.

My phone rang, snapping me out of my thoughts. It was Benja. I spoke to him in Swahili. The brain was not really caffeinated enough to speak in Maasai, so Swahili would have to do. He had heard I was off home and wanted to say goodbye. It was nice to speak with him. We seemed to have a reasonable friendship. A lot had been damaged by the events in April, but we were very much in context now, something which felt good and correct. I could be friends with my Maasai. I could have them in my life along with my special people. It didn't have to be more than friends. This felt good. In my recent days of desperation to get home, I hadn't felt much of anything, so to feel my boundaries once more was very refreshing.

I finished speaking with Benja, and carried on with my food. While I had been speaking to Benja I noticed 2 of the patrons of the hotel looking at me. As a Mzungu in Africa, this was not something unusual. One of them spoke to me, commending me on my control of the Swahili language. I felt a sense of pride in the compliment. I had always wanted to speak languages, and to be fluent in Swahili was something about myself I enjoy. It was not the most usual language to hold as a European, it was also not as bizarre as being able to speak Ki-Maasai! It was that little something different about my life. Something good?

The sun was now up. I decided to take a walk around some of the streets. I didn't think I looked like much of a tourist, I did have cargo pants on and a vest, but still, my actions and walk were not that of wangeni (tourists) so I thought I would blend in reasonably well, and not be the robbery target most Mzungus are in Nairobi.

I left the hotel and walked across the road to take a look at the church which was in full swing and bigging it up African style. I was very attracted to go and take a look. There was a small road running along the side of the tin church. I couldn't find the door into the church compound so took the street, thinking it was the most logical place to find the door.

Walking along, I was completely unaware of being followed. A car was behind me. I was surprised to hear the engine, mainly because this street was so narrow, but hey, this was Nairobi. Road rules were in a league of their own! I squeezed myself along the side of the tin church, finding a space so I would not get hurt by the vehicle that was intending to pass. The car went past me, stopping just after where I was positioned. The back door opened and a man got out. It was one of the guys that I had spoken to in the hotel restaurant that morning. He asked me if I knew where I was, I replied that I did. He started walking towards me. I felt fear grip me. Just before he got close I felt intense terror. My instincts aware something was very wrong with this situation. I wanted to run, but it was too late. He held something over me, it had the aroma of a hospital. I felt sick. Dizzy. Wasted. He pulled a knife on me, I think. I didn't actually see the knife, he said he had one, I just felt something in my side, pushing me along, and into the car. Everything went black.

When I came round, the first thing that hit me was the smell. A damp, mouldy and festering one. The second thing to hit me was a fist. Reeling from the force of the punch, I flopped down. My head was fuzzy and recollection was vague at best. I appeared to be on some kind of foam mattress. It stank. The room I was in was putrid and dark. I couldn't really get any sense of size or bearings. It was hard to focus my eyes. I felt tears rolling down my face. I tried not to make any sound. Over and over in my head, I was saying to myself "please don't cry, please don't cry". I cried.

Somebody came to stand near me. He seemed so tall, like a giant. My head felt very drunk and perception was not really working well. The man knelt down beside me. He turned me over on my back. One of his hands touched my breasts. Roughly. He squeezed them. It hurt. I tried not to show anything. He shouted in my ear. "Are you enjoying it?" I cried. He saw my tears and slapped my face. In his anger he tore my trousers down and off me. Then my vest. I was naked. Ripping open my legs, he climbed on top of me and tried to put his hard penis in me. At first he couldn't do it. He was hard, but I was too dry and scared. My muscles were not going to let this happen. He didn't care. He just kept hammering away until he got it in. I couldn't move. He raped me. Hard. It didn't last for a long time. He soon came in me. I cried. He slapped me and got off.

I was stinging everywhere. My vagina felt so sore. I was shaking all over. I must have fallen asleep, because the next thing I remember was waking up to find somebody had draped a blanket over me. There were four people in the room now. I couldn't make out any features of them, but their voices were distinctly different from each other. I had no concept of time. One of the men realised I was awake and came over, quickly followed by another. One sat by my head, the other near my feet. I could see the one near my head rubbing his crotch, before unzipping his jeans. He got out his penis and told me to hold it. I did. He told me to rub it, I tried to, but obviously didn't do it good enough because he took it back from me and began to rub himself furiously. The other man, positioned near my feet opened my legs and started to put his fingers up my vagina. He then raped me. He didn't come inside me. The other man who had been pleasuring himself while watching the rape swapped positions and took me that time, giving me his wicked liquid.

It finished. They got off. A sickly smell seemed to fill the room. I think it was crack cocaine, I'm not sure why. I have never tried crack but I know people who have, they had explained it had a sickly sweet smell when people were getting their rocks. Whatever it was, something was definitely being taken. These men were off their faces, spaced out and possessed by some kind of drug, madness and demon.

I couldn't stop shaking. They hadn't killed me yet, which I guessed meant either they hadn't finished with me or were not planning to. At that point I couldn't see which was the better option. From somewhere deep within me I seem to find a focus and the thought that as I had survived rape once before. I could do it again. I was younger then, so it would be easier now.

I could get through this, as long as the cunts were not planning to kill me.
I was raped over and over again. In the missionary position and by violation of objects into my vagina. I was so hurt, so damaged and so

degraded. I would sleep, they would wake me up and fuck me, then give me something to drink, which seemed to make me sleep. It just went on and on. They were high and revelling in the fact of what they were doing. Just when I thought these bastards could stoop no lower, and they could not damage me anymore, they did.

One of them, a Luwyah man, came to me. I had not heard any of the other voices for a while and had drifted off into another, I guess, drug induced sleep. He woke me violently, his crazed eyes demanding more from me. He punched me in the stomach and told me to turn over. I did. He pulled me up on to all fours by my arse. I wanted to fall. Fear made sure I couldn't. I thought he was going to take me from behind, until he tried to enter me. I was wrong. He wanted me anally. Trying to push his well-endowed penis into my rectum, he found it was going to be difficult. He got off. I felt relieved and flopped down. Until he came back.

He was mad, and angry. Pulling me back onto all fours, I thought he was going to try again, but this was different. This was not him. This was not his penis. He had something. It was cold and hard. It hurt. He opened my anus with it, then with an almighty push rammed something up me so hard it caused me to howl. I heard the sound coming from me, I had absolutely no control over it. I howled and howled until I couldn't even speak anymore and my screams were just silent. Held together by my tears. Sobbing I pleaded with him to stop.

He wouldn't and laughed carrying on and on. The pain was unbearable. I heard voices. The others were coming. He stopped. I sobbed. I couldn't control my sobbing. The pain was too much to take. I broke and fell unconscious.

The next time I opened my eyes, there was one of the men on the mattress with me. The man from Greton hotel. The man from the car. The man who had pleasured himself in my pain so very much. His face had changed from evil to concerned. He was stroking my hair telling me how sorry he was and begging me to forgive him. I tried to take in everything. I felt sticky. I felt sick. I remember asking if he was going to kill me. He said No. I asked him to.

He told me to get up. I did, and on doing I fell back down. He gave me my clothes. I put them on, then after managing to get up, was led by his hand to the car which had brought me here. The bastard drove me to the Greton Hotel. He threatened me to say nothing, I nodded. Anything just to get away. He kept saying sorry. I said OK, I forgave him, knowing that I never would.

The hotel staff were pleased to see me. My blue bag had been here and they had kept it safe, for the almost 3 days I had been missing! 3 days! Amazingly the little money I had was still in it, as was my passport. I took a shower, blood was pouring from my vagina. I must have started menstruating. I then grabbed my bag and ran. I was not sure what to do. I had no ticket for Emirates, I had no reason to be in Nairobi, and I just had to run and run and run. Forrest Gump had nothing on what I was feeling. I had to run. I grabbed a taxi and asked to go to Nairobi Central Police, thinking I should report. Remembering the unhelpful attitude of Kenyan police from a previous matter, I changed my mind and headed for the Akamba stand, boarding the first coach with a destination I knew. Dar es Salaam.

Sitting on the coach from beginning to end of the massive trip, I didn't even notice the time go past. We must have stopped at the border. I must have gone through immigration control, because there was a stamp to show it. I had no recollection of the process or even the journey. Everything in me ached. I was bleeding. Was it just my period or something else? Why was I heading for Dar? What would I do in Dar?

I planned I would get medical help and try to call Mr. Kavindi. Mr. Kavindi was actually a friend of John's, not mine, but we had met in Karatu when he came to set up the business documents for the tourism company.

I knew he had money. He was a business consultant. I arrived in Dar and couldn't find Kavindi. It is easier to find someone if you even have a number for them! I had no details of Kavindi! I also had no money, and not even a phone. I managed to get a room saying I was waiting for my bank card to work. I wasn't, however the hotel staff believed I was, and even let me use their phone. I called John, who wanted an explanation I could not give, then got the number for Kavindi. I called and we arranged to meet.

I then called Andy. I couldn't speak. He called me back, with such an anger in his voice. He wanted reasons and the whole story. I couldn't even think properly let alone talk. I put the phone down in tears. I was unsure of time, of space, of anything. I was alive but felt dead. I wished into the air that I would die. I couldn't wish to God. My God had forsaken me.

Chapter 25

Days passed in a blur. I was in Dar, had been to a Dr. there, but didn't have enough money to pay for the care needed. The man I was looking for had gone on safari to Arusha. I decided to go to that town also.

The wounds inflicted on me throughout my Nairobi ordeal were extremely painful, especially in my rectum. The journey to Arusha was very long and painful. My arse was so sore, my vagina weeping, my mind a blur.

In Arusha I went to the Marie Stopes clinic to be examined and checked over. Swabs and samples were taken from everywhere for testing. Within an hour the results started to come through. I had Gonorrhea and Syphilis. It was also suspected I had pelvic inflammatory disease. My HIV result was negative, but this did not really mean much apart from the fact that I did not have it prior to the attack. It can take up to 3 months for the disease to show in the blood.

My vagina would recover and already was healing from the prolonged abuse, but my bum was in a terrible state. There was glass stuck up it and embedded in the sides of my rectum. I was cut to pieces and needed to have surgery to remove the glass and repair the insides. I was booked in to the Mount Meru hospital, where there a surgeon who could perform the procedure, at a realistic price. I had little money to eat or pay my medical bills.

Surgery took place, but had to be redone 3 times over the next month. Until it finally started to heal.

All throughout this time, I felt myself sink into a lower state of mind. Every passing day was so pain filled. I could barely sleep, I was desperate to get home. I wanted my babies, but with every step deeper into low I was experiencing, I felt myself closing and pulling further away.

Andy had accused me of making up the whole attack situation, both in an e-mail to me and to the face of my friend Delphine. His words will forever be with me. This was the guy that had read through the abuse support website and had read that the worst thing you can tell a victim of abuse or rape is that it is not true. He did and I felt my whole life crumble to a new depth.

I was alone. In the most awful situation and facing it by myself. I couldn't think or focus properly, and was scared to even live. I sent away my friends, scared to let them close to me. I also could not afford to have them around me. If they had no work or money there was no way I could afford to feed them as well as myself. Everything was an absolute mess.

I tried to keep a focus, but it was fake, and I couldn't act anymore. All throughout this time, my situation became more and more desperate. All I wanted was to get home, yet to go home filled me with such fear. I needed rest and help not accusation. I started to see no point to being alive. The thoughts grew deeper every day. I didn't really even have much memory of days and times. Everything was a blur. One time, in Endallah, a week had passed without me realising. I needed help. Or to die. Whichever would come first.

I reached a new low. I received test results from the Marie Stopes clinic that my HIV result was now +. This was based on a rapid test, so I went to have an anti-body test to confirm the status.
It was true. I had contracted the very worst of all the STI's. The killer disease. I freaked out losing all sense of life and time. What was the purpose to my being? Had I not tried to help and live a decent life? Had I not been punished enough? Was the rape not an ordeal in itself to go through, without becoming a fatal incident?

Of course I was suicidal, but suicide would be my choice, not inflicted on me by 4 guys high on crack. Suicide. It was the only option coming to my mind.

I wanted to see my children. Yet how could I ever be a Mother to them now, with this death sentence hanging over me. How could I be a wife to Andy? How would I ever have sex again, or be able to have a period without hating my blood? How could I ever be human again? How could I stay? How could I go home? I felt sick, disgusted, ashamed, alone. Ready to die.

I wanted to go to Endallah. If I was going to die, it was going to be there, surrounded by nature. I left Arusha, writing some notes for people and instructions for them to be posted after my death.

Sitting in the dala dala, I felt waves of peace. It was soon going to be over. I closed my eyes, happy at the acknowledgment that the pain would soon be over. I was seated in the middle section of the 2nd row of seats. Squashed either side by someone with either an aversion to washing, or an allergy to soap. I hadn't noticed anybody that was of any recognition to me as. I climbed in the dala dala. On a normal journey, I would have many people to speak to. Not this time. I noticed nobody and didn't want anyone to see me. When I heard somebody say "Hi Sam." I wanted to ignore them. The voice sounded of no importance to me and I just wanted to be left alone. Then the person who had tried to greet me tapped me on the shoulder. Turning around, shock and anger took me once more. The person trying to communicate with me was Alex!

Alex. The man who had stranded me in the desert. I think he caught the anger in my eye, and knew to back off. He tried to greet me. I turned to him and told him to leave me alone. He had caused me enough pain and damage. He looked surprised, as were most of the other passengers. How dare this man greet me like a friend! Then I exploded. If I was going to die tonight, then let me have my say. Bus full of people or not. So I did. I absolutely let rip into Alex. Who sat there dumbfounded, staring at me, and getting the brunt of my pent up anger and frustration. Initially Alex could not even speak back to me. Then when I stopped to take a breather, he spoke. Telling me I had it all wrong. 'I' had it all wrong? What? The fact that he had left my family and I broken and stranded, taking money and so much more from us?

He denied everything. Which of course he would have! He wasn't about to admit what he did to me to a load of passengers on the dala dala was he?

I had to stop the discussion. I was about to burst into tears and didn't want him or them to see that. I shut up and told him I was no longer in this conversation. Trying to grab some sort of slippery control. I couldn't compose myself. The 'dala dala' was driving through Ilkisongo and I made a snap decision to get off. Ilkisongo is a Maasai/Mwarusha town about 35 kms outside of Arusha. Karatu was still about 3 hours away. I decided to get myself composed and jump on a different dala dala a bit later. Away from Alex, away from those passengers who had heard what we had said. I wanted to cry and scream. I got off. In my haste, I never looked back, never saw my bag, or Alex holding it, when he got off the dala dala just after me.

I went to a hotel and ordered myself a cup of chai. I had never liked chai, until I realised I didn't have taste buds anymore. Months of eating bland food seemed to have taken away my desire for tantalizing tastes, and now chai, a sickly sweet version of milky tea, was something I could take quite easily.

I reached down into my bag, to get the 150/- to pay for my drink, then realised I didn't have it. Panic gripped me again. No bag, would mean no passport, would mean no ID, would mean no nothing. Not a huge deal considering I hadn't planned on ever needing my passport again, but I needed to pay for this drink and my dala dala fare. What was I going to do? Then I saw Alex. Walking up to me with my bag on his shoulder. First of all I thought he had stolen it from me, then I thought again, he had probably seen me leave it on the bus and brought it to me. Which was exactly what had happened. I was happy and angry. I now had to speak to and even thank my enemy. I managed it with gratitude and clenched teeth. Quite a considerable effort in combination!

I managed it. I thanked Alex. He wanted to speak, and sat down opposite me. Top on his agenda was what I had said to him on the dala dala. Looking at me, across the wobbly plastic table, he asked me to repeat again. I was somewhat calmer now, and knew that I would not have another chance to get my hatred towards this man off my chest. I poured out all of the emotions I had carried with me since I had last seen his face, when we broke down in the Serengeti. He sat and took everything I had to say, which was remarkable especially considering the fact that when I had finished my venting session, the first thing he said was "you've got this all wrong!"

Wrong? Me? 'I' had it wrong? I could hardly believe my ears. How dare he! I got up to walk away, angry and hurt. He asked me to sit down. Not really having anywhere to walk to, I did. He went on to tell me his version of what happened. The man he had gone with had told him to go to Arusha to get the part, when Alex had returned to Karatu, the guy had already left, leaving a message for Alex at the garage that he had the part and had gone back to the Mzungu. Somewhat confused Alex, had headed out to the Serengeti, aware that we needed a driver to get the Pajero back to a garage. By the time he got to the remote section where we had broken, my children and I had gone. The Pajero was there, and it was he who, over the next few days had arranged it to get towed back to Karatu. Paid for the car and a guard for it until I returned. Alex was speaking with such a passion. Such a need to be heard, that I instantly recognised as truth. I had been wrong. All this time, I had such negativity to this man, yet he hadn't done what I thought he had. I asked about my bags, again, with truth in his eyes, he said he had taken his bag only. Sometimes the impossible is proved possible. I told Alex I believed him.

There was silence, which brought with it a healing between us. I felt drawn to Alex, he was very open in his body language to me. I needed a friend more than ever at that time, somehow Alex sensed this and was there with me.

Sitting in the hotel Engigwana in Ilkisongo, I was able to open up to Alex in a way I have never opened to anyone. Through a tirade of tears I was able to tell him how fucked up everything was, including myself. I even shared with him my suicidal intention for that evening.

He didn't say much again, which I guess is one of the best things about him. He only speaks if it is necessary. He let me empty, then took me outside for some air, where we sat, absorbed in the African night, and I emptied some more. I felt like Alex was really capable of understanding my pain, I guessed he had been on the edge before and knew how it felt to feel you have lost everything and are worth nothing.

Alex asked me if I was really going to kill myself. I said "yes, I have every intention." He said "OK, do you want me to help you." I was shocked, I didn't feel as if I had had much help in life, and now I was going to get some in my death. I refused his offer, but asked him if he would call Andy when it was done. He said he would, I gave him the numbers needed. There was something nice about sharing this strange dark moment with him. I felt so close to this man. This day I had woken with him listed as one of my enemies, now my heart and soul melted near him. Thankful for someone to talk to. Thankful for the non-judgement. He put his arm around me and told me he would be with me until the end. The end was nigh.

From Ilkisongo, I never made it back to Karatu. Alex and I got on a dala dala heading for Arusha. Booking into a cheap guest house, in separate rooms. Saying goodbye that night was not hard. It was refreshing. I thanked Alex for his assistance. Checked he had the numbers and letters for my family. Then went into my room.

I called my Dr. at the clinic, we spoke, catching up on life, I then asked again for my test results, They hadn't changed. The suicide would continue.

I found a space to sit down. This wouldn't take long. The choice had already been made. My choice. It felt good to think such a thing. I was doing this. Nobody, no man, no nothing was inflicting it on me. Soon I would be free.
Opening the tablet bottle, I smiled. Relief would soon come. Then I started.

1 lithium, 2 lithium, 3 lithium, 4. Accompanied with tequila shots.

These tablets had taken me so far into being like a zombie, they could have the rest of me. I carried on taking them. At number 10, the tears started. I thought of my children, of how I had let them down in life. I hoped I wasn't doing that by my death also. My death. How had it come to this point? How had I got to this level? From being a normal mum of 4, with a career, a family and a life, to this ghastly shell of a being, popping the last pills, ending her pathetic existence.

I had been so sure of what to do. I didn't want to hurt other people and decided the least painful way would be an overdose. Blood looks nasty. Jumping would leave squashed remains for other people to clear up. An overdose would be perhaps some vomit and a corpse. The much better option. I didn't want to hurt any more people.

11, 12, 13.

I started to feel light in my head. The effects coming. At least it wasn't going to hurt. Maybe I could just sleep and drift away into oblivion. Then I could rest. The pain would be over. I shut my eyes, breathing in my last sensations.

My mind wouldn't shut from images of my children. I pictured myself pregnant with them, them as new born babies, of our once happy family life, of my Sons, my Daughters, growing
from little helpless beings into the people they are today. The beautiful children. I wondered what they would look like in the future. I knew their Father would be good to them.

I knew they would have a normal life. Probably much better than with me around. Their Mum. The one who was seen as fun and adventurous, vibrant. The one who life had pretty much destroyed. The one they had not seen for 6 months.

My tears would not stop falling. 14,15,16.

I didn't deserve them and there was no way I could have a future with them now. What could I do for them? I had gone from being Mum the adventurer, to Mum the wasted and infected.
I would much prefer them to have a good memory of me. Not one of me falling away from them day by day.

17, 18, 19, 20.

My Daughter. I could not get her out of my head. I felt her, she was crying for me. She needed me. It was as if I could see her and feel her pain. I pictured myself in her room. She was lying in bed. I reached out, she fell from my grasp.

I have to stop. I can't, it is done. I am slipping. I wanted to stop, I need to see my Daughter.

Stop the pills! Reaching for my phone, I called the last number. Who was it? My head was gone. I had no thoughts.

The blackness came.

Chapter 26

Dr. Karanga picked up his phone to a sound of nothing. It disturbed him. He could see it was my number calling. The line between us was connected. As much as he tried to speak to me, no sound was coming from my end. Given that I am not one for prank calls. He sensed something was wrong and rushed to the guest house I was staying in.

The door was locked, Karanga knocked again. Raising up Alex, who was in the room next door. Alex, finding out I had called the Dr. ran to the managers room to get the spare key, hoping that an establishment such as this would keep one. They did.

According to the Dr. and Alex I was in the bed on my side. Unconscious. Tequila on the floor, tablets by my head. They took me to the clinic. Unaware of how many tablets I had
taken, his only choice was to do a full stomach pump. Alex at this point said that I would not want this, I had wanted to die, and therefore I should be left to die. Karanga argued back that
I had called. I had probably changed my mind. They would never know, so a decision had to be made. Karanga won. I was pumped out of the poison I had willingly put inside.

I don't have a recollection of the procedure, just hazy memories, but the pain from my stomach afterwards was awful. I would like to say awful enough not to consider doing that again, but one can never be sure.

Over the next few days, I stayed at the house of Karanga, to try and recover from the events of that night. Alex stayed in Arusha and was with me most of the time, being my shoulder to cry on. I told him to go away but he wouldn't. I was even abusive to him. I wanted to be left alone but I wanted to feel wanted, did I really know what it was I needed?

I needed to get home for medical care and to just get home I guess. The thought of it was both horrible and terrifying. Why should I go home if I can be no good to anybody? What am I going home to? My children? They are better off without me. Surely it is better for them to have a memory of a good Mum then the reality of an ill and depressed one who is going to fade away slowly from life and existence? Still, I should get home.

I had been let down by everybody who had said they would assist me with a ticket. I wish they had just said they could not help rather then let me think there was a hope. No hope is better than false hope.

In desperation I contacted my Brother to ask for help. I told him I was HIV+ and needed to get home. He never replied, but showed my e mail to my parents and Andy. Great. I had wanted to tell Andy when I was able to face to face, something which was now not possible.

Something positive did come from this though. Andy said he would get me home. Hope? A few weeks was needed to get the cash together for the flight. I needed a similar amount of time to psyche myself up for the journey and going home. The fear I felt at going back to London was deep. I knew that setting myself a target day was the only way I was going to manage it and stick to it without disappearing into the wilderness somewhere. So I did. I gave myself the date 1st October.

Survival is something we achieve through struggle and problems. To survive the child abuse I set myself targets. If I got to such a day I would feel better. If I made it to my 10th birthday everything will be OK, and so on. It was the same formula I had applied in my adult life. Especially now. Since the attack in Nairobi, this was the only thing I could do. It works to some extent. Except when you don't meet the target or somebody else takes it away from you. Then the whole strategy collapses in your mind and screws you up a bit more.

Alex had to go to see his Grandfather in the Kilimanjaro hills. I was sad to see him go, he had helped me so much just by being there. Even on the days when I had demanded him to fuck off and leave me alone, he had stuck with me. He had seen me crying, vomiting, suicidal, desperate, yet had not walked away from me. My one time enemy had turned into the only ally I had and I loved him greatly for it. He asked if I wanted to come. I did. I had never spent time in that region, I had no reason to be in Arusha and the thought of being here without Alex scared me more. So I went.

I bid farewell to Karanga. He had assisted me so much by just being with me. With promises of never letting go of me and making sure I was supported and well, he hugged me goodbye.

I didn't really believe what he had said. Most people here had lied to me, that the element of trust of anybody had gone. Even seemingly nice people. Mbokuma is situated next to the might Kilimanjaro mountain. The rooftop of Africa. It is home to the traditional Chagga people. The citizens of Kilimanjaro who still live the old way. Chagga are not as extreme or as steadfast in their culture as Maasai, but they still live in the traditional houses, eat the same way as they have for hundreds of years.

The Grandfather of Alex lived in Mbokuma. To get there we had to get bus to Moshi, a dala dala to the main road at the foot of Mbokuma, then a landrover taxi up the hill, which was as well maintained and carefully driven as most rural vehicles in Tanzania, with no regard for speed or road. Probably given the fact that there was indeed no road, what did I expect?

Meeting old people for the first time is something I always find either daunting or amusing. I don't quite know how to take them and vice versa. Sometimes old people have reached a glorious stage in life where they just don't care for social protocol any longer and say things as they are.

Much respect to the oldies who can do this! If I do get old, which is something I doubt very much, I would much rather be an oldie who can get away with being as blunt and out there as possible! The Grandfather of Alex, Jasper, was one of these oldies.

On the day we arrived, the old man welcomed us into his hut, we sat down, he prepared fresh coffee for us. By fresh I mean fresh. As in picked a few days before from the adjoining garden to the home, roasted by little iron pot, crushed by hand made pestle and mortar, and now bubbling away on an open fire. Fresh? Jasper's Kilimanjaro brew could certainly teach 'Costa (lot) Coffee' and the likes a few things! We drank the said coffee. Feeling somewhat more relaxed, we started to hold a conversation, just a 'how is life' sort of thing, then Jasper comes out with the most amazing question. He said "who are you both?" I was surprised.

Alex was more than surprised! His own Grandfather had not recognised him, yet had invited us in given us coffee, chatted with us. It was so funny, and after formally introducing himself as a member of the family, Jasper recognised him, giving away to laughter in abundance from us all. What a fantastic welcome!

The village was like a paradise for me. From the moment we arrived there to the day I left, I found myself far more peaceful than I had been at any other time during the past 3 and a half months. There is something truly magical about that mountain, and living in its shadow, surrounded by the forest and natural springs helped bring an energy to me. I was so comforted by the natural energy that I never returned to Arusha to stay.

I had to go back a few times to see the psychologist at Mount Meru hospital. However, I no longer found her of any benefit as she had broken my trust and the confidentiality oath between a Dr. and patient. My family had contacted her. She had contacted them. The damage was irreparable. By speaking with them I felt she had crossed over to their side. I had been getting somewhere. Opening up slowly. Making sense slowly.

Then the family and the Dr. were in contact. My parents of course tried to show themselves to be the caring people they are not. They ruined my only source of professional assistance out there.

So my last home in Tanzania was deep in the Kilimanjaro hills. Where I was blessed with evening and night views of the overshadowing mountain, in all its glory. I managed to find some sort of healing.

Some peace and definite energy to come back home. Alex, through his actions had helped me to get to the point where I felt I could leave. Of course I was scared. I didn't know what I was coming back to. It was obvious everything had changed. 6 months do not go by without change. I had changed. I was far more bitter than I have ever been. Sick. Hurt. Depressed. I wondered how much everyone else had been affected by the last 6 months.

Andy booked me a flight for the 9th October. Having a date to fly was reassuring. I was flying from Kilimanjaro. Andy had understood I could not get back to Nairobi. Something I was thankful for. I didn't know how I would be at the flight, especially at the transfer stage when reaching Amsterdam. I have this eternal instinct to run away when stress is coming, would I do this again? Would the freedom of a European Union passport actually make me leave Schipol?

I tried to relay my fears to Andy. He tried to help, but I don't think he really understood the state I am in.

The day came. I met John Perasso to say goodbye. So much had happened since April. He thanked me for my work, said he was sorry I had faced so many issues while here, and gave me some money! Some small assistance for my trouble. Too late. Why could I had not had that on the day I was hungry? John asked when I would be returning to Karatu. I couldn't answer. Not even with a maybe.

Alex and I then got in a car heading for KIA. He stayed with me until I could wait to check in no longer. This man seemed to just know what to do. He knew I was distressed and traumatized. He might not be a Dr. but he was the best help I could have possibly had in those final days in Africa. Thanking him for everything, I gave Alex the money John had given me. He refused it. Alex only had work here and there, he had never asked me for anything, it seemed right to do so, but he wouldn't accept it. Telling me to go and change it and give it to my children. I did as I was told.

On 09/10/06, after 193 days inside, I left Tanzania. I left Africa. Knowing that I would probably never set foot in my land again.

Chapter 27

I arrived at Heathrow. Nobody was waiting for me. Andy had said he might be late, and I didn't have anyone else I could call to meet me.

For half an hour I stood in culturally shocked fear before he came. The meeting was frosty to say the least. He just said "you're home now."

We drove home. I barely recognised where we were. A place I have known for so long seemed so alien to me. The children were at school when I had arrived, so I had the day waiting to see them. The welcome I received was beautiful. Such unconditional love poured from them to me. They had not judged me. They did not hate me. They were not even that angry. Whatever they had felt had gone because I was home and with them. Of course we would work out any problems with time, but right then, as I hugged my daughter, I couldn't thank her enough for coming to my rescue that night in Arusha.

Life seemed just as normal as ever. This was so wonderful to see. These people had existed fine without me. In some ways that made me think about my whole point of being here. I was very pleased though that life had been as near to normal as possible for everybody.

One thing which was never going to be normal again was Andy and I. This was painstakingly obvious from the time I was in Tanzania, and even more so now. One of the thoughts which had sometimes kept me going at my bleakest moments, when I was crying alone and in need of some real love and support, was the fact that if Andy was here he would help. He would hold me and make it all better. Even on the flight home, I thought to myself that this is the last night I will sleep alone unheld. Andy would hold me from tomorrow. My Andy. I will feel safe once more. Andy didn't hold me. Andy, initially, stayed as physically away as possible. My first night back in the house of my children, I was dumped in the spare room to cry alone.

Andy didn't hear me. Or ignored me. Delete as you think appropriate. I realised over the next few days that Andy did not think I was coming back. At the time I was getting my passport in Dar Es Salaam, he was writing to various people telling them I had left him.

He does not think I was attacked, he came into my single room one day and asked me what had really happened, which to me shows his true thoughts. Also, he told me that he had even thought perhaps it would be better if I didn't come back, because everything was settled. 'Everything was settled' meant that life was comfortable. Andy had his work and social life, the children could go to school. Everything was settled came across to me as if a ' we don't have a place for you here'. I told Andy previously that I thought I wouldn't have a place here, and you know, I was right. I don't. It is as if there is no room for me.

I looked at the calandar. Catching up with what had been happening over the past few months. It struck me with some degree of pain that my birthday was not even marked. There were the dates for new friends, my family, most other people, except me. No date. No place, no position within this family. The doors are closed to me.

A Poem
I am spare
To this world I don't belong
I am spare
I walk around with others
Though alone
Never belonging, never being.
I am spare, in the spare room.
Spare, not needed.
Spare I do not exist.

I know I should say my place is with my children, but what can I do for them? My parents have too much involvement for me to even be effective. They also have Andy where they want him regarding me. They don't believe my childhood abuse or how it has affected my life, he doesn't believe the later issues.

The pain, loneliness and torture I went through out there, only to come back home, where I am meant to be safe and loved, yet all I feel is more alone and more desperate than ever.

Diary Entry
Life and punishment - 1st night home
He couldn't even kiss me goodnight. The first night we have been in the same country, let alone the same house for nearly 7 months. All we have gone through – alone. Separated by continent, circumstance, money, everything. Yet here we are. Upstairs, downstairs.

I need him more than I have ever needed him, tonight. I don't want anything sexual. That is impossible. I just need to be held tight. To be reassured. To be loved. I have cried so often
alone into my pillow, alone. Longing for him to be there. I cannot truly give words to how this is feeling. It is as if any hope I had was false. I have held out in the bleakest of moments and blackest of nights with thoughts that one day I would be back in his arms and he will soothe this pain. Like his words promised me. Make it better somehow?

How can I recover from this added slap. Is the rest I have endured alone not enough? Why can't he hold me? Why can't he love me? I need him tonight. I feel so low. So sad. In Africa I had a reason to be lonely. There was nobody with me to wipe away my tears and fears. Here I don't have the same reason, but tonight is more lonely than any night I spent there. My tears fall and there is still no-one. No-one holding. No-one helping. He there, and I here. Separate rooms. Separate floors. Will this pain never stop growing?

My son heard me crying and brought his 12 year old body downstairs to ask what was wrong. I said nothing. His Father must have also heard me. Why did he ignore me? I had a hope in him, it was false.

It is better no hope than false hope. It is easier to swallow and won't let you down.

When my un-parents found out about my childhood abuse. I felt like they had a chance to help and pick up my pieces with me. Now Andy has the chance to help me rebuild, but he just pushed me away into the spare room.

I am also feeling angry. I did not ask to be treated in this way. I did not ask for what happened. I did not want this. I only wanted to get home. I am a rape victim. I suffered alone and in great pain. I had to be repaired. My fragile mental state collapsed. I had to endure surgery, tests and an eventual positive result, all while being away and far from my family, and trying to get home. I did not want any of this.

Yet I am being punished for it. I don't understand. If no one held me there and no one holds me there, then I am truly alone in this world and have no place with nobody.

Grave swallow me now.

I have come to the conclusion that suicide really is my only option. The depression I feel is far too much to cope with. The pain of life is immense and the option of ending this trauma becomes the only light I can see. I am starting to receive help for this depression, but it is everything else. It is the nightmares, the pain, the mental prison I am in, the loneliness, the fact that everything does exist fine without me, and I believe in a better and more realistic format.

I am not good for my children. I adore them but I am not good for them. I am not good for my husband, he has other people who make him smile in a way I used to. More than anything I want him to be happy. I want him to smile. I hear of the summer and what fun everyone had without me, and it hurts. I wanted to be here, but here moved on without me and left me behind.

Everybody else is part of something I will never belong to. There is a family which I do not have. A few days after I arrived home, my Father managed to get into the house when Andy was not here. He proceeded to verbally abuse me in a most despicable format. Knowing full well how sick with this depression I am, he called me all the names under the sun and clearly showed his distaste for me and disbelief of what I have said and done, before ending his tirade of abuse by declaring me a non-entity. A few days later a letter from my Mother arrived telling me stop this stupid behaviour, that I had been away for no reason, my actions were not very Christian. What actions? Being raped? Living with a crippling depression? Or perhaps it is the fact that I have now exposed my childhood trauma to them and as I refuse to back down from the only truths I have. Would it be more Christian to cover up and pretend nothing had happened? If so, then I fail as a Christian. Such is life.

The depression consumes me and will devour me. This I know. I am losing the struggle against it. I don't see a future for my family with me in it. I want to, but in my heart I know it will never be. I cannot give, I cannot provide, I cannot be. All I am is a depressed Mum, a shit wife and a bad friend. I wish I had died that night. I wish I had not called Karanga.

The pursuit of self? Sometimes I wish I had not bothered. Bombarded with media pressure and desires to 'just be yourself ', we often think we can, but the reality of far more twisted than that. When we find our true selves we have to face the reality that the truth sometimes sucks. When we hide and bury our lives in career and other people, perhaps we are merely masking our own problems and pain. When we uncover what lies beneath, the corpses of our past appear like the evil dead ready to capture us once more.
If I had not bothered to be myself, have an adventure, leave and live, would I be in this mess now? Would it have all come to the surface at some point or could I just have existed.

Pretending in the family I was in, having a part of something, as fake as it was, and looking normal, like everybody wants one to be?

Regrets? I always wanted to be like Edith Piaf. She sang a song entitled 'Je Ne Regrette Rien', I regret nothing. I wish I was like that. Regrets? I have many. Lies and situations caused by lying. While there are reasons, it does not change the actions, and what is done is done. I can change nothing.

Despite what happened, living in Africa was the best thing that happened to me. The meeting of new people, living a new culture, escaping my past, the pursuit of my self. I guess it is just sad that my real self is such a mess and I guess everything opened at once. The freedom I found in myself perhaps gave me enough rope to hang myself.

Andy will always be my all time love. The only person who has stuck with me and knows as much about me as I can give out. Yet even he is not my Andy now. I don't have anything. I don't have anybody. My Maasai family are far. My blood family are gone. There is no future with Andy and the children are all fine without me. I have gone from finding my truth, living life with a freedom, enjoying my growth, to nothing but pain and a battle with myself to live. My self is the loneliest place I have been and it is the only place I wanted to go.

I give up.

Can extraordinary things happen to ordinary people? Can wishes or dreams come true? Is everything just locked into patterns of yes and no, or are there grey areas in life which truly exist and are not just based on indecision?

I was sitting in the waiting room of the sexual health centre, wondering on my whole point of being there. There wasn't much. I was attending the clinic for a cell count. While I was out in Africa, I tested positive twice. Once with a rapid test, the second time with an antibody count.

Having 2 positive results is a very certain diagnosis, however, on the advice of my friend Sheila who is a Dr. in Tanzania, I went for a retest a few months after my arrival back in the UK, even though I knew it would just be a cell count for me. There would be nothing new to tell. I was HIV positive and that was that.

Sexual health clinics are really quite bizarre places. Their waiting rooms are like none other on earth. People attend for various reasons under the umbrella of sexual health, such as contraception, advice, counselling and tests. The clients seem to range from extremely embarrassed to very nervous, or proudly loud about how and why they are there, and making arrangements for maybe meeting up again same time same place next week! I couldn't help but look at my fellow silent clinic users and wonder why they were here. I wonder if they were doing the same. Did I look like I have HIV? I wonder how many would guess my problem correctly?

I was finding life in the UK hard to adjust to after my time in Africa. I had spent so long trying to get here, that now I was back, it was as if I had lost focus and was in some sort of culture shock. I didn't seem to understand anything. Not how things worked or why they are as they are. A numbness took hold of me most of days, which I guess is how I got through them.

The nurse called my name snapping me out of the thoughts which consume me. She then showed me into Dr. Desmond's room where I would find out my count and if I needed to go onto medication or *not. The thought of medication everyday was not something I was looking forward to, so I hoped my blood was still strong enough to go without.*

The Dr. came in with her file. Smiling, she said " I have some news for you Samantha ".Great . News? What kind of news? Why was she smiling so much? There is nothing that could be that happy in this situation? I figured that maybe she was mad or just an over-the-top positive thinking kind of type. "You're test results are negative " she said. My what? My test is negative? I am not HIV+? The Dr. kept smiling. I couldn't smile back. Tears fell down my face, confused, desperate for an explanation but not being able to speak, I just sat there. The nurse fetched some water for me. It had no effect. I was completely numb.

The previous months flashed before my eyes. From the time I was told I was infected with HIV to that very morning, when I had cursed my menstruation once more, for showing itself and my infected blood to me. All the confusion, pain, attempted suicide, loss of hope, depression, and it was all for what? It was too much to take.

A taxi was called. I spoke with Andy. He was ecstatic. I should have been. I knew that. I should have been jumping for joy, that would be the correct thing to do right now, wouldn't it? Or maybe be angry, or something? Yet, I had no feeling. I was not happy or sad. Just somewhere.

This is the day I realised that I had to get help.

Chapter 28

The sounds of a hospital are always disturbing. Sick people making sick noises. The stench, which is a mixture of home smells and hospital disinfectant is enough to disturb even the strongest of nostrils.

The sound of a psychiatric ward is particularly disturbing, every morning so far this week I woke up to the realisation that I was indeed in such a place. The psychiatric ward of my local hospital!

I had got here through giving up on my life. I couldn't find any reason to be alive so considered the logical next move to be death.

Some people say suicide is selfish. At my suicidal times I have found it to be logical. As if there is no other choice. I balanced out my life and my death. My death won because I was not worth my life. It was not selfish, it was right, or so I thought. I had come voluntarily under threat of being sectioned under the mental health act. There wasn't really much volunteering in the whole episode, but I guess the word is placed in the midst of the act to make one think they actually have some control over what happens. Which you don't, when a life has gone so far down.

My GP got in contact with the mental health team, who saw me straight away, asked questions, got answers, and asked me to come here or be brought here. Am I really that bad?

I have been diagnosed with having severe depression, Bi-Polar disorder and post traumatic stress disorder. None of which really came as a surprise. The Dr. in Arusha had suspected I had Bi Polar due to my rapid cycling mood swings. He had even given me some medication called Lithium, which was perhaps irresponsible on his part because I had not had a full psychiatric evaluation done, and tried to commit suicide with it, but hey, at least it was the right medication for the disorder. So his diagnosis was correct!

I don't know how I feel about being diagnosed with this. Part of me feels satisfied that I have an explanation for what has been wrong, then the other side of me fears exactly how much of my life has been influenced because of this illness.

I mean, have I really ever experienced anything over the past few years? Were all of my times of adventure, actually just mania? Was my sadness and loss actually depression? Was it real? Did I feel? Does it all have to be labelled as something? I am pleased that I now have a reason, some sort of explanation as to why I am as I am. Yet, it scares me. Have I actually lived anything naturally, or have I forever been a nutter?

The hospital feels and sounds surreal. I can hardly wait to get out of here. The level of care is ok, apart from the odd God squad pushy nurse, or the OTT evangelical Christians who seem to be in abundance on the ward.

One evening, in the lounge room, while being preached to about becoming a 'fisher of men' by a schizophrenic, heavily overweight, pot holed faced, 6 ft, ginger haired, dirty with dribbles Manchester United T shirt wearing right wing Christian, I asked his opinion of why there are so many Christians admitted into the Psychiatric ward, in comparison to say, Muslims? Living in the south east of England, especially Slough. From a population perspective, one would expect to see far more Muslims/Eastern religions represented in the hospital. It would make sense. Of course, the dribbler had no answer, and proceeded to tell me that Babylon fell. Well, really. The conversation couldn't have got much worse, when praise be to the highest (sic) the drugs trolley came round. Mind numbing medications for all and off we go to sleep until the next day, where pottery classes, papier mache and drawing with pastels could be on the agenda. If we're lucky!

How the hell did I get here?

I managed to avoid the occupational therapist the next morning. I am sure that these people do wonderful work, but, not with me. I don't want to learn pottery, I want to get better and struggle to find the link between clay and healing. Expressive art form could be it perhaps, but it is not my art form so why should I have it inflicted on me?

After my questions with the Christian guy yesterday, something had twigged in my mind. Perhaps my way out of here was to become an instigator? Not of violence or fire alarms. Just by popping little, um, life questions into a forum shall we say! It seemed pretty harmless, and in some ways almost fun. Forget 'The Jeremy Kyle Show', which seemed to be on constant play on the television in the lounge room. I had my own people, real people we could get to the bottom of issues with. Of course, the fact that we were all mentally ill in one way or another might add or take away the pleasure, but all things considered, it was worth a shot.

One of the most misunderstood things about mentally ill people, is how intelligent the majority of them are. What is lacking in social capability is often more than made up for with a locker full of information on some of the most bizarre subjects one could wish to hear about. The lounge room is a fabulous source of information ranging from misunderstood children, to conspiracy theories, and of course, the very popular, religious debates. OK, if I was going to do this, I had to be subtle. As the only pagan person in the ward, I was probably under suspicion for every psychosis caused hex and curse going!

So, one evening after dinner, but before the sleep inducing medications were on offer, we patients were sitting in the TV room, and my chance came. Somebody mentioned they were hoping to be out for Christmas. So, as one would, I asked if they celebrated Christmas? The patient said "yes". I replied with a "why", and so it began. My justifying of Christmas as Yule, a Pagan festival to the Christians and Muslims who were planning to celebrate.

A heated debate got going, apparently it lasted a long time, until the nurses had to put a halt to it. I wouldn't know, I had slipped out of the room not long after it got started, got my medication and went to bed. Goal achieved!

The next morning, after managing to avoid occupational therapy once again, I was due my medical review. I was hoping, to be discharged, but I was not. A compromise was reached, where I could go home in the afternoon, but come back to the hospital for medication and sleeping. The reason being I had to be stabilised on the drugs for bi-polar, before release. I was kind of ok with this plan, I knew I wasn't ready for discharge, but my hatred of hospitals, especially psychiatric wards was fuelling my desire to leave.

I often sat wondering about Bi-Polar. I had read all the information, asked all the questions I could think of, yet still had little idea of what had been real in my life and what had not. What did I feel?

Did I love people or was it mania? Did other Bi-polar people go through this? Other people's reaction to my mental state was strange. Andy was amazingly supportive. It was as if having a reason for my behaviour, and some level of understanding what had gone wrong, helped him to understand. I guess it comes to responsibility taking. We now had a place to apportion blame for some of what had gone wrong in our lives. I guess the hard thing will be to not blame everything on the Bi– Polar! It could be tempting to just say ' this caused it', when we actually have to question our own actions and motives also!

Andy coming with me for tests, maybe seeing scars on my body, and seeing my reactions in psychologist appointments when speaking of the Nairobi rape, has shown him how very real the experience was. Andy visits me every day, once by himself, and another time with the children. It is wonderful to see them, but I wonder if it is good for them to see me here. They have become my motivation to get out, and I will. Just a few more question sessions, and a week of ' good ' behaviour and I'm sure I'll get out on probation at least!

There is a Kenyan nurse working on the ward. After she found out from my notes, I had been in Kenya she keeps speaking to me in Kiswahili, which is a bit disturbing. I understand what she is saying and normally answer her in English, which should give her the realisation that I don't want to speak in Swahili. It doesn't. Today I have decided if she starts again, I'll answer in Swahili and tell her to naff off and shut up; which I am quite capable to do! One of the most important things to do when learning any language is learn the offensive and swear words. That way you know when people are insulting you.

She did it.

Nurse – Habari Samantha.
(Hi Samantha)
Samantha – Habari yako?
(How are you?)
Nurse -- Aah! We hongea kiswahili leo!
(Aah, so you will speak in Swahilli today!)
Samantha – Ndio
(Yes.)
Nurse – Mzuri sana. Sasa Wewe tunajua Mungo anapenda sana. -
(Very good. You know? God loves you very much.)
Samantha – Mungo ana acha sana -
(God has forsaken me.)
Nurse – Hapana, Mungo ana baraka wewe, anapenda wewe -
(No, God is blessing you. He loves you.)
Samantha – Hapana, achana na mimi. Sitaki we hongea mimi swahili, pia sitaki we hongea mimi
kwa mungo. Kwendo ouko!
(No, he has left me, I don't like you speaking to me in Swahili, also I don't like you
speaking to me about God. Leave me alone.)

Nurse leaves.

Victory! I was then called to a review meeting, where I found out I could be discharged under the care of the home assistance team. I felt so excited. It meant having a nurse come to see me at home for a while, but as I sat there something stirred in me. I think it is just possible I may have a future?

It might be a manic and weird one, or drug controlled, but it is a future none the less. Isn't it?

Karanga has kept his word. When I had last seen him, after the suicide attempt in Arusha, he had promised to stay in touch and check on me. He did. While I was in hospital, he kept calling and sending sms, providing me with some much needed moral support. I also heard often from Alex, who, it seemed had not forgotten me either. It was nice to feel I had some friends out there, who knew what a state I was in and hadn't run away from me.

I guess that is the strangest thing. With the entire situation, sickness, time away, relationship problems, I have truly seen who my friends are and are not. The sad reality that I can count my total friends on one hand, hits me hard in the heart. This time a few years back I had a whole tribe of a part of north eastern Tanzania to call family and friends, a few people here and there in Europe, and of course my Andy. I was speaking to my family, so there was some sort of relationship, in a bizarre kind of format, but now, there is nothing. No family and the majority of the fingers on my hands spare. I should stop counting with them and reflecting like a child. It would probably ease the mental state.

Sickness is hard to comprehend; mental illness is the most difficult, because you can't actually see the problem. Telling someone with depression to ' just cheer up ', is perhaps the worst thing you could come out with, but then again what is the right thing? It is a very intense problem for the sufferer and their families to go through, and there is no short term easy solution, because, it is often the case that the roots of the problem go far deeper than the surface can ever allow to show.

Yet, what if the problem is something else? Something like Bi-polar. Little is known in the general sphere of knowledge about this disorder. Often non-sufferers will dismiss it as a nothing, proclaiming, as my dentist did when I had to list my medication for him, "we all get ups and downs, that's life, not a disorder".

Well, really? When did your little 'up' assist you to jump on a plane and run to Africa? Or, on the flip side of the coin, when did your slight down cause you to attack yourself and attempt suicide? It is not an up or down. It is an uncontrollable swing between a massive up and a destructive down which makes Bi-polar different to what is accepted as a normal mood.

Andy and I have told the children about Bi Polar, Depression and Post Traumatic Stress. We have sat with them, hugged them, spoke with them, answered their questions, and offered to get a professional in to help them. They all seem to understand and cope quite well. For me, coming from a family where important issues like, what was happening, were swept and hidden away, it is so important for us to communicate with our children and give them some level of understanding as to the situation and what is wrong.

Fear is a breeding ground for ignorance. Dispel the fear and ignorance won't grow seems like a good theory, which I guess is all we are doing. Taking the advice of the nurses and the theories of professionals, together with our ideas and finding some kind of balance and normality which applies to my family.

Andy is holding us all together fine. I know he struggles with me. I struggle with me, so for anyone else it must be even more of a trial! I know he has considered walking away, or getting me moved out. The letters from relevant authorities, and everything being put into his name kind of proved that to me.

I can understand it. He wanted to make sure his and the children's security was ok, regarding the house and everything. I just think he was was perhaps a little early to be doing so. The dates show his actions to be before the rape, before the suicidal tendencies, before my Birthday, when I was just struggling to get home to my family.

There are massive divisions between us. I hope they can heal. He wants to, I want to. I want to give him the normality he craves, yet I fear I will never be enough. I cannot do normal. I don't understand what it is? It is something that everyone has their own interpretation of, so how can there be a universal normal? Is normality just conformity? But then, what are we conforming to? I don't understand. Just be normal? Tell me what it is and I could probably play the part....... I wish I could stop thinking!

I am not actually doing anything right now, except write, when my concentration allows. Take medication, and try to work out life. The children are at school most of the day, my nurse calls in to check I am still alive, then goes leaving me alone until Andy gets in from work. I think. I drink coffee. I think. I drink herbal tea. I hurt. I think. I drink coffee. Andy comes home, followed a few hours later by the children. C'est la vie.

On many of my thought paths, I am led to Africa. A place where so much of my real life was lived. There are painful memories and fantastic ones. Such as the first time I crossed the Serengeti, the animals, the people. Living a different culture for a while. I mean actually doing it. Not just fantasizing and day dreaming, but actually getting out there, and doing something. OK, so it all went a bit tits up in the end, but I do have the experiences. Positive ones and negative. There is something grounding in that thought. I did it. We did it.

I am soul tied to Africa which is something very few people can understand; especially when you consider the fact that my last few months in the continent were so full of pain. It is easy to just run away from the location where you are. However, it was not a location which caused my problems, it was people. Why should I feel more connected to Africa then to Europe? I am European, but my pain was as much in Europe as it was in Africa. When the problem is the past, cutting it away is a lot easier than dealing with it.

I get the impression I am meant to be living in some sort of shame, but I do not. I am learning to cope in a strange, almost new world.

When you have taught yourself to live in one place, it becomes a hard chore to find all new strategies, to cope in the real world, and sometimes seems easier to not bother and just go back to the coffee couch, sit, and think, and hide from life, The fight against the depression is difficult, often devoiding me of myself. Then I manage to spark.

Something in me clicks, and from deep within I remember something positive. Thank you Prozac! Yet, I did it. Despite, and perhaps fuelled by Bi Polar, I did get off the couch of life, and did get something done in my life. I did try and help. I did learn new culture and languages. I did fuck up. I also did immensely well to survive it all! I praise myself and loathe myself all at the same time. I guess the diagnosis is right!

I haven't heard from any of my Maasai since coming back to the UK. I miss my Maasai. I miss Samwel. I guess in life there is a time and a season for everything, and my season of the Maasai has finished, which means that the part of me that felt like a piece of that tribe should close, shouldn't it? Then why can't it? I look at pictures and long to see them, I look at my few bits of Maasai clothing and jewellery, remembering the times I adorned them, and scared of the wish I feel to wear them again. Do you think I would look odd in Windsor High Street in an Esouce and Esiankiki skirt?

My Maasai at one time became such a part of my everyday life. I am thankful for the experience and times shared. For the good times and the bad. I wish I heard from them, and I hope one day I will see some of them again. Especially my Sister Samwel. Until then I have a few photos and other memorabilia of my Maazungu experience.

When my family and I were living in Kisumu, our home often had Maasai visitors. They accepted me as their friend, it was normal for some to call on me, just as a friend is welcome home in pretty much any culture. Many of them worked night shifts as guards in the city, so the most popular time for visits was in the morning hours. Leaving home on the school run was an adventure in itself most mornings. The children would get ready, leave the house to get in the car, and more often than not a few Maasai would hop in the car with them. Unable to communicate in Maasai and presuming they wanted a lift to town, Andy would drive off with them in tow. However it was often the case these guys wanted nothing more than a ride in the Pajero!

Maasai and water are not a normal combination. Kisumu is a city on the shores of Lake Victoria. I love the water, so would often go down to Hippo Point in Dunga. A few years previously, Andy and I had made a couple of friends there, who worked as fisherman on the lake. Titus and John.

When we arrived in Kisumu, we arranged to have a boat built for them. The deal was that they could work the boat, as long as we could go out in it for free whenever we wanted. It was good for both parties, we got to experience the nature of the second largest freshwater lake in the world, and Titus and John could earn a living without having to hire a boat first.

The boat only took a few weeks to build, from start to finish. We had watched it and admired the craft as it turned from lumps of wood into something that with every day resembled a lake worthy boat.

On the day of the maiden voyage, a group of people from the community centre, including Andy and I all went down to the lake to watch the launch. My Father was also visiting from the UK. It was nice to have him there there to witness the occasion.

I also had the Maasai Morans, Samwel and Laata with me. Samwel had finished working at my house, but had decided to hang out for the day with us. Laata had just turned up to visit in the morning. I told them what we were doing, and he came along with us. So there we were, on the shore of lake Victoria, launching the boat. It was an absolutely fantastic moment, especially when Andy and Titus encouraged the Maasai to get in the boat! They were fearful, but as Morans, could not show fear. It was so funny, and very interesting from a sociological point of view, watching them balance between the urge to run but the need to stay and be brave. Samwel and Laata got in the boat, both shaking from their braided Maasai dreadies to their tyre strap shoes!

It is said to overcome a fear one must confront it. I guess that day Samwel and Laata were doing ok. Until a family of five hippos emerged from the water to see what was going on! Give them a lion and a spear anyday. As Maasai warriors they would know what to do, but armed with nothing but their small warrior knives and facing a massive hippo while in a boat was not their idea of fun. I wonder why?

I have so many stories and memories of my every day life made bizarre by my co-existence with Maasai. I treasure them, laugh at them, cry with them. Hurt with them, and smile. Thankful for the life, both good and bad I was exposed to.

They kind of keep me company. When I am alone, and the children are not here. In a place where no-one really understands who you are and what makes you tick, delving into thought and memory often feels far safer than reality.

Chapter 29

Disability. Apparently I have a disability! I read on a document about me, of which I was sent a copy. I have a severe mental disability. Fucking great. I hate that word. As it rolls of my tongue and resounds in the air around me I feel reviled at myself. Disgusted. How did I become disabled? I am able, am I not? Will I ever be free from this disability and seen as able? How can just one word fill me with such fear, anger and sadness?

Being disabled, for me, means other people have more control over your life than you do. I don't particularly feel as if I have any control at all right now. Only in my writing. What I want is not listened to, what I feel is not affirmed. It is as if everybody around me is talking about me, making decisions on my behalf despite what I think. I also feel I can't communicate very well to my mental health team about this, as I would probably then be disabled with another label. Paranoia perhaps?

It is getting close to Christmas. I can compare my notes from last year to this, and it makes me feel more down. I was desperate to get away then, I want to be home now, but I feel so scared of what the future will bring. Do I want it? Am I needed in it? If I have no voice, no say, no choice in my own life then what is the point of it? I feel ashamed for feeling suicidal, and called selfish when I communicate about it. Selfish is what they say. Logical next step is often what I think.

I am managing to try and find coping strategies which work for my life right now. This has helped tremendously. When I feel the need to hurt myself or kill myself I touch a bowl of ice cubes. It causes a painful sensation but does not leave me with a scar, and distracts the mind off the thoughts. It might sound weird, but it works!

Christmas will be strange. Christmas is strange. I am not even really a Christian, yet in some fusion of Solstice and Christmas, we celebrate as others do. I am so thrilled to be here with my family which is something I didn't think was going to happen.

However, Christmas without Mum & Dad is going to be so awful. Time to face the reality of true life I guess, which is sadly painful and full of hypocrisy.

Why do people send Christmas cards? Isn't the thought meant to be to greet the recipient? To send wishes of cheer and appreciation of their involvement in your life? Is that the reason? I am sure back in primary school we studied the whole history of Christmas card sending, and it was along those lines. A nice greeting. This years deposit of so called 'greetings' have been used as emotional weapons against me. I thought it was just me being over sensitive when the cards started coming through the door, were not addressed to me. Then I read them. A continuing succession of Brother and family. Andy and 'Andy-lings'. Andy and children. Then I realised, out of all the cards received, from both Andy's family and mine, only a bare few mentioned my name or existence.

I have never been close to Andy's family, and the distance with between me and my own people is vast. These actions were just plain nasty. To be completely pushed out of the scene? Of course they would favour Andy in any situation, that is natural, but to outcast me with such emotional violence at my most vulnerable, makes me sick to the core. I hope one day they can forgive themselves, because I don't. If we live our actions how we want to treat others and the laws of karma really are in effect, then they will get theirs. I will get mine. Let it be.

On Christmas Eve, I was feeling all negative about the times, present, past and future, what had been and would never be again, I guess watching a dose of Dicken's 'Christmas Carol' on channel 4 fused me or something because a thought occurred to me like a revelation.

If I wanted change. I had to be the change. If I wanted to get better I had to stop letting myself hurt. If I wanted to grow , I had to stop restricting myself. Simple concepts, probably thought of millions of times before by billions of people around the world, but that night, they blinded me like a torch in the eye. I had to change this pattern of pain.

There is no time like the present. Or so they say. But what could I do at Christmas Eve, about 8 p.m.? What was there to possibly do to improve and heal this situation which was so old? Sitting pondering this thought over a coffee, I recalled Andy had told me that my parents were going to be calling round that evening to drop in the children's Christmas presents. I formulated a plan that I would go and greet them and say thank you for the children's presents. I didn't want to be thought that I was causing the problem anymore than what they already thought I was. I also wanted to show I could rise above the situation. In truth I couldn't, but I started to psyche myself up for a confrontation/greeting of some kind. Arming my body with a lorazepam, I waited for them to pull up on the drive. They did, but by the time I got downstairs, they had gone! Aaaaagh!

My best attempt at moving forward was thwarted by my slow psyche up. Not to be put off and in desperate need to use the momentum I had gathered, I picked up my mobile phone and sent a text message to my Mother. Thanking her, and telling her I was sorry to have missed her when she called in. The next thing which happened took me by surprise. My phone rang. It was her number calling. I had to make a choice there and then to answer or reject. It felt like so much more than it was, and I realised that my action would have a profound effect on my forthcoming months.

I picked up the phone and said " hello". The first words I had uttered to my Mum in nearly a year. It was a very awkward and tearful conversation. I sat with my hand in a bowl of ice cubes trying to control myself and not throw the phone down and run from the situation. A whole spectrum of emotions arose in both of us. Some good, some bad. All painful.

My Mother and I had crossed the ' not speaking' threshold. It was no Christmas miracle. It was a rational decision, based on information, lorazepam, and a desire to move forward. Ultimately, we have to get to that place ourselves. The spot in life or a situation where it is us who want to move on. Nobody can do it for us. We will play around and skirt the problem until it will not move, and it is either a case of do it now, or never go forward. I chose to move on and live my life. I guess that is the key. You have to want the change and be in the position where you have accepted situations enough to want to not be in the same place anymore. Not wanting to run or hide anymore, I knew the time had come to finally face and beat the negativity which had took so much of my life. It was the best decision I had made in about 25 years!

Over the next few weeks communication was slow, but there. Sometimes the tortoise approach is better, in order to walk the correct path, and I don't want to rush any foundation building stage, and allow everything to crumble around me again. I also don't want to expose myself too much. Pole pole, as we say in Swahili. Which translates as slowly, slowly.

Medications have finally seemed to stabilise me, I am not sure how I feel about that. I want to get better, but I want to be natural. I want to be in control of the Bi-Polar, but I don't want to pop pills everyday. I scare myself with thoughts of the damage it could do. This condition holds a grip on my mind so much. I am slowly seeing a future, where I thought there was none. I am seeing a life. People. University, Holidays. My career. My life. A real life? And, the biggest change came from within me. It is always easier to expect other people to battle our demons for us, but we are the ones who must face our life and fight for it. No one else can be in that vulnerable and special position but ourselves.

I am not HIV +. This fact seems to have just hit me. The revelation that I had some three months ago has just come to me like a ton of bricks and the joy it brought was immense! Oh my God! I am NOT Hiv +! The Dr. in Arusha had been so right to tell me to retest.

I am so stupid! She had cited that the quality of most medical tests in Tanzania could not compare with what we have in the UK.
She also complained about the electricity supply, and the labs. Electricity is extremely temperamental in all areas of Tanzania,

especially so in Arusha. I didn't really make a connection with what she had said then and how it could affect me. In some ways I still don't fully understand, but I guess the electricity breaking and bad generators could have something to do with it? I have known 'Mount Meru' hospital to be without power, so? Anyway.

I am not HIV +. I am not, I am not! My eyes and mind have finally been opened to this fact and it feels so good! How can I have missed it? I do have a life!

When one feels alive to such a degree as this, you can find yourself needing a desire to fully experience life. I have seen before how people, when faced with the news of a terminal illness suddenly find the energy and motivation to face the World they never saw. In some ways, having being misdiagnosed and undiagnosed with this sickness has led me into this state of happiness.

No amount of leaflets entitled 'positive about being positive' were going to get through to me at that stage in my life, this I know, I was too far gone, but now I am back in the grip of reality and life. Working out the next steps, and pushing forward.

I know I am not meant to say this, but I want to go back to Africa. Now I have started to heal from the previous and ongoing pains, I find myself thinking more and more on life there. I find myself longing for the African landscape, some of the people there, and just life there. I love England, but I don't feel as if I am made for here. Does that make any sense?

There is a little piece of my heart missing that seems to come alive when I think of the Savannah life.

I will give myself some time before thinking more seriously on Africa, this is because right now whatever I do is either labelled as manic or depressive. In the eyes of others I can no longer be happy or sad, which is amazing really. I mean when undiagnosed and suffering, I was thought of as anything but ill. Now we are aware of what is wrong, it is considered I am sick with this condition every day, at every minute, and in every possible way.

I won't even get close to mentioning what I am really thinking, probably for at least a year. As doing so would probably get me committed into the Psychiatric ward again! I am realistic enough to know this! If nobody understands my passion for Africa, then nobody would understand my life in it? So, for now, like the good girl I am meant to be, I'll shut up.

In the new year, I shall be taking a university course, aiming for a degree in 'Modern Language Studies.' This should keep my mind a bit more occupied. I have been advised to not even think about working again for at least two years, which is awful. I thought I should occupy my time and learn something new to improve my life skills for when I am given the all clear to work again.

However, I don't think writers actually stop working. Only during a block. Writers, are among the strangest breed of human there is. To cease our ' work ' often suffocates us. It is often only during a block that a writer cannot write, and will hit probably the lowest points of their lives in not being able to do so. The rest of the time our lives we are thinking, remembering, taking notes and writing. In our created Worlds or the rest of the Earth. Whichever time, mentality and life will allow!

Languages show me a future. They are not just words. The ability to communicate in different languages gives one the chance to explore and live life in a further capability than your average Joe abroad. To speak the language of the people I am visiting, to me, shows a mark of respect to the place you are exploring. The ability to speak Spanish opens up South America to me in my mind. I have an ambition to see 'Machu Picchu' in Peru. I will go and I will understand what is being said.

Though the reality I may be surrounded by other tourists from London or America has struck me several times!

As the books arrive for the course, I feel excited by what the future will bring. I am feeling
challenged. I have a chance to prove to others that I am not completely mind fucked, though I do acknowledge that the ability to run somewhere else could be behind the desire to learn! We'll see how it goes!

The last months has been an extreme roller- coaster and vertical drops of emotion and life, and now, as I sit, life is calming down and settling. The books are poised; mind ready, I claim back my life.

On a rock with the Maasai